Government and Economic Growth in the 21st Century

This book offers an alternative view of the economy – and indeed, society – that does not rely on an ever-expanding government to address the problems which individuals typically face during their lives.

The book is a Classical Liberal response to the way leading economies have been (mis)managed in the last three decades and the principles and models that have guided such policies, particularly since the outbreak of the Global Financial Crisis in 2007–09, which has resulted in enlarged government deficits and public debt, as well as more intrusive government regulation and virtually no economic growth. The book does not only criticise the current dominant view which favours ever-growing governments but also puts forward an alternative set of policies and institutions compatible with long-term growth in a free(er) economy. The book is structured around three major themes: (1) what classical liberalism is (or should be) and why it still matters, (2) how state-sponsored capitalism hinders the well-functioning of the market economy as well as being a bad recipe for economic growth and individual freedom, and (3) which are the essential Classical Liberal institutions necessary for a free market economy to flourish.

This volume will be accessible not only to specialists in the subject but also to a well-informed audience interested in current economic issues, the role of government in the economy, and how history, traditions, the political system, and economics shape the institutions that help us to explain how markets function and their outcomes.

Juan E. Castañeda is Director of the Vinson Centre for the Public Understanding of Economics and Entrepreneurship and Senior Lecturer of Economics at the University of Buckingham, UK.

Routledge Frontiers of Political Economy

Inequality and Stagnation
A Monetary Interpretation
Capraro, Panico and Torres-González

Political Economy of Post-Capitalism
Financialization, Globalization and Neofeudalism
Richard Westra

The Political Economy of Mediterranean Europe
A Growth Models Perspective
Luis Cárdenas and Javier Arribas

Economics for Humanity
Integrating Well-being, Community, and Practical Philosophy
Mitsuaki Okabe

Sustainable Economic Development
Perspectives from Political Economy and Economics Pluralism
Edited by Giorgos Meramveliotakis and Manolis Manioudis

The Myth of the Global Market
A Marxist Critique of Neoliberalism
Giulio Palermo

Government and Economic Growth in the 21st Century
A Classical Liberal Response
Edited by Juan E. Castañeda

For more information about this series, please visit: www.routledge.com/Routledge-Frontiers-of-Political-Economy/book-series/SE0345

Government and Economic Growth in the 21st Century

A Classical Liberal Response

Edited by Juan E. Castañeda

Routledge
Taylor & Francis Group
LONDON AND NEW YORK

First published 2025
by Routledge
4 Park Square, Milton Park, Abingdon, Oxon OX14 4RN

and by Routledge
605 Third Avenue, New York, NY 10158

Routledge is an imprint of the Taylor & Francis Group, an informa business

British Library Cataloguing-in-Publication Data
A catalogue record for this book is available from the British Library

Library of Congress Cataloging-in-Publication Data
Names: Castañeda, Juan E., editor.
Title: Government and economic growth in the 21st century : a classical liberal response / edited by Juan E. Castañeda.
Description: Abingdon, Oxon ; New York, NY : Routledge, 2025. |
Series: Routledge frontiers of political economy | Includes bibliographical references and index.
Identifiers: LCCN 2024030628 (print) | LCCN 2024030629 (ebook) |
ISBN 9781032824192 (hardback) | ISBN 9781032824215 (paperback) |
ISBN 9781003504412 (ebook)
Subjects: LCSH: Economic policy. | Economic development--Government policy. | Free enterprise. | Liberalism--Economic aspects.
Classification: LCC HD87 .G688 2025 (print) | LCC HD87 (ebook) |
DDC 338.9--dc23/eng/20240815
LC record available at https://lccn.loc.gov/2024030628
LC ebook record available at https://lccn.loc.gov/2024030629

ISBN: 978-1-032-82419-2 (hbk)
ISBN: 978-1-032-82421-5 (pbk)
ISBN: 978-1-003-50441-2 (ebk)

DOI: 10.4324/9781003504412

Typeset in Times New Roman
by KnowledgeWorks Global Ltd.

Contents

List of Figures

List of Tables

Authors'/Contributors' Information

Editor

Juan E. Castañeda is Director of the Vinson Centre for the Public Understanding of Economics and Entrepreneurship and Senior Lecturer of Economics at the University of Buckingham.

A Doctor of Economics since 2003 (Universidad Autonoma de Madrid) and lecturer in Economics at the University of Buckingham since 2012. He was the Director of the Institute of International Monetary Research from 2014 to 2023. He has collaborated with the European Parliament's 'Committee of Economic and Monetary Affairs'. He has been an Honorary Senior Visiting Fellow in Cass Business School (London) and a visiting researcher at the Centre of Monetary and Financial Alternatives at Cato (Washington, DC) and at Universidad Francisco Marroquin in Guatemala. Before moving into the UK in 2012, he worked for 14 years as a lecturer in Economics at UNED University in Madrid. He has been awarded a Bank of Spain annual scholarship to develop research on monetary history, and he has authored and edited academic books and research articles on money, monetary policy, and central banking. He is the review editor and deputy editor of *Economic Affairs*. Since September 2018, he has been a member of the Institute of Economic Affairs' 'Shadow Monetary Policy Committee'.

Contributors

Christian Bjørnskov is Professor of Economics at Aarhus University in Denmark.

He is an affiliated researcher at the Research Institute of Industrial Economics (IFN) in Stockholm. He is a trustee of the board of the Institute of Economic Affairs (IEA) in London and the Center for Political Studies in Copenhagen and the 2024–25 President of the Public Choice Society. He is also a regular columnist at the Danish financial newspaper Børsen. Christian received his PhD from the Aarhus School of Business in 2005 and has since published more than 100 articles in international peer-reviewed journals, including the *American Journal of Political Science*, *Journal of Development Economics*, *Academy of*

Management Perspectives, *Public Choice*, and *Journal of Law and Economics*. He is also the author, with Stefan Voigt, of the recent book *State of Emergency*. His research interests are situated at the intersection of public choice and political economy and development economics, and mainly focus on the long-run influence of formal and informal institutions and economic freedom.

Forrest Capie is Professor Emeritus of Economic History at the Business School, City, University of London.

He has taught at the London School of Economics, the University of Warwick, and the University of Leeds. He has been a British Academy Overseas Fellow at the National Bureau, New York, a Visiting Professor at the London School of Economics, and a Visiting Scholar at the International Monetary Fund. He has written widely on money, banking, and trade and commercial policy. He was Head of Department of Banking and Finance at City from 1989 to 1992 and editor of the *Economic History Review* from 1993 to 1999. His commissioned history of the Bank of England was published by Cambridge University Press in 2010. He is a Governor of the National Institute of Economic and Social Research.

Stephen Davies is Senior Education Fellow at the IEA.

He graduated from Saint Andrews University in 1976 and gained his PhD from there in 1984. He taught for 30 years in the Department of History and Economic History at Manchester Metropolitan University. He has published many articles and books including *Empiricism and History*, *The Wealth Explosion: The Origins and Nature of Modernity*, *The Economics and Politics of Brexit*, *The Streetwise Guide to the Devil and All His Works*, and *Apocalypse Next: The Economics of Global Catastrophic Risks*. He has also written about political realignment, the economics and politics of virtual worlds, and the economics and politics of the home. He is interested in popular culture, especially popular fiction genres and musical subcultures, and is a keen Manchester City fan.

Julian Jessop is an independent economist.

He graduated with a first-class honours degree in Economics from Cambridge University (Clare College) in 1987 and has further qualifications both in economics (an MPhil, also from Cambridge) and in law (the post-graduate diploma from the College of Law). He was Chief Economist at the IEA until 2018. He holds the honorary position of IEA Economics Fellow, member of the IEA's Academic Advisory Council, and member of the IEA's Shadow Monetary Policy Committee. He works with Speakers for Schools, and he is a Fellow of the Royal Society of Arts. Previously, he was a Director, Chief Global Economist, and Head of Commodities Research at Capital Economics, where he worked from 2004 to 2017. He often appears in the media, including TV and radio, and writes for a variety of websites, newspapers, and magazines. He has also provided expert testimony to many parliamentary select committees.

Daniel B. Klein is Professor of Economics and JIN Chair at the Mercatus Center at George Mason University.

He leads the Adam Smith Program at George Mason University Economics. He is the chief editor of *Econ Journal Watch*. He holds degrees from George Mason University and New York University, where in both cases he studied the classical liberal traditions of economics. He is the author of *Knowledge and Coordination: A Liberal Interpretation*, *Smithian Morals*, and *Central Notions of Smithian Liberalism*.

Alberto Mingardi is Professor of History of Political Thought at University Institute of Modern Languages (IULM) in Milan.

He is also a Presidential Scholar in Political Theory at Chapman University (Orange County, CA). He was one of the founders and is the Director General of the Italian free-market think tank, Istituto Bruno Leoni.

He published monographs on F.A. Hayek (2020), Thomas Hodgskin (2016 and 2020), and Herbert Spencer (2011). He edited critical editions of works by Richard Cobden (*Scritti e discorsi politici*, 2022), F.A. Hayek (*La presunzione fatale*, 2023), Thomas Hodgskin (*Crimine e potere*, 2014), Elie Kedourie (*Nazionalismo*, 2021), Herbert Spencer (*L'uomo contro lo Stato*, 2016), and Vilfredo Pareto (*L'ignoranza e il malgoverno*, 2018). He translated into English Antonio Rosmini, *The Constitution Under Social Justice* (Lexington Books, 2003). With Deirdre N. McCloskey, he authored *The Myth of the Entrepreneurial State* (2020). With Maria Blanco, he edited *Show and Biz. The market economy in TV series and popular culture (2000–2020)* (2023), one of the first investigation of economic narratives in pop culture. He writes frequently for the popular press. He is an adjunct scholar at the Cato Institute, a member of the Royal Historical Society, and the current Secretary of the Mont Pelerin Society.

Mark Pennington has been Professor of Political Economy and Public Policy in the Department of Political Economy since January 2012.

Prior to joining Kings' he taught for 12 years in the School of Politics and International Relations at Queen Mary, University of London. He holds a PhD from the London School of Economics and Political Science. Mark is currently Director of the Centre for the Study of Governance and Society. He works at the intersection of philosophy, politics, and economics with a particular focus on exploring problems of limited knowledge or bounded rationality and their relationship to 'ideal' and 'non-ideal' theorising in economics and political theory. This approach was exemplified in his 2011 book *Robust Political Economy: Classical Liberalism and the Future of Public Policy* (Edward Elgar). Mark has written widely on the political economy of urban planning, environmental governance, social capital, and the relationship between markets and democratic citizenship. He recently completed a major project on the 'political economy of knowledge and ignorance'. One output from this project was his newly completed book *Foucault and Liberal Political Economy: Power, Knowledge, and Freedom* (forthcoming, 2025 with Oxford University Press), which makes the case for a 'post-modern' liberalism.

Martin Ricketts is Emeritus Professor of Economic Organisation at the University of Buckingham.

He is Emeritus Professor of Economic Organisation at the University of Buckingham. He is a trustee of the IEA and is Chairman of its Academic Advisory Council. A graduate of the University of Newcastle upon Tyne (1970), he has a DPhil from the University of York (1980). He was a Research Economist at the Industrial Policy Group (1970–72), a Research Fellow at the Institute of Social and Economic Research, University of York (1974–77), and was Economic Director of the National Economic Development Office (1991–92). He joined the academic staff of the University of Buckingham in 1977 becoming Dean of the School of Accounting, Business and Economics (1993–97) and then Dean of the School of Humanities (2002–15). He has published in professional journals on the New Institutional Economics, the Theory of the Firm, Entrepreneurship, Public Choice, and aspects of Public Finance and Housing Policy. He has authored books on Business Enterprise and Ownership Structure and co-authored books on the Economics of Energy (with Michael Webb) and Government and Industry (with Alan Peacock).

Pedro Schwartz is Emeritus Professor of Economics at Camilo José Cela University in Madrid.

At the London School of Economics (LSE) he studied under K. Popper. His thesis on J.S. Mill was supervised by Lionel Robbins. He also critically took a welfare economics course by A.K. Sen. He has held chairs in the History of Economic Thought at four Spanish Universities and has taught monetary economics at the University of Buckingham. He is a member of the Mont Pelerin Society. In September 1990, HM Queen Elizabeth II made him an Honorary Officer of the British Empire. In February 2003, he was awarded the Rey Jaime I Prize for contributions to economics in Spain. In February 2005, he became a member of the Royal Academy of Moral and Political Sciences of Spain. In November 2010, HM the former King of Spain handed him the Rey Juan Carlos Prize for Economics.

Aris Trantidis is Senior Lecturer of Politics and International Relations at the University of Lincoln.

He previously held research and teaching positions at King's College London, the European University Institute (EUI) in Italy and George Mason University in the United States. Aris has a multidisciplinary background with studies in politics, law, and political economy and holds degrees from King's College London, the LSE, the University of Surrey, the University of Athens, and the Aristotle University of Thessaloniki, Greece. Aris' research focuses on democratic theory, clientelism, climate politics, economic policy, foreign policy analysis, semi-authoritarian regimes, and the epistemology of social sciences. His work has been published in leading international journals such as the *Journal of European Public Policy*, *Political Research Quarterly*, *Politics*, the *British Journal of Politics and International Relations*, *Polity*, *Public Choice*, *International Studies Review*, and *Democratization* among others. His book, *Clientelism and Economic Policy: Greece and the Crisis* (Routledge, 2016), develops a novel approach of how the practice of clientelism affects the design of economic policy and the provision of public goods in a democratic system.

Cento Veljanovski is Managing Partner and founder of Case Associates.

Cento Veljanovski is Fellow in Law & Economics at the IEA and Senior Fellow at the GW Competition & Innovation Lab, George Washington University. Cento has degrees in law and economics and over 40 years of experience as an academic, as consultant on competition and regulatory economics, and as an expert witness in competition litigation. He has held academic appointments in economics and law faculties in the UK, Australia, and North America including at Monash University, York University, University of Toronto, and University College London and adjunct/visiting positions including at the universities of New York, Miami, Buckingham; the Australian Law Reform Commission, Centre for Economic Policy Research, and Centre for Policy Studies. He was the first economist appointed to a UK law school at University College London. Cento was Editorial and Research Director of the IEA following Arthur Seldon's retirement. Cento has published extensively including most recently 'Cartel Damages: Principles, Measurement, and Economics' (Oxford University Press, 2020), 'Hayek on Antitrust' (IEA, 2023), and in leading academic journals such as the *Economic Journal*, *Journal of Competition Law & Economics*, *The Antitrust Bulletin*, *Journal of Empirical Legal Studies*, and *Singapore Economics Review*.

Geoffrey Wood is Emeritus Professor of Economics at City University Business School in London and Emeritus Professor of Monetary Economics at the University of Buckingham.

A graduate of Aberdeen and Essex Universities, he has worked in the Federal Reserve System and the Bank of England. Overseas he has advised several central banks and national treasuries. He is an adviser to several financial institutions and two pension funds and was an adviser to the Treasury Select Committee of the House of Commons and to the Parliamentary Banking Commission until the Commission ceased to exist on the publication of its report. He has authored, co-authored, or edited over 30 books and has published over 100 academic papers. His fields of interest are monetary economics, monetary history, and financial regulation.

Preface

Every book has a story behind it. This one is no exception. On 19 July 2023, the (first) annual conference of the Vinson Centre was held at the University of Buckingham. We decided to advertise the conference under no specific theme but to stress very clearly that it would be 'in the Classical Political Economy tradition'. This is very much the approach to political economy we follow at the Vinson Centre, and we regularly engage with like-minded institutions and individuals in this tradition in the UK and elsewhere; among them is the Institute of Economic Affairs in London, the main partner of the Centre. This is important to note so that the reader knows that the book is not intended to cover other traditions of political economy, although we do not disregard their relevance in the academic and policy debate.

The conference assembled a group of economists, political scientists, and political philosophers from the UK and abroad, all of whom were concerned about the state of classical liberal institutions, in particular the exercise of individual freedom and individual responsibility in a free market economy. A preliminary version of some of the chapters in this volume were presented at the conference, in particular those by Daniel B. Klein (though on a different topic), Martin Ricketts, Pedro Schwartz, Mark Pennington, Aris Trantidis, and Christian Bjørnskov. You will be able to find their presentations on the Vinson Centre's YouTube channel. I am very grateful to them all and to those who attended the conference for the lively discussions which followed the presentations at the conference. But the book is more than an edited collection of the papers presented at the conference. I invited other colleagues (Alberto Mingardi, Cento Veljanovski, Stephen Davies, Julian Jessop, Forrest Capie, and Geoffrey Wood) to contribute to the book on key topics, with a special emphasis on why state-sponsored capitalism and ever more stringent regulation have not seemed to have produced greater growth in recent years but rather quite the opposite. The book offers an alternative to the way leading economies have been (mis)managed in the last three decades and the (flawed) principles that have guided such policies, particularly since the outbreak of the Global Financial Crisis in 2007–09. More details in the book.

My sincere gratitude to all the contributors to the book, for their generosity and continued support of this project.

Juan E. Castañeda
In Buckingham, on 26 May 2024

Introduction

On the Principles and Policies to Foster Long-Term Economic Growth

Juan E. Castañeda

In the book we offer an alternative view of the economy – and indeed, society – that does not rely on an ever-expanding government to address the problems which individuals typically face during their lives. Moreover, whenever there is a severe crisis – whether brought about by flawed policies, government regulation or supposed failures of 'the market', the cry goes up from the media and other institutions for the government to intervene more and 'do something about it': in the forlorn hope that it will be able to solve the current problem. People often forget that 'the government' is just a collection of politicians and bureaucrats with their own goals and careers, whose interests are rarely aligned and who suffer from a fundamental problem; the 'fatal conceit' of believing that they have the knowledge and the information needed to change the economy and improve our standards of living. In so thinking, they take for granted that information is given as a sort of a 'manna from Heaven' and that they have the expertise to make the appropriate policy changes required to improve the economy. Take, for example, the Treasury or national central banks when they, respectively, put the budget together or make a monetary policy decision. Hundreds if not thousands of well-trained economists work in the policy and research departments of governments and central banks but a factual assessment of the outcomes of their decisions in the last two decades sadly reveals all too many shortcomings. The reaction to the Global Financial Crisis (2007–09) and the COVID-19 pandemic (2020–21) has resulted in enlarged government deficits and public debt, as well as more intrusive government regulation. And none of their initiatives have led either to greater economic growth or improved public services. Quite the contrary, for nearly two decades stagnation and lack of productivity growth have been the norm. This is a tragedy that reflects a very poor understanding of the institutions and policies that led to the extraordinary surge in economic growth in leading economies back in the late 18th century. In this volume, the reader will see that we do not only criticise the current dominant view which favours ever-growing governments, but we also put forward an alternative set of policies and institutions compatible with long-term growth in a free(er) economy.

The book focuses on three major themes: firstly, what classical liberalism is (or should be) and why it still matters, including the distinction between modern economics and political economy as related though separate disciplines; secondly, how state-sponsored capitalism, including industrial policies, hinders the

DOI: 10.4324/9781003504412-1

well-functioning of the market economy as well as being a bad recipe for economic growth and individual freedom; and thirdly, which are the essential classical liberal institutions necessary for a free market economy to flourish. These three themes correspond to the three parts of the book.

Part I on 'Classical Liberalism: A Re-statement' consists of three chapters. In Chapter 1, Stephen Davies (Institute of Economic Affairs) defines Classical Liberalism as a historical term with its origins in the late 18th century. Though open to controversy, he defines Classical Liberalism as 'the various kinds of liberal thought and politics found between roughly the 1770s and the 1880s or 1890s'. However, he notices that in recent decades leading classical liberals seem to have narrowed the scope of Classical Liberalism excessively; for example, many focus too much on the economic tradition of this school and very much disregard other significant aspects in this tradition as developed in the 19th century. The challenge for Classical Liberalism today is how to revert to a broad(er) tradition of liberal economics and thought as detailed by the author in this chapter.

In Chapter 2, Pedro Schwartz (Universidad Camilo José Cela) criticises a very narrow definition of liberalism, usually defined as the right of individuals to live their lives as they wish, without judging other people's choices. This narrow definition of liberalism paves the way to the critics of liberalism who claim that it results in individuals and society being focused on the market and the pursuit of wealth at any cost, as if liberalism were devoid of a moral code. According to Pedro Schwartz 'such a mistaken conception of liberalism originates in a failure to distinguish between the ethics of the open society and the morality of the individual'.

In Chapter 3, Martin Ricketts (University of Buckingham) explains the differences between political economy, as the prevailing discipline in this area in the 19th century, and economics, as the new discipline resulting from the Marginal Revolution at the end of the 19th century. He explains that the difference between these two disciplines is in the method(s) used to study how markets work; in particular, the way they address how information and knowledge are generated and used by individuals when making a decision. Modern economics uses highly formalised models to explain the firms and individuals' decisions and impose a set of assumptions on the availability of information. Whereas 'In the world of political economy it is recognised that to study the process of exchange is wider than the study of "the price system", important though the latter might be'. Therefore, political economy provides a more comprehensive approach, as the study of institutions such as markets or the rule of law are part of the discipline, and not assumptions added to a model.

In Part II on 'State-Sponsored Capitalism – A Critique' the reader will find several chapters focused on a critique of *new* (or rather, rejuvenated or re-labelled) proposals for the state to have a greater role in the economy. In Chapter 4, Alberto Mingardi (Istituto Bruno Leoni) addresses a recurrent form of state intervention through 'industrial policies' (now usually put under the more fashionable umbrella of 'green policies' or similar) and innovation policy. As the author argues, these policies rest on the assumptions that governments know which sectors and technologies need to be championed, while disregarding the inescapable limitations the government bureaucracy faces to achieve its goals in real-life scenarios. Even more, because of the discretionary nature of these policies, 'Such an activist State in the realm of production is not compatible with the rule of law', which means that these policies will not only be inefficient but also harm individual freedom.

In the same line, in Chapter 5 Aris Trantidis (Lincoln University) describes in detail how a state-sponsored economy can erode the basis of a liberal democracy through the exercise of clientelism. Aris Trantidis uses a model to explain the conditions under which a state-sponsored economy can lead to greater 'autocrasitation', as well as how we can avoid it. As he puts it, 'autocratisation is a conceivable development for consolidated democracies to the extent that the socioeconomic structure allows the government to build a comprehensive system of clientelist rewards and sanctions. (…) democratic backsliding and ensuing autocratisation is less likely to occur in an economy that retains its autonomy from state sponsorship and clientelism'.

In Chapter 6, Mark Pennington (King's College London) continues the discussion on what he terms as the 'Missionary Theory of Industrial Policy', an approach and a development of the role of government in the economy that, if not new, have become more prominent with governments' reaction to the COVID-19 pandemic. The author summarises this mission-oriented view of the government as '(…) having a government with the willingness to make bold and strategic investments that goes beyond tinkering at the edges of existing markets is the key to reducing uncertainty and to giving entrepreneurs and investors the confidence to act'. Mark Pennington addresses the main theoretical flaws of this view of the government and uses the responses to COVID-19 pandemic as a case study, one of the flaws being the suppression of dissent. This links with the next chapter (Chapter 7) by Daniel B. Klein (George Mason University) on '"Misinformation" as Censorship Stratagem'. The author explains how propaganda can only survive if accompanied by censorship of dissent. However, in recent years critics of an open or a liberal society frequently claim that those opposing their views use 'misinformation', as a strategy to silence dissenting voices. In the author's view, in so doing they are committing a category error 'because people do not argue fervently over mere information. That is especially plain when things are taken to the point of censorship, cancellation, or criminalization'.

Part III on 'Market Institutions and Economic Growth' consists of several chapters which discuss the determinants, policies and institutions needed to achieve greater economic growth; including how to enhance productivity growth, stable money and sensible market regulation. In Chapter 8, Juan E. Castañeda (University of Buckingham) discusses money, the central bank and the government. The author criticises the general trend in monetary policies in recent years, though he focuses on central banks' reactions to the Global Financial Crisis and the COVID-19 pandemic, resulting in greater monetary instability, macroeconomic instability and discretionary policies. Taking the principles governing the Classical Gold Standard as a benchmark, Juan Castañeda puts forward a rule-based monetary policy to tie the hands of the central bank and the government regarding their ability to make monetary policy decisions.

As he puts it: 'In this framework, the central bank's primary concern should be fundamentally of a financial nature, namely how to increase the demand for its currency on a long-term basis'.

In Chapter 9, Christian Bjørnskov (Aarhus University) addresses a fundamental empirical question on growth. According to the available evidence, there is a negative correlation between the size of the government and economic growth over the long term. The author addresses two questions: (1) Which elements of big government are responsible for this? (2) Does the analysis hold when applied both to a liberal democracy or an authoritarian state? The author concludes that '(…) the size of government and particularly larger transfers and subsidies hold back long-run growth in electoral democracies. Subsidising some voters and some interests therefore comes with a price tag for all of society'. Based on these empirical results, Christian Bjørnskov concludes that the recent surge in government spending under the COVID-19 pandemic could harm economic growth substantially in the future.

In Chapter 10, continuing on the discussion on growth (or the lack thereof), Julian Jessop (Independent Economist) addresses one of the main problems affecting leading economies since the outbreak of the Global Financial Crisis in 2007–09 – the return to secular stagnation or as it has been put in recent years, the 'productivity puzzle'. Julian Jessop addresses this puzzle by explaining how increased government intervention in markets in the last 15 years has led to slow economic and negligible productivity growth. The author focuses on the role played by innovation in free markets as the main driver of growth, and how stringent regulation has stifled innovation in recent years, which explains why the USA has outperformed the UK and other OECD economies. The author concludes that we should '(…) revert to these basic principles, including: lower and simpler taxation, especially of investment; reforms of the tax and benefit system to make work and entrepreneurship pay; deregulation (…); reducing barriers to international trade and cross-border investment; maintaining flexible policies on migration; market-based reforms of public services (notably the NHS in the UK), and the return of "sound money", with central banks re-focused on monetary stability'.

In the final two chapters of the book, we focus on regulation and the regulatory state. In Chapter 11, Cento Veljanovski (Case Associates) explains F. Hayek's 'competitive order' and the principles Hayek put forward to limit the growth of the regulatory state. The author explains the crucial role played by free competition in markets to address a fundamental information problem: 'Free competition gives rise to a "spontaneous order" which coordinates buyers' and sellers' actions to produce an efficient outcome over time. By "order" Hayek meant "system" rather than some stable state of affairs; what today would be called an "ecosystem." Instead of decentralised decisions causing chaos, free competition generates a "spontaneous order" in which the expectations of buyers and sellers are rendered mutually compatible, and which adapts quickly to the continuous changes in circumstances and new information and allows for experimentation and entrepreneurship'. Cento Veljanovski reflects on whether the limits and principles suggested by Hayek to limit the growth of the state (mainly the rule of law and the application of a cost-benefit analysis) are effective constraints or not.

In Chapter 12, Forrest Capie (Bayes Business School) and Geoffrey Wood (University of Buckingham) propose an alternative to government regulation in order to promote economic growth. The authors argue that 'this can be best achieved by reliance on governance not regulation, not by telling people what to do but by establishing incentives to induce them to behave in a desired manner'. Capie and Wood apply this distinction to the world of finance where firms spend a considerable amount of resources to comply with regulation and to innovate in order to circumvent regulation. They use three contemporary examples to highlight the flaws of the regulation in finance: the regulation of bank capital ratios under the 'Basil accords', the regulation of investment trusts, and the regulation of accounting standards.

Part I

Classical Liberalism

A Re-statement

1 Classical Liberalism Today

What It Must Be

Stephen Davies

1.1 Introduction

The term 'classical liberalism' is a widely used one, by both historians and analysts of contemporary politics. As such it has a generally agreed on referent although that is contested, not least by those who think it is unjustified. It is also a self-adopted identity or label for a current type of politics and political theory, so there are people who think of themselves as being classical liberals. What though does this actually mean in today's world? What kinds of outlook and beliefs would classical liberals have (assuming that this is an accurate of justified label or identity) at this historical conjuncture? If we are speaking of an intellectual and political tradition, then does it still make sense or is it something from a past era, no longer relevant?

Classical liberalism is a kind of politics both in theory and practice that has simultaneously a historical and a current meaning and referent. As such, it has changed and developed over time, but the core elements have remained constant, so we may speak of something that has persisted through time. The ideas and the approach and policy that they lead to are now needed more than ever before. This is despite, or even because of, the rise of a kind of politics that explicitly rejects it and its legacy. The need also comes from our being in a critical conjuncture, a moment of history in which a kind of politics and economy that has lasted for almost a century and a half is now drawing to a close. However, for classical liberalism to survive as an effective analysis and practice it will also have to change – or rather to revert, to rediscover much of what it once was. This involves abandoning or discarding much of what classical liberalism has come to be associated with and even identified with in the last 30 years or more (since roughly 1990).

1.2 Historical Classical Liberalism

The term 'classical liberalism' is contested (Losurdo, 2014). There is disagreement about exactly what it refers to and, in particular, as to whether it is an appropriate label for anything existing now. There is one meaning that is widely accepted, which is as a historical term. Used this way, classical liberalism refers to the various kinds of liberal thought and politics found between roughly the 1770s and the 1880s or 1890s. There was a great deal of variety within that, not least the contrast

DOI: 10.4324/9781003504412-3

between more cautious and limited types of liberal politics and more impatient and radical ones. Another difference was over the relation between equality and liberty. There were also definite variations at a national level, reflecting the specific circumstances and traditions of different parts of the world. All that said, there were a number of very pronounced commonalities so that we can reasonably speak of a single movement in ideas and politics but with several distinct manifestations.

What we should avoid is the kind of sectarianism found in the writings of later liberal writers such as Friedrich Hayek (1996). For him, classical liberalism was a movement found primarily in Britain in the late eighteenth and very early nineteenth centuries and marked by a sceptical view of knowledge and the capacity of human reason. By contrast, other movements, such as the Benthamite Philosophic Radicals and most continental liberals (especially the French, with a few exceptions such as Tocqueville), were not classical liberals for him and barely liberal in any sense. His view meant that he ignored the whole of nineteenth-century liberalism in Britain and elsewhere as a kind of falling away from the earlier, Whig, form. Hence, the absence of any attention to people such as Cobden, Spencer, or even Gladstone in his writings. This is a preposterously narrow definition of who should count as historical classical liberals, akin to the kind of sectarianism found among socialist sects more recently. His mentor Ludwig von Mises had a similar, if less stringent, kind of exclusivist definition (Mises, 2005). The reason was that people like Hayek were participating in an early to mid-twentieth-century debate as to what counted as true liberalism and their strategy was to define it very narrowly, in a way that excluded many people who were regarded as liberals, both by themselves and by others. This kind of sectarianism is not helpful for either historical understanding or clear thinking about what the core elements of liberalism were at that time and continue to be.

The main reason for seeing liberalism in the 1770 to 1890 period as a singular intellectual and political phenomenon is that there was a large body of ideas, programmes, and outlooks that were shared by all of the thinkers, movements, and individuals who either self-defined as liberals or were regarded as such by their contemporaries. In terms of taxonomy there are enough common features that are distinct and peculiar for us to count liberalism as a genus, if not a species (Bramstead and Melhuish, 1978; Salvadori, 1978; Rosenblatt, 2012). This in turn reflected another reality. Throughout that period all liberals faced opponents or interlocutors who were also identifiable as a singular category. These were what we may call 'classical conservatives'. The divide between conservatism and liberalism at that time was a single issue, with several aspects. This was whether to welcome the changes and novel phenomena that we collectively call modernity, or to resist them while trying to sustain or restore the historic old order (Weiss, 1977; Fawcett, 2022). The liberals supported modernity to a greater or lesser degree while the conservatives sought to resist it, again to a varying degree (Ruggiero, 1961). In this classic left-right divide the radical egalitarians concerned with the social question were on the same side as the liberals. They were however more impatient, less committed to constitutional politics, and believed that liberal modernity required major changes to a number of legal and social institutions. They were not however a substantial interlocutor for the classical liberals in the way that conservatives were. Liberalism before the 1880s was thus defined to a great extent by its opposition to the established old order and its defenders.

So, in the aftermath of the French Revolution and the wider 'Atlantic Revolution' of the later eighteenth century, a self-aware politics took shape in most parts of Europe. It is those movements and their ideas that the term 'classical liberal' refers to in the most widely agreed sense. To repeat, it makes sense to describe all of these movements, ideas, and individuals as being a single if varied entity or phenomenon because of certain common shared commitments and basic ideas. The most notable were the belief that liberty was the primary or central political good, and its realisation and instantiation the central purpose of politics; that this was because it was essential for a range of social and political goods, notably self-realisation and human flourishing, intellectual, social, and individual progress and improvement; and that politics as an activity should be defined by open discussion and debate, the deployment of reason, and the rule of law as opposed to either power or privilege (Kelley, 1990; Fawcett, 2018; Kahan, 2023). The last was associated with a distinctive kind of class theory, which drew a distinction between productive or industrious classes and idle or exploitative ones, the latter being those who owed their income and property to government power (Hart, 2016).

All of these were associated with specific values and institutions: freedom of speech and of conscience; the separation of church and state; free exchange and a more open market economy; constitutional and limited government along with reform of the institutions of government; a firm defence of civil rights for individuals, with strong support for property rights in particular; opposition to both peculiar rights or privileges and also legal disabilities for certain groups; political and religious pluralism; the so-called 'voluntary principle' in which the ideal social order was one formed by the free association of individuals and the further association of the groups and institutions so formed, in a bottom-up type of federalism (Bradley, 1980). All of this came to be developed or even discovered through a series of campaigns around specific issues, such as anti-slavery, free trade, peace, and anti-militarism, in favour of religious toleration and pluralism, and against censorship and restrictions on the dissemination of knowledge (as in the British case of the campaign against 'taxes on knowledge').

1.3 Later and Contemporary Classical Liberalism

The second common use of 'classical liberal' is as the label for people and movements that carried forward the original ideas and analyses of the classical period, after the 1890s. This is done by both friends and foes to distinguish them from the other forms that the original classical liberalism evolved into between the 1880s and the 1920s. During that period liberalism as both movement and idea underwent a number of intellectual changes and as a result the original singular classical liberalism developed into several novel or distinct forms. Simultaneously two other things happened. One was the emergence of socialism as a major political and intellectual force, along with a transformation in how the politics and practice of socialism were commonly understood (Wolfe, 1977; Clarke, 1978). This meant its emergence as a serious opponent of continuing liberalism, so liberals now had to confront more than just one kind of opponent. The other was the transformation of conservatism. With the clear and obvious failure of the classical conservative project by the end of the 1870s, a novel kind of right-wing politics emerged, one that accepted modernity, democracy, and the modern state but sought to use them for conservative ends (Klemperer, 2015). Liberals thus had to confront a different kind of right-wing politics, as well as a new one opponent on their other flank.

The intellectual and political shifts of the later nineteenth and early twentieth century produced two major liberal traditions, depending on which of the two interlocutors liberals chose to define themselves against. One was so-called 'New' or social liberalism, which defined itself against the new kind of right-wing politics and became supportive of both a more expansive role for government and an egalitarian redistribution of income and (sometimes) property. This kind of liberalism can be hard to distinguish from the non-revolutionary varieties of socialism (Freeden, 1986, 1988). The other major liberal tradition defined itself primarily in opposition to socialism and took on many moderate conservative arguments and sensibilities. Here it can be hard to distinguish such liberals from moderate conservatives, and, to add to the confusion, liberals of this kind were often found in nominally conservative parties (Green, 2002; O'Hara, 2011). There were other less prominent varieties of liberalism that emerged at this time (notably the combination of liberalism and nationalism) but these need not detain us here.

There were though liberals on both sides of the Atlantic who did not go down either of the routes just described. Instead, they attempted to carry forward the politics of the original classical liberals while adapting them to the novel conditions that had become clear by at least the 1890s, if not sooner. For some this was a matter of preserving the ideas and approach of the earlier period, but increasingly, during the 1920s and 1930s, this meant adapting and developing those ideas. The point though was to try and carry forward a kind of liberal politics that while new in some ways had clear continuity with the older classical liberalism and did not lean so strongly towards either socialism or the new right-wing politics as the two main varieties of post-1880 liberalism did. These are the self-defined classical liberals in the second sense.

Not everyone outside their own circles accepted this however, which is why this second use of the term is more controversial and contested (Robin, 2017). The critical take comes from socialists and (many) social liberals, who argue that despite their protestations the classical liberals are simply examples of another type of right-wing politics and should be put in the same basket or large category as conservative liberals and outright conservatives. This comes though from making the question of equality the defining one in politics, alongside the related question of the role of government in economic life. If one takes that perspective, then since both conservatives and classical liberals are anti-egalitarian (or at least opposed to redistribution), it makes sense to put them both on the right, since politics is seen as egalitarian left versus non-egalitarian right. There are however other questions in politics, which means that a one-dimensional spectrum of that kind does not capture reality. On these other questions, notably that of cultural conservatism versus ethical individualism and also innovation versus preference for the traditional, there are equally sharp divisions between the classical liberals and the conservatives and conservative liberals.

Classical liberalism therefore has a real meaning as the name of a current and continuing kind of liberal intellectual enquiry and politics, one distinct from both socialist egalitarianism and traditionalist conservatism and also from the other varieties of liberalism that lean towards one of those two other positions. It has been however a difficult position to maintain, both intellectually and politically, because of the gravitational pull of those two other positions. That in turn comes from a central feature of the politics of most of the last century, the way that issues of economics came to dominate political argument. All of that however is now changing. Just as the old world of the conflict between the classical right and left drew to a close at the end of the nineteenth and start of the twentieth century, so the politics of the twentieth century are fading. Given that, what kind of future is there for classical liberalism as both enquiry and political project?

1.4 The Situation Facing Contemporary Classical Liberals – The Politics

The starting point for addressing that question has to be an examination of the situation the world and, therefore by definition, classical liberals find themselves in. The short answer is that things are bad and clearly getting worse, by a number of metrics, and in ways that pose huge challenges for all kinds of liberal. We can identify eight constituent elements of the present situation of mounting crisis for liberals. Three of these relate to current politics and geopolitics. The other five are structural factors or forces that are driving the first three. Their structural quality makes them more troubling and challenging because they represent changes at the level of the *longue durée* which means they are barely amenable if at all to being changed or redirected by human effort. It is rather a matter of coming to terms with them and making the best of them.

The first political phenomenon we can see has been given several labels, but the commonest is 'the crisis or death of neoliberalism'. This refers to a major shift in the position of the median voter on a number of issues and collectively a repudiation of the policy consensus that came into being during the 1980s and which has dominated politics since the early 1990s (Bowman et al, 2014; Wolf, 2024). This includes such things as a growing support for protectionism and national industrial policy and a rejection of free trade and exchange, rising support for public ownership of large parts of the economy and for a more interventionist and activist government generally, and, most strikingly, vehement hostility to both the phenomenon of migration and towards actual migrants. This is often combined with a cult of a 'strongman' leader (Rachman, 2023). All of this translates into support for an increase in authoritarian measures and a growth in state power in all areas, not just the economic (in fact a growth in state power in economic areas inevitably means its increase elsewhere, as classical liberals have always argued) (Kukathas,

2021). Neoliberalism is the label given to the dominant policy suite of the last 30–40 years. Sometimes it is used as a synonym for free-market capitalism, but it has a more precise and substantive meaning. In particular it refers to the idea of markets and market relations not as spontaneously arising out of voluntary human action and interaction but as a kind of technical construct, designed and created by governments or rather by expert technocrats, and to a policy position in which governments should engineer or create markets in as many areas of life as possible (Steger and Roy, 2021). The problem for classical liberals in particular is that this outlook and set of policies is thought to come from a capture of the policy process by classical liberals when in fact it comes from a very different kind of ideas and politics. To add to this problem many contemporary classical liberals themselves agree with that identification and it is true that the policy regime of the last 30 years or so was initiated by people inspired by classical liberal thought, although it was not what they intended or anticipated. This all comes from a misreading of recent history, as we shall see.

The second political phenomenon of the present conjuncture is related to the first and is no less threatening. This is the breakdown or increasing deliquescence of the international order. This order, which governs everything from trade to investment flows to international travel and migration to international law and regulations of all kinds, was created slowly after World War II, through a series of international treaties and agreements and the creation of a number of institutions, notably the General Agreement on Tariffs and Trade (GATT), the World Bank, and the International Monetary Fund (IMF). It was driven by the deliberate policy of the United States but with active support from Western Europe and Japan. Initially this took place in the context of the Cold War competition with the Soviet bloc, but after 1990 it became truly global and was intensified and extended by a number of agreements such as the North American Free Trade Area (NAFTA)and the creation of the European Union at Maastricht, and the creation of the World Trade Organization. All of this is now clearly coming apart and the Economist magazine has warned that it is now so fragile that it could suddenly completely collapse at any moment (Economist Magazine, 2024).

The crisis of the supranational legal and regulatory order is partly driven by the decline of its counterpart in military affairs and international relations, which was a set of security arrangements underpinned by the power, military, political and financial, of the United States and NATO. This has faced a number of increasingly serious challenges in the last two decades due to a number of failed ventures in nation building and remaking of the social and political order in several parts of the world. It now faces an existential challenge in the war in Ukraine with an even more threatening one on the horizon in the shape of a possible confrontation between the United States and China over Taiwan. At present (Spring 2024) the signs are not good as to the outcome of this challenge. The war in Ukraine has exposed the weakness and limitations of many of the military systems of NATO and even more in the manufacturing base behind it. It has also conclusively demonstrated the weakness of the supposed financial supremacy of the US-Europe-Japan alliance (Ferguson, 2004; Todd, 2004).

None of this means that a new paramount power or alliance is about to emerge. It does not mean for example that if the supremacy of the dollar ends then a new reserve currency will appear. Far more likely is what is often called a multi-polar world. This will actually be a reversion to the historical norm, of European history since the Renaissance and of world history since the early eighteenth. It will be, in other words, a return to the kinds of conditions and relations found in the nineteenth century up to 1914 – but with the added spice of nuclear weapons. In monetary terms, if the dollar ceases to be the general reserve currency the likely outcome is not its replacement but a reversion to the conditions of the inter-war period, when there was no dominant currency.

The third aspect of the present world political conjuncture, which grows out of the previous two but also drives them, is the emergence of an explicitly and foundationally anti-liberal politics (Rose, 2021). Since the defeat of fascism in World War II liberals of all kinds saw the main threat to liberal values and principles as coming from the revolutionary socialist/communist left (they disagreed about how to respond of course). After the fall of the Berlin Wall some assumed that now there were no true systemic opponents left and that we had arrived at the 'end of history'. That belief did not last long. Now though, a novel kind of politics is appearing in one country after another, not least the United States. This kind of politics is in many ways a recrudescence of a much older type of politics, the kind of novel right-wing politics that emerged after the defeat of classical conservatism, during the Belle Epoque and later. It combines popular majoritarian democracy with cultural traditionalism, nationalism, economic dirigisme and collectivism, authoritarianism, and rejection of a supranational rules-based order in favour of national sovereignty (Hazony, 2018, 2022). As found in the speeches of people as different in other ways as Viktor Orban and Narendra Modi all of these themes appear and are explicitly presented as being 'post'- or 'anti'-liberal.

1.5 The Situation Facing Contemporary Classical Liberals – Structural Shifts

What then are the structural factors? The first, which people are only starting to become aware of, is the decline and fading away of economic growth, in one part of the world after another. Economic growth rates in the G7 and the OECD countries have been declining for about two decades. In several wealthy developed countries, it appears to have effectively stopped – Japan, Italy, and (since 2008) the United Kingdom are examples (Martin, 2017). The figures for the growth that we do have are also misleading because of the way different regions and sectors are aggregated to arrive at a national figure. In the United Kingdom, for example, almost all of the growth that took place in the decade before 2008 happened in just one place – Greater London – and in a very small number of sectors. These were basically FIRE (finance, insurance, real estate) plus tech and communications. That has now stopped. In the United States right now the average growth figures look impressive but much of this comes purely from (often wasteful and corrupt) government spending and the rest is again sectionally and geographically limited. This explains the finding, which baffles economists, that most Americans are depressed about their economic state and prospects, despite the headline figures saying that the economy is growing rapidly.

A number of observers, notably the OECD and the World Bank, have predicted that economic growth will cease or be very low in most of the developed world (Kose and Ohnsorge, 2023). There are a number of reasons for this, none of which are easy to reverse. One is the combination of very low birth rates (and hence a declining population absent immigration) with an ageing population. Another is a decline in innovation, particularly if it is measured per capita (Park et al, 2023). Related to this is the reality that while quite radical innovations continue to be made in some areas, these do not appear to have the productivity enhancing and transformative effects of earlier waves of innovation, notably the one that took place at the end of the nineteenth century and created the world we live in (Cowen, 2011). The world economy as a whole will continue to grow to the end of this century and beyond, but most of this growth will happen in lower-income countries. There are two main reasons for this: there is a great scope there for catch-up growth, in which relatively small investments and introduction of technologies bring major productivity gains; these parts of the world still have a growing and youthful population (although their birth rates have declined even more precipitously than elsewhere, the age distribution means they will still grow for some time). This all suggests that East Asia will continue to grow for a while before stagnating and that the last two areas where we can expect growth to persist are South Asia and Sub-Saharan Africa.

This though leads on to the second structural phenomenon shaping today's world and that of the next few decades. This is mass migration from the South of the planet to the North. This is already driving much of the political turn described earlier and will do so even more in the coming decades, unless the phenomenon itself is understood and responded to effectively and in a way that preserves the liberal settlement. Right now, a popular trope on the emergent right is that this phenomenon of migration is the product of deliberate political choice and therefore in some sense designed. This moves rapidly on to the conspiracy theory of the 'great replacement', that there is a nefarious and deliberate conspiracy by 'globalist elites' to replace the indigenous population of Europe and North America by people from the global South (Camus, 2011). The reality is that this is a spontaneous emergent phenomenon and not the product of design or policy. It is the aggregate or collective outcome of millions of individual decisions made by particular human beings, to move and relocate themselves and, ultimately, their families, and by other people to employ them and trade with them. The only conscious political choice is to not resist this spontaneous process. What though creates the incentives that lead so many to make such decisions? There are two reasons. One is entirely bad, the other is the effects of something that most would correctly say is good, at least from a liberal or progressive perspective.

The first is the progressive collapse of political authority and civil order in a range of countries in a huge arc, stretching from Central Asia across the Middle East and then right across the Northern third of Africa. In this region many states have failed and many that still function have limited capacity and are fragile and deteriorating (see https://fragilestatesindex.org). This displaces large number of people. The point is that even if conditions in developed countries are made as hard and unwelcoming as possible, they will still be more attractive than living in a part of the world with no functioning infrastructure and where the rule of law has broken down. The other factor is the consequence of something good, which is the transformation of agrarian economies over the last 50 years. This is commercialising agriculture and the wider rural economy right across the global South. It is this that caused the dramatic and unprecedentedly rapid decline in global extreme poverty since the 1960s, so that the proportion of the world's population living on an income of $1.75 a day or less has gone from over 50% to less than 10%.

The problem though is this. Firstly, the increased productivity in agriculture, which is the main process driving this, means that there are far fewer farmers needed. Right now, there are about three billion people who depend upon some form of subsistence or near subsistence agriculture either directly or indirectly. As agriculture becomes more productive almost all of them will become redundant. They will no longer be able to support themselves in the global countryside, the rural South of the planet (Amin, 2019). They will migrate, most of them to the rapidly growing urban areas of the South. A minority, but very large in absolute terms, will look to move to the developed world. Secondly the commercialisation and marketisation of rural society in the poorer parts of the world fundamentally changes the living conditions and incentives of the people who live there. The bulk of the people living on very low cash incomes by the World Bank's estimates were not living in total destitution. Rather, most of them were living in a non-cash and non-monetised economy – so not having much of a cash income was not such a serious matter in terms of access to vital resources such as food, clothing, and shelter. This way of life was very restrictive in terms of personal choice, but it was relatively secure. The move to a market exchange and cash-based economy expands horizons and increases the range of opportunities, but it also means that not having much of a cash income becomes something really bad, a literal matter of life and death. A very small number of subsistence farmers will become successful commercial farmers. Most though will have to move into other kinds of activity. The lack of fixed capital and the dysfunctionality of many states in these parts of the world means that there is a very strong push factor for migration to the developed parts of the world – for now at least.

The third structural factor is increasingly acute Malthusian constraints. This is not a matter of running out of resources such as metals, water, or most prominently, oil. Rather it is that the marginal cost of the production needed for a range of activities to continue at their present level and certainly for them to grow continues to rise. The problem is that the price required to generate the level of supply needed for a range of activities will destroy demand, plus many of the activities in question do not make sense at the margin at the price level that generates enough supply. The result, which we can see very clearly in oil and other energy prices since 2007, is for any uptick in global activity and growth to trigger price rises which then lead to a slowdown in growth which then in turn triggers a price crash. The big problem is that because stable and higher prices cannot be confidently expected there is no incentive for the kind of investment needed to sustain an expanded supply. All this in turn feeds into both recurrent economic disruption and the slowdown in growth mentioned earlier.

The fourth structural factor is getting a great deal of attention right now, with a surprisingly wide consensus across the ideological spectrum as to both its nature and what needs to be done (even if that is difficult). This is the social and cultural transformation that began in the later 1960s with mass television and has progressed since then with 24-hour programming and multiple channels through cable and satellite, to the internet and thence to social media in all its guises. When linked to the other aspects of the computing and information revolutions, and emergent technologies such as AI, the result is a transformation of the social life of humans in a profound way. The results of this were predicted with astonishing prescience by a number of observers in the 1960s, notably Marshall McLuhan, and the Situationists such as Debord, and later by others such as Postman (Postman, 1987; Debord, 1994; McLuhan, 2001). The growing consensus is that many or most of the effects of all this have been malign, from an epidemic of stress and anxiety among young people, to the hollowing out of politics as a process and activity, and the corruption of public discourse (Haidt, 2024).

The final structural force we can observe is an increasingly acute problem of excessive complexity in most developed societies. In simple terms life and the institutions through which it is organised are too complex and also too efficient. The point about complexity is the one made by Tainter in his now-classic work (Tainter, 1988). Social complexity, arising in response to challenges, enables society to surmount those challenges and become more productive. However, it also brings costs and is subject to a process of diminishing marginal returns. Eventually greater complexity actually brings negative returns for society as a whole, even if it still gives benefits to a minority. Excessively complex systems and processes in this sense are also typically dysfunctional, they simply do not work effectively in terms of getting things done, because of knowledge problems and delayed or even non-existent decision-making. The problem with excessive efficiency is that if a system has no slack or redundancy/spare capacity it will not be able to cope with any kind of departure from the medium to long-term average of pressures or challenges. This became very clear in a range of areas from healthcare and hospitals to supply chains and 'just in time' production systems during the COVID-19 pandemic, when they were unable to deal with the challenges posed by an abnormal stress or shock and, in many cases, simply seized up.

The structural forces briefly described pose a massive challenge to any kind of political process and to liberal politics in particular. The stresses that are mounting are leading to the political developments laid out before that. What all of this means is that liberalism of all kinds faces a profound and difficult challenge. That is to address the structural challenges in a way that deals with the more immediate political threats at both the national and international level and to do so in a way that preserves the system of modern liberty created by the classical liberals of the nineteenth century. The challenge is particularly acute for the continuity classical liberals because they are blamed by many for the mounting crisis. This is unfair and inaccurate, for several reasons, but it is plausible because of the way politics developed during the Cold War in most Western democracies and the turn it took after the 1970s. What though was this and how did we arrive at a situation of mounting challenges to classical liberalism in particular and increasingly liberal politics of all varieties?

1.6 How We Got Here – The Cold War and the Homogenisation of Ideologies

One way of answering that question would be to examine the way the structural shifts briefly set out have developed and exerted increasing stress on the system, since roughly the 1970s. We do not have space for that however; so the main focus is on the way liberal thought and policy responded to those challenges as well as those posed by the rival totalitarian system of Soviet communism. This led to apparent triumph, not least, it seemed, for resurgent classical liberals, but in fact it led to the current political impasse.

The prolonged confrontation between liberal democracies and their Soviet rival was thankfully not resolved through a military confrontation (which would have been truly catastrophic) thanks to the successful policy of containment. However, the Cold War had a profound effect on political thought and practice in the democratic west, which was to their detriment, even if they were ultimately victorious (Moyn, 2023). The Cold War led to a flattening out and homogenisation of politics, found in all countries and affecting all ideologies and political traditions, including classical liberalism. The great variety of ideologies that had appeared at the end of the nineteenth century was dramatically reduced with several of them, such as radical individualism and libertarian socialism, effectively disappearing. Others lost their distinctive quality and became assimilated to the mainstream of Cold War politics. This happened for example to Christian Democracy, which lost its distinctive Catholic elements and became merely another indistinguishable form of liberal conservatism. Among conservatives and socialists, the distinctive forms of those traditions, traditionalist conservatism and classical social democracy, faded away and they became essentially forms of moderate and social liberalism, respectively.

A similar process happened on the side of anti-systemic politics with the result that by the 1960s there were only two broad kinds of politics left – Soviet style socialism and Cold War liberalism. The latter could be divided into three subvarieties, a left-wing variant influenced by social democracy, a right-wing one influenced by moderate conservatism, and a small continuing tradition of classical liberalism that carried forward the traditions of liberalism from before 1914. This process of homogenisation was if anything accelerated after the end of the Cold War, so by the 1990s politics in most democracies was dominated by a uniform kind of deracinated liberalism with politics as an activity reduced to a debate within that tradition. The intensity of those debates should not hide from us the narrowness and limited nature of the field of conflict.

The classical liberals were a minority tradition in all of this, but they did not escape the effects of the processes described. The pressure of the bipolar politics of the era pushed most towards an assimilation with the moderate conservative wing of Cold War liberalism, no matter how they resisted it. At the same time, they like all of the other democratic forms of politics were affected by two other aspects of the homogenisation of politics that happened after roughly 1950. One was the steady movement towards a kind of technocratic managerialism. In this way of thinking, politics as a process was about meritocratic experts analysing defined social problems and devising policies (various forms of the exercise of state and managerial power in other words) to address and resolve them. This suppressed or concealed the normative element of politics and also the reality and extent of social conflicts that politics should aim to resolve. It made it a debate over which precise tool kit or approach the managerial class should use.

Alongside this was the way that economics and economic issues came to totally dominate politics as both an intellectual and practical activity. Other kinds of political question, which had also been a part of public and intellectual debate before the 1950s, faded away or were recast as economic questions – or more often challenges of economic management. This can be seen for example in the way that welfare politics were discussed where the economic arguments about things such as costs and incentive effects overshadowed and replaced the kinds of ethical and sociological arguments that had featured in earlier debates, between for example the Webbs and the Bosanquets (McBriar, 1995). The emphasis on economics and on questions of production and distribution and economic management made growth the central and dominant question in politics. The debates came to focus on the questions of how to achieve economic growth, how to increase it, and how to distribute the products of that growth. Everything almost came to be seen through that lens.

The continuing classical liberal tradition was deeply impacted by this, not least because so many of its leading figures were economists (as opposed to people from other disciplines such as history, or activities such as art, music, and literature). The primary effect was that much of the tradition inherited from the earlier nineteenth- and early twentieth-century liberals was forgotten or discarded. In particular, radical ideas and insights such as the voluntary principle and radical federalism, classical liberal class theory, and the classical liberal theory of peace and international relations developed by Cobden and others were allowed to fade from memory. Classical liberal thought, particularly among economists and philosophers, came to be dominated by a strong defence of free markets as opposed to central planning, and resistance to arguments for redistribution of the products of growth deriving from models of social justice. It came to be seen as identical with and defined by its economic component so that economic liberalism and classical liberalism became for many complete synonyms. The rest of the tradition was pushed into the intellectual equivalent of a large locked wardrobe, like discarded clothing, and mostly forgotten.

1.7 The Neoliberal Project and What It Became

This matters for the current position of the classical liberal tradition in the context described earlier. During the 1970s classical liberals benefitted from the crisis of the Keynesian post-war settlement, which confirmed the criticisms they had made of it as economic policy. This enabled them to exert greater influence on the right side of the divide within Cold War liberalism (Cockett, 1994). At the end of that decade governments came to power in Westminster and Washington that were motivated by the economic agenda of the surviving classical liberals, to a considerable extent. What though were they trying to achieve and what did they actually end up bringing about? The danger here is to look at what resulted from the revived classical liberal turn in politics and policy in the 1980s and to conclude that this was what the politicians and intellectuals involved had intended and aimed at. This was not the case. Rather, after initial success, they found that they had acted as midwives for a political turn of a different kind, one that intensified the trends of the Cold War era.

The initial aim of politicians such as Thatcher and Reagan, and their intellectual mentors, was to reverse the shift in policy that had taken place with the New Deal in the 1930s and the Attlee government in the 1940s and to return to an updated version of the settlement that Attlee and Roosevelt had overthrown – the 1920s in the American case, the 1930s in the British. The initial idea was that this would involve a rolling back of state power, a reduction in state functions. This, it was thought, would leave a space for free private activity. The whole process was conceived of in largely negative terms – it was a case of government becoming smaller and getting out of the way to that spontaneous social and economic processes could take place – with no predetermined idea of what they might produce. Another important aspect of their politics was that it aimed at a reversion to the kind of national based capitalism that had been predominant from the 1920s up to their own time (the 1970s) but with less government as part of the mix.

This is not what happened. By the end of the 1980s and early 1990s it became increasingly clear that the reforms of the 1980s had produced something unexpected, not what people like Thatcher and Reagan or Friedman and Hayek had anticipated or intended. In the first place the size of government, as measured by the share of GDP accounted for by government spending, had not declined (Burton, 1985). This had a number of causes, but the main one was that while the economic classical liberals had won the argument about how best to organise production, they had lost the debate over the rules for the distribution of the product. This meant the triumph of the egalitarian social liberals, such as Dworkin and Rawls and, in practical terms, the extension of state welfare into a massive and costly system of income transfers.

Secondly, the project underwent a profound change in its nature from the later 1980s. We may capture this by saying that it shifted from being a (limited) classical liberal one to a neoliberal one. What we can see is the emergence of the kind of neoliberal policy suite and set of arguments described earlier. This was fully rolled out and implemented not by administrations such as those of Thatcher and Reagan but by their successors, Blair and Brown in the United Kingdom and Clinton in the United States. It was at this point also that this kind of neoliberalism succeeded in a range of other countries, notably Germany under Schroeder, and became embedded in a range of international institutions, such as the IMF and the World Bank in the shape of the so-called 'Washington Consensus' – the 'Golden Straitjacket' as Thomas Friedman dubbed it (Friedman, 2000).

How though was this a departure from the initial project of Thatcher and Reagan and the intellectuals who inspired them? That project was about undoing the social democratic turn of the mid-twentieth century and 'getting government out of the way' of spontaneous market processes. The reality after about 1990, both intellectual and practical, was of the deliberate use of political power through legislation and regulations to design and create market processes and institutions. These were now seen not as natural or spontaneous phenomena but as designed and created institutions and regimes. It was a shift from the classical liberal idea of a spontaneous social order with a limited sphere of politics to a social order designed and administered by technocratic experts and managers. The sphere of democratic politics was still drastically reduced but politics as such (collective decision-making backed by power) was not. It simply became the domain of civil servants, regulators, central bankers, and experts rather than politicians and the voters they represented.

Some would argue that this trajectory was always implicit in the original classical liberal project. The most radical version of that argument is the one made by Karl Polanyi, that right from the start the liberal project involved the use of political power to create a market economy (Polanyi, 2002). The more limited one is that the original project of people like Hayek, in the 1938 Colloque Lipmann and later the Mont Pelerin Society, was one of that kind. The work of Burgin suggests that for Hayek and others this was not true but that this was a strong element in the thinking of others, notably many of the German Ordoliberals and, on the other side of the Atlantic, the Chicago School as represented by Milton Friedman. The point though is that by the early 1990s it was the constructivist thinking of the Chicago School that had become the public face of classical liberalism (Burgin, 2015).

This partly reflected intellectual developments within the academy, such as the rise to dominance within academic economics of a highly abstract neoclassicism. It also came from social developments that were facilitated by some of the policy changes the governments of the 1980s had brought about but which were not the anticipated or intended outcome of those changes. The main one was the transformation of global capitalism that followed the collapse of the Bretton Woods system and the response to it inspired by people such as Milton Friedman. The two main elements were a move to floating exchange rates and the abolition of controls on the movement of capital. The thinking was that this would lead to a stable but dynamic relationship between national economies and to a stable monetary policy within countries with monetary sovereignty. In reality it enabled two quite different things.

The first was a movement away from the national capitalism of the first two-thirds of the twentieth century to a truly global and networked capitalism, built around flows and exchanges between metropolitan city regions. Increasingly these had closer connections with each other than with their own geographical hinterlands. This process was also driven in part by the communications revolution alluded to earlier but the freeing up of financial flows and the abolition of fixed exchange rates was a necessary condition for it to happen. The second phenomenon was the process usually described as 'financialisation', in which pure finance and the manipulation of money became the central activity of capitalist economies (as opposed to an important part). This again was helped by technological innovations but would not have happened without reforms of the financial system and in particular allowing private banks vastly expanded scope to create credit and to monetise an ever-wider range of debts and assets.

All of this has had results that would dismay Friedman if he were alive now. In particular, it has severely undermined the integrity of the price system and the validity of the prices of major asset classes. It has also led to an increasing movement away from profit and towards rent as the most desirable kind of income, transforming many kinds of business activity from profit seeking to rent seeking. In this process business organisations and activities are redefined simply as assets rather than as activities and institutions that organise factors of production towards the defined end of producing a good or service. It is worth emphasising that this was all predicted at the time by other classical liberals who were critical of Friedman, notably Charles Kindleberger, Jacques Rueff, and Alan Mundell (Kindleberger, 1981). We now retrospectively see the policy debate of the 1970s and 1980s as a two-way one between Keynesians (social democrats) and Monetarists (classical liberals) when in fact there were at least three other groups – other classical liberals such as Kindleberger, radical post Keynesians such as Hyman Minsky and Wynne Godley, and Friedrich Hayek who had a distinctive position of his own.

These changes have interacted with the slower structural shifts outlined earlier to produce the three political features of the contemporary world, particularly the first one, the demise of neoliberalism. The great danger is that classical liberalism itself or even all kinds of liberalism will be dragged down by the rise of the anti-liberal politics that are arising as a response (the third political feature). In addition to the issues already alluded to we can add several others. The most significant are firstly a worldwide crisis of real estate valuations in major metropolitan areas. This is made worse by the deadly combination of high demand and restricted supply but these only exacerbate the ultimate cause, the financialisation of metropolitan housing and its transformation into an investment good not a consumption one. The second is the whole array of issues associated with energy policy and climate change while the third is a growing crisis of the meritocracy due to elite overproduction – the appearance of what is now called 'woke' and used to be called 'political correctness' is a by-product of that (Turchin, 2023).

1.8 What Should Classical Liberals (and Liberals Generally) Be and Do Now?

All of this means that liberals of all kinds are facing a very challenging future, the darkest for the cause of a free and open society since the 1930s. The central reality is that all kinds of politics are moving into a world defined by limits, above all the fading away of growth. This poses challenges which, so far, no political tradition has confronted. Events though will leave them no choice. In that situation what should classical liberals become? What should they do? The classical liberal project and liberalism more generally going forward will have to be built around the following main elements.

The first is coming to terms with the nature and legacy of the neoliberal project with which liberalism and classical liberalism in particular have come to be identified. The analogy is with the challenge for traditional socialists and social democrats of clarifying their relationship to the Soviet project and critiquing it or for Keynesian liberals of recognising the intellectual and policy problems of the immediate post-war settlement. This means a clear-eyed evaluation and understanding of exactly what happened during the years after 1979–80 and how it came to produce a policy regime that everyone can now see has failed and is also clearly not in accord with the central philosophy or principles of classical liberalism. In particular, there has to be a repudiation of the monetary policies followed since the mid-1990s, and a recognition of the disastrous consequences they have had. More generally, there must be a repudiation of the move to a regime of technocratic expertise, and expert and procedure led governance. Instead, there needs to be a rediscovery of collective popular agency, whether political in the form of representative democracy or more widely in the shape of voluntary collective action of all kinds (Ostrom, 1994; Ostrom and Ostrom, 2014; see also Wall, 2017; Nordman, 2021).

The second is reemphasising the nature of classical liberalism as a politics of scepticism and acceptance of limits. Fantasies of remaking the world to a liberal design should be firmly set aside. This means giving up on grand designs but also questioning or abandoning notions of automatic progress or teleological evolution in history. The acceptance of limits means coming to terms with the structural constraints described earlier, as they press with increasing force on the room for manoeuvre of human beings, and humanity in general. It means thinking seriously about how to make sense of and live well in a world in which growth has become difficult or impossible to achieve and in which, because of the excessive complexity identified earlier, the experience of politics (and much private life) is that 'nothing works' (Calafati et al, 2023). Improvement rather than progress should become the new guiding idea.

This may seem difficult, not least because of the ways in which classical liberalism has come to be justified mainly by its economic results, as a way to achieve growth and rising living standards. In fact, as generations of liberals of all kinds have argued, that is not the real justification for liberalism, it is rather a pleasant bonus. Moreover, the classical liberal tradition in particular is well suited to the challenges of a world of limits, scarcity, and the increasing recognition of the limits of human capacity and reason. The third element of a renewed classical liberalism today is in many ways a reversion to the original classical liberalism of the nineteenth century and the insights of people like the classical economists. This is a renewed concern with the questions and analyses that were central for liberal thought before economic growth and large managerial and procedure guided institutions became manifest. It will also mean recovering many of the ideas, arguments, and insights that were abandoned or forgotten during the years of the Cold War such as class theory, radical ideas about international relations, and the wide implications and application of the 'voluntary principle'.

The central part of that, which should be the fourth ingredient for a revived classical liberalism, is scepticism about the effectiveness of and need for large, hierarchically structured, and procedure-driven organisations of all kinds and not just government (Yadav, 2023). This is an extension of Hayek's insights about the nature and limitations of human knowledge beyond their original target of government and economic planning to large institutions in general. This involves a critique of both the ideas and practice of managerialism (not the same thing as management). The other side of this is rediscovery and reassertion of the idea and practice of radical bottom-up federalism on the voluntary principle. It also means rediscovering the original classical liberals' thinking about social welfare and ideas about mutual aid (collective self-help and mutualism) and effective philanthropy.

Another insight of earlier classical liberals, including Hayek, is the fifth element. This is scepticism about scientism, the mistaken application and extension of the techniques and models of science to areas of life where that is not appropriate, and the conflation of scientific hypothesis with judgment (Hayek, 1991; Hine, 2024). Even more widely there is the need for greater scepticism about the very idea of scientific progress as a simple 'good thing' and a questioning of the unexamined belief that if something is technologically and economically feasible, then it must happen. One part of this is recognising the threat that certain feasible technological developments pose to the humane or the very concept of humanity (Fukuyama, 2006).

This connects to the sixth element, the recovery of classical liberal social thought (as opposed to strictly economic). As an intellectual project with practical applications this involves, inter alia, a fundamental critique of meritocracy and the related idea of social mobility. The positive aspect is the rediscovery of the classical liberal argument for the equal respect and dignity for all kinds of work and for all non-predatory ways of living (Lasch, 1991). Related to that is another idea and practice that should be disinterred, that of the 'democratic intellect', the idea of an elevated culture and conversation that is open to all and which is not confined to a specific place (mainly the academy) or the preserve of distinct and supposedly superior social groups (academics and experts) (Davie, 2013; Rose, 2021).

Finally, and following from that, classical liberals need to rediscover the interest, once central, in the study and exploration of forms of culture and ways of living at a personal and collective level, including norms and models of personal conduct (Jarvis, 1997). This requires the development or rather the rediscovery of something once central but long abandoned, a cultural politics or metapolitics concerned with sensibilities and ways of living that operate at the level before explicit politics. Since the 1920s only a few people and tendencies within liberal thought and practice have sustained an interest and concern with this, most notably Objectivists, but this is an area of vital importance, not least because of the way much of the emergent rival politics of the right is focussed on it.

What all of these, along with the emerging political challenge, means is a reunification of liberalism, with a rapprochement between the different varieties that the original singular liberalism of the classical period fractured into between roughly 1890 and 1920. Another way of thinking of this is a reconciliation of classical and moderate liberalism with the social liberalism that formed at that time. On the other side, moderate or conservative liberals as both a political and intellectual movement are already at a moment of decision as the new kind of politics consolidates. Many will choose the conservative part of their heritage and become part of the new right-wing and anti-liberal politics that is emerging strongly everywhere. Others will reaffirm their liberal identity. With the social and classical liberals, the key to this process of intellectual reconciliation is a rethinking on both sides of the issue that was at the root of the original divergence and has remained so ever since – the debate over equality, social welfare, and private power. Recently a number of scholars such as John Tomasi have argued from a classical liberal perspective that the differences (between for example Hayek and Rawls) are not as great as often imagined (Tomasi, 2013). Similarly, Jacob Levy has made the case from a classical liberal perspective for rethinking the liberal view of the position and standing of institutions and ways of life that are not created by government and have spontaneously developed but which restrict human flourishing (Levy, 2017). These are difficult questions for liberals, but their resolution is essential to the continued existence and development of a liberal politics in the world we are now in.

The practical political aspect of all this has to have one thing at its centre for classical liberals. This is realising and accepting that the century long alliance with conservatives and the democratic right, which was intensified during the Cold War, is over. The new kind of anti-liberal politics is now the main opponent and interlocutor, for liberals of all kinds – as its prominent advocates and theorists make clear (Deneen, 2019; Ahmari, 2022; Hazony, 2022). This is another way in which we are returning to something more like the politics of the nineteenth century but updated. The very acute practical questions that this politics will revolve around are ones to do with migration, the ideas of national identity and sovereignty, and the question of international relations and international order. It is clear that the attempt to create a supranational order underpinned by a hegemonic power or empire is close to failure. The pressing need to is to understand this and to achieve a different response to the challenge of competing and clashing national sovereignties otherwise the kind of collapse that happened after 1914 will be revisited. In this connection, the time is ripe to revive another element of radical classical liberal thought, one that was further developed by many democratic socialists, that of personal cultural autonomy and the separation of territory and sovereignty, or radical political pluralism.

The goal of any classical liberal politics now has to be modest. The goal must be simply to conserve and preserve the liberal civilisation and institutions created and sustained by earlier generations of liberals. This means coming to terms with the recent past and rediscovering arguments, insights, and principles that have been forgotten or obscured by the twentieth century's focus on the economic. This is needed more than ever.

References

Ahmari, Sohrab (2022) *The Unbroken Thread: Discovering the Wisdom of Tradition in an Age of Chaos*. London: Hodder & Stoughton.

Amin, Samir (2019) *The Liberal Virus: Permanent War and the Americanisation of the World*. New York, NY: Monthly Review Press.

Bowman, Andrew et al (2014) *The End of the Experiment? From Competition to the Foundational Economy*. Manchester: Manchester University Press.

Bradley, Ian (1980) *The Optimists: Themes and Personalities in Victorian Liberalism*. London: Faber.

Bramstead, E. K. & Melhuish, K. J. (1978) *Western Liberalism: A History in Documents from Locke to Croce*. London: Longman.

Burgin, Angus (2015) *The Great Persuasion: Reinventing Markets since the Great Depression*. Cambridge, MA: Harvard University Press.

Burton, John (1985) *Why No Cuts?* London: Institute of Economic Affairs.

Calafati, Luca et al (2023) *When Nothing Works: From Cost of Living to Foundational Liveability*. Manchester: Manchester University Press.

Camus, Renaud (2011) *Le Grand Remplacement*. Paris: David Reinharc.

Clarke, Peter (1978) *Liberals and Social Democrats*. Cambridge: Cambridge University Press.

Cockett, Richard (1994) *Thinking the Unthinkable. Think Tanks and the Economic Counter-Revolution, 1931–1983*. London: HarperCollins.

Cowen, Tyler (2011) *The Great Stagnation: How America Ate All the Low-Hanging Fruit of Modern History, Got Sick and Will (Eventually) Feel Better*. London: E. P. Dutton.

Davie, George Elder (2013, 1st pub 1961) *The Democratic Intellect: Scotland and Her Universities in the Nineteenth Century*. Edinburgh: Edinburgh University Press.

Debord, Guy (1994, 1st pub 1968) *The Society of the Spectacle*. London: Rebel Press.

Deneen, Patrick J. (2019) *Why Liberalism Failed*. New Haven, CT: Yale University Press.

Economist Magazine (2024) "The Liberal International Order Is Slowly Coming Apart: Its Collapse Could Be Sudden and Irreversible", 9 May 2024. https://www.economist.com/leaders/2024/05/09/the-liberal-international-order-is-slowly-coming-apart#

Fawcett, Edmund (2018, 1st pub 2015) *Liberalism: The Life of an Idea*. 2nd Edition. Princeton, NJ: Princeton University Press.

Fawcett, Edmund (2022) *Conservatism: The Fight for a Tradition*. Princeton, NJ: Princeton University Press.

Ferguson, Niall (2004) *Colossus: The Rise and Fall of the American Empire*. London: Penguin.

Freeden, Michael (1986) *The New Liberalism: An Ideology of Social Reform*. Oxford: Oxford University Press.

Freeden, Michael (ed.) (1988) *J. A. Hobson: A Reader*. London: Unwin Hyman.

Friedman, Thomas (2000) *The Lexus and the Olive Tree*. London: HarperCollins.

Fukuyama, Francis (2006) *Our Posthuman Future: Consequences of the Biotechnology Revolution*. London: Profile Books.

Green, E. H. H. (2002) *Ideologies of Conservatism: Conservative Political Ideas in the Twentieth Century*. Oxford: Oxford University Press.

Haidt, Jonathan (2024) *The Anxious Generation: How the Great Rewiring of Childhood Is Causing an Epidemic of Mental Illness*. London: Penguin.

Hart, David M. "Classical Liberalism and the Problem of Class". *Liberty Matters*, 1 November 2016. https://oll.libertyfund.org/publications/liberty-matters/2016-11-01-david-m-hart-classical-liberalism-and-the-problem-of-class-november-2016

Hayek, F. A. (1991, 1st pub 1952) *The Counter Revolution of Science: Studies on the Abuse of Reason*. Indianapolis, IN: Liberty Fund.

Hayek, F. A. (1996, 1st pub. 1946) "Individualism: True and False" in *Individualism and Economic Order*. Chicago, IL: University of Chicago Press.

Hazony, Yoram (2018) *The Virtue of Nationalism*. New York: Basic Books.

Hazony, Yoram (2022) *Conservatism: A Rediscovery*. New York: Forum.

Hine, Dougald (2024) *At Work in the Ruins: Finding Our Place in the Time of Science Climate Change Pandemics & All the Other Emergencies*. London: Chelsea Green.

Jarvis, Adrian (1997) *Samuel Smiles and the Construction of Victorian Values*. Stroud: Sutton Publishers.
Kahan, Alan S. (2023) *Freedom from Fear: An Incomplete History of Liberalism*. Princeton, NJ: Princeton University Press.
Kelley, Robert (1990, 1st pub 1969) *The Transatlantic Persuasion: The Liberal-Democrat Mind in the Age of Gladstone*. Englewood Cliffs, NJ: Transaction Books.
Kindleberger, Charles P. (1981, 1st pub. 1969) "The Case for Fixed Exchange Rates, 1969" in *International Money: A Collection of Essays*. London: Routledge.
Klemperer, Klemens von (2015) *Germany's New Conservatism: Its History and Dilemma in the Twentieth Century*. Princeton, NJ: Princeton University Press.
Kose, M. Ayhan & Ohnsorge, Franziska (2023) *Falling Long-Term Growth Prospects: Trends, Expectations, and Policies*. Washington, DC: World Bank.
Kukathas, Chandran (2021) *Immigration and Freedom*. Princeton, NJ: Princeton University Press.
Lasch, Christopher (1991) *The True and Only Heaven: Progress and Its Critics*. New York, NY: Norton.
Levy, Jacob T. (2017) *Rationalism, Pluralism, and Freedom*. Oxford: Oxford University Press.
Losurdo, Domenico (2014) *Liberalism: A Counter-History*. London: Verso.
Martin, Fernando M. (2017) "Why Does Economic Growth Keep on Slowing Down?". *Federal Reserve Bank of St. Louis*, 9 February 2017.
McBriar, A. M. (1995) *An Edwardian Mixed Doubles: The Bosanquets versus the Webbs: A Study in British Social Policy, 1890–1929*. Oxford: Oxford University Press.
McLuhan, Marshall (2001, 1st pub 1975) *Understanding Media: The Extensions of Man*. London: Routledge.
Mises, Ludwig von (2005, 1st pub 1962) *Liberalism: In the Classical Tradition*. Indianapolis, IN: Liberty Fund.
Moyn, Samuel (2023) *Liberalism Against Itself: Cold War Intellectuals and the Making of Our Time*. New Haven, CT: Yale University Press.
Nordman, Erik (2021) *The Uncommon Knowledge of Elinor Ostrom: Essential Lessons for Collective Action*. Washington, DC: Island Press.
O'Hara, Kieron (2011) *Conservatism*. London: Reaktion Books.
Ostrom, Vincent (1994) *The Meaning of American Federalism: Constituting a Self-Governing Society*. Washington, DC: ICS Books.
Ostrom, Elinor & Ostrom, Vincent (2014) *Choice, Rules and Collective Action: The Ostroms on the Study of Institutions and Governance*. London: ECPR Press.
Park, Michael, Leahy, Erin & Funk, Russell J. (2023) "Papers and Patents Are Becoming Less Disruptive Over Time". *Nature*, 613, 138–144.
Polanyi, Karl (2002, 1st pub 1944) *The Great Transformation; Social and Economic Origins of Our Time*. Boston, MA: Beacon Press.
Postman, Neill (1987) *Amusing Ourselves to Death*. London: Methuen.
Rachman, Gideon (2023) *The Age of the Strongman: How the Cult of the Leader Threatens Democracy around the World*. London: Vintage.
Robin, Corey (2017, 1st pub 2011) *The Reactionary Mind: Conservatism from Edmund Burke to Donald Trump*. New York, NY: Oxford University Press.
Rose, Jonathan (2021, 1st pub 2001) *The Intellectual Life of the British Working Classes*. New Haven, CT: Yale University Press.
Rose, Matthew (2021) *A World After Liberalism: Philosophers of the Radical Right*. New Haven, CT: Yale University press.
Rosenblatt, Helena (2012) *The Lost History of Liberalism: From Ancient Rome to the Twenty-First Century*. Princeton NJ: Princeton University Press.
Ruggiero, Guido de (1961, 1st pub 1927) *The History of European Liberalism*. Boston, MA: Beacon Press.

Salvadori, Massimo (1978) *The Liberal Heresy: Origins and Historical Development.* New York, NY: Saint Martin's Press.

Steger, Manfred B. & Roy, Ravi K. (2021) *Neoliberalism: A Very Short Introduction.* Oxford: Oxford University Press.

Tainter, Joseph (1988) *The Collapse of Complex Societies*. Cambridge: Cambridge University Press.

Todd, Emmanuel (2004) *After the Empire: The Breakdown of the American Order*. London: Constable & Robinson.

Tomasi, John (2013) *Free Market Fairness*. Princeton NJ: Princeton University Press.

Turchin, Peter (2023) *End Times: Elites, Counter-Elites, and the Path of Political Disintegration.* London: Penguin.

Wall, Derek (2017) *Elinor Ostrom's Rules for Radicals: Cooperative Alternatives Beyond Markets and States*. London: Pluto Press.

Weiss, John (1977) *Conservatism in Europe, 1789–1945*. London: Thames & Hudson.

Wolf, Martin (2024) *The Crisis of Democratic Capitalism*. London: Penguin.

Wolfe, Willard (1977) *From Radicalism to Socialism: Men and Ideas in the Formation of Fabian Socialist Doctrines*. New Haven, CT: Yale University Press.

Yadav, Vikash (2023) *Liberalism's Last Man: Hayek in the Age of Political Capitalism.* Chicago, IL: University of Chicago Press.

2 Liberalism as an Incomplete Ethic

Pedro Schwartz

Among the reasons why the better part of conservative opinion is shunning liberalism is that it does not enjoin individuals to cultivate any other virtue but mere toleration. The view that individuals have a right to lead their lives as they see fit and that liberals should refrain from judging other people's conduct is seen by critics as the single defining element of liberalism. This narrow definition of the moral life also gives free rein, it is said, to an absolutist view of the economic market, which many condemn (for the wrong reasons) as the locus of material utility, hedonism, selfishness, and greed. This elementary view of human nature and society attributed to liberalism is charged with leading to the destruction of civilisation. My thesis today is that such a mistaken conception of liberalism originates in a failure to distinguish between the *ethics* of the open society and the *morality* of the individual. It is urgent that we should correct it.

2.1 Three Kinds of Liberty?

In his influential essay "Two Concepts of Liberty" (1969) Isaiah Berlin presented not two but in fact three concepts: negative, positive, and communal – harking back to the cry of the French revolutionaries: *Liberté*, *Égalité*, *Fraternité*. Calling the classical idea of liberty "negative" – the ability of individuals to resist the undue interference in their persons and property by other individuals, especially those in positions of authority – was unfortunate. I would prefer to call it "formal liberty" as based on laws and traditions that defend minorities from overbearing majorities or authorities. Then he defined a second view of freedom as "positive liberty", which has the means for functioning according to one's capabilities, again a name that is inexact. I would prefer to call it "patrimonial" or "paternalist". As an afterthought he brought in a third kind of liberty: what I would call "fraternal liberty", the recognition of status demanded by downtrodden nations, races, and sexes. The crucial form of liberty is classical or formal liberty, the one needed to protect individuals from undue coercive interference. It is the one I wish to study from the point of view of morality or virtue, because a sub-thesis of mine is that *Égalité* and *Fraternité* of the revolutionary slogan observably and spontaneously follow from *Liberté*. The countries that have shown respect for formal liberty have progressed in prosperity and have maintained their independence with unexpected success.

DOI: 10.4324/9781003504412-4

We must first see whether classical liberty is safe in our open societies. Karl Popper pointed out a weakness in our democracies, which he called "the paradox of freedom": that liberty can be used to destroy liberty. This self-reference paradox must be guarded against. Popper proposed regulation against such enemies of freedom as extremist parties and their propaganda (see Popper, 1945). This is the method used in Germany today against a revival of Nazism – with mixed results it must be said. An element of my thesis today is that we need more. We need the virtue of responsibility and other virtues such as a respect for truth and striving after excellence to strengthen institutional barriers against totalitarianism.

2.1.1 The Impossibility Theorem

But before we proceed, we must find our way through a thicket of seductive ideas.[1] Distinguished political philosophers have proposed that we start by defining the perfectly just society and then try to realise it. Such striving for political perfection was the aim of hallowed thinkers such as Plato, Descartes, Hobbes, Locke, Kant, Rousseau, or today, John Rawls. This is not the path freedom lovers should follow. The perfectly just society is not definable, in fact it is logically impossible, as Ken Arrow showed in (1950, 1963). With his path-breaking impossibility theorem Arrow proved that the idea of a just society, even if defined in the simplest and least demanding terms, necessarily leads to dictatorship. I suggest that for inspiration we look at other less transcendental thinkers, such as Adam Smith, Hume, Condorcet, J.S. Mill, Tocqueville, Popper, Hayek, who prefer to ground classic liberal policies on an essential respect for freedom.

Here again we must tread carefully. We should resist the attraction of mere empiricism, for principle it is only abandoned at the cost of consistency. The impossibility of political perfection could tempt us to recommend looking at social arrangements case by case, following the original example of the economist Nassau William Senior in the 1830s, when he opposed John Stuart Mill's principled defence of *laissez faire* and modified it by proposing a flexible look at its immediate consequences. This is the way chosen by Amartya Sen in his seductive book *The Idea of Justice* (2011) and more recently in (2014). He fully accepts the Arrow impossibility theorem (see Sen, 2014). Instead of transcendental ideas of justice, which are strictly impossible, he prefers to evaluate and debate on the possibility of social welfare or justice case by case, by the democratic comparison of human development and its failings in different societies.

2.1.2 Sen and Bhagwati

This I think is not the way to react to Arrow's impossibility theorem. Jagdish Bhagwati, an unyielding defender of the rule of free trade, argued that India should further reduce State intervention and use the market to foster growth and fight poverty (see Bhagwati, 2013).[2] During the last general election campaign Indian voters were treated to a clash between Bhagwati and Amartya Sen over the best policy to reduce poverty: Bhagwati with his defence of the free market and the reduction of the "Permit Raj" and Sen with his advocacy of public intervention and planning, as applied in the State of Kerala. This is an instance of the contrasting strategies of the rule-based freeing economy that has transformed the Indian economy in the last decades and a piecemeal case-by-case tactic of economists who doubt the power of the market.

My point is that we should indeed base liberalism on the principle of formal liberty, positively confirmed by historical experience. The ethic of formal liberty has had a wondrous effect for the progress and welfare of human societies. However, formal justice is a necessary but not a sufficient condition of a free society. The ethic of formal freedom needs to be complemented and defended by personal and political morality. Without this moral grounding, our formal liberties are in danger.

2.2 Adam Smith on Moral Sentiments

As Sen himself has stressed, Adam Smith has been caricatured by us economists as the moralist of selfishness. Remember the ever-repeated quotation from *The Wealth of Nations*:

> It is not from the benevolence of the butcher, the brewer, or the baker, that we expect our dinner, but from their regard to their own interest. We address ourselves, not to their humanity but to their self-love, and never talk to them of our own necessities but of their advantages.
>
> (1776, vol. I book I, chr. 2)

Smith reinforces this feature of individual rationality when he proceeds to point out that even the beggar will take part in economic exchange, when he uses the coins given him in alms to purchase food or when he trucks the old cloak given him, for a more convenient one.

However, self-regard is not the only trait of human nature on which Adam Smith dwells. The self-regard analysed in *The Wealth of Nations* (1776) must be placed within the framework of sympathy as he did in *The Theory of Moral Sentiments* (1759). The very first phrase of this earlier book tells another story.

> How selfish soever man may be supposed, there are evidently some principles in his nature, which interest him in the fortune of others, and render their happiness necessary to him, though he derives nothing from it except the pleasure of seeing it.

Smith goes so far as to say, "that the most hardened violator of the laws of society, is not altogether without it". This I think is more than saying that the utility function of individuals, as we would put it today, includes that of his fellow human beings. The mention of "pleasure he derives" may make one doubt that he has abandoned *homo oeconomicus* as clearly as Sen says. In the moral choices he supposes an individual makes, is he not including those of the Good Samaritan, who succors a wounded man though he derives no utility from it? As Amartya

Sen (2011, ch. 8) comments, the master seems to be going further in his *Moral Sentiments* than self-interest and sympathy and extolling active commitment to the welfare his wounded brother.

Adam Smith famously internalised the sources of morality flowing from sympathy. In the second edition of his treatise, he supposed an "Impartial Spectator" in our breast, an imagined man within, who watches our actions from a "Sense of Justice", helped by "Remorse" and "the consciousness of Merit" (*TMS* II.ii.2.2). Smith is faithful to his individualist philosophy, but seems to build an edifice of social commitment on it. In any case, Sen derides the "Rational Fools" (1977) of neo-classical economics who are supposed to be moved exclusively by narrow self-interest. For Adam Smith in *The Theory of Moral Sentiments* morality must not be reduced to the material benefits. He underlined the fact that one of the aims individuals pursue is a good name: an important goal of man's endeavour, he said, is "to be observed, to be attend to, to be taken notice of with sympathy, complacency, and approbation"; but note that in the detailed study of Virtue that Smith added to the last and sixth edition of *The Theory of Moral Sentiments* in 1790 he showed no inclination to abandon self-interest as a crucial impulse of man in the economic world. True, Smith does consider other motives for human action.

He always did so from the point of view of the individual. However, the question is not whether Smith moved from self-interest and sympathy in *The Theory of Moral Sentiments* to what we today would classify as a consideration of collective choice and social welfare. The crucial question is whether we his followers, when maintaining formal freedom and the free economic market, must only behave as quintessential *homini vel mulieres oeconomicae*, whatever Smith may have intended. In an exchange economy,[3] there is room for a diversity of human motivation without renouncing the formal rules of freedom. Are we forced to set aside a formal Constitution if we want to pursue individual welfare? Not so. A variety of human motives for action is compatible with respecting formal legal, political, and economic rules. We should place liberty at the centre of our preferences.

2.3 Becker's Economic Approach to Human Behaviour

If we want to discover how societies function, we should start from Gary Becker's canonical paper "The Economic Approach to Human Behavior" (1976) and then proceed to apply the knowledge so gathered to the processes of a free society. Becker there summarises his individualistic methodology with two principles, to wit: "Maximizing behavior, and market equilibrium". There could not be a more neo-classical approach to the explanation microeconomic behaviour. Surprisingly this methodology as applied by Becker allows him to include a variety of material and non-material motivations in the analysis of the economy. The individual, the family, or the firm are not constrained in their material aims, but by their knowledge, approximate though it may be, of economic incentives. The individual starts with a panoply of possibilities and then takes account of the prices and costs he faces, and the income he gets. This kind of analysis is not mechanical, in that, based on the said incentives, it leaves room for different and even contradictory political choices and so can be applied to explaining both why free societies deteriorate, and why they prosper.

This application of economic analysis to the explanation of diverse social phenomena is based on a contrarian and unusual anthropology. Becker and Stigler ("De Gustibus non est Disputandum", 1977) argued that making predictions of market behaviour must be based on a model different from the textbook model. They started by assuming that fundamental preferences such as health, sustenance, are comparatively stable and common to all men and women. Then they refrained from seeing the household as a black box. They presented it as a small factory where people tried to combine market resources or commodities and internal activity for the best, after taking account of changes they experience or foresee in prices and incomes. This model permits a wide variety of observable tastes and decisions (1977, pg. 185), which is precisely what we need to show when speaking of possible political preferences. We can try to live either in Athens or in Sparta.

2.4 Two Levels of Human Action in Society

As I say, our democratic societies should move on two levels: on the Constitutional level where formal freedoms are agreed and established unanimously and on the day-to-day political level, where decisions are taken by majority (Buchanan and Tullock, 1962). This is the way we apply the traditional distinction between what is right (the framework of freedom) and what is good (individual moral choices).

Liberalism is not a morality or not enough of a morality to help conduct one's life. It is an ethic that defines rights, negative or formal rights, and traces the frontier that others must not cross and also determines the limits of what we can do to our neighbour. Liberalism is a framework within which moral virtues can flourish. In his almost agnostic essay *On Liberty* (1859) Mill did have something to say on the morality of public discussion, such as eschewing intolerance or refraining from attributing intentions to a rival or misrepresenting the beliefs of the other. He also said something, not very much, on cruelty, malice, and bad character. But there should be more.

That short list of vices to be avoided is not sufficient to lead a fruitful and dignified moral life. Rasmussen and den Uyl (1997) have used convincing words on the incomplete personality of a merely tolerant person who counts no friends and lacks integrity, courage, and respect for truth.

A notable addition to the catalogue of virtues is the sense of duty, on which Smith wrote in detail in Part III of *The Theory of Moral Sentiments*. The captain of a sinking ship, who decides to die with it, benefits no one except his sense of honour. He pays tribute to what MacIntyre (1981) calls "internal excellence". Further on the road of personal morality is "external excellence", the dedication of a person to an outside aim or achievement: the mathematician who, not so much in search of fame, successfully achieves the proof of an unsolved theorem, or the musician dedicated to his art who finishes a composition. They are not moved mainly by self-regard but by the love of an ideal outside their person, the love of mathematics, or music.

What we consider as personal moral virtues may not be found in the same degree in different persons: the virtues of Mother Theresa and those a racing driver, those of a musician and of a bullfighter, are very different and even contradictory, but they all have a place in a society that respects formal liberties.

2.5 The Moral Bases of a Free Society

One of the founding texts of the free society is the funeral oration of Pericles in the wake of the soldiers killed during the first year of the Peloponnesian Wars, as recounted by Thucydides. It is said that Pericles had the help of his lover the beautiful rhetorician Aspasia of Miletus, a foreigner in Athens. The *Oration* is a document well worth reading in its entirety, but let me give a brief summary. He extols the courage of the dead in itself, but also for their service to Athens. The Athenians pursued their different callings but also enjoyed their leisure, partook in sports, cultivated the life of the mind, created objects of beauty. Trade allowed the consumption of "foreign goods as of our own local products". Athenians sought riches but were not ashamed of poverty, only of not taking measures to escape from it. They showed deep respect for the personal affairs of the other.

> We do not get into a state with our next-door neighbour if he enjoys himself in his own way, nor do we give him the kind of black looks which, though they do no actual harm, still do hurt people's feelings. We are free and tolerant in our private lives; but in public affairs we keep to the law.

Pericles gave much thought to the political Constitution of the *Polis*. Citizens mind their own business but also take part in political life. Citizens were equal before the Law, written and unwritten, which they obeyed, especially those laws that protected the oppressed. Authority is respected, he adds, because Athens is a democracy, "because power is in the hands, not of a minority, but of the whole people".

The final lesson he imparts is striking: "Make up your minds that happiness depends on being free, and freedom depends on being courageous".

2.6 Public Choice and Majority Voting

Formal liberties are of the essence of a free society, but they will not endure in a vacuum, and this leads me to fear for liberal democracy. Liberalism without competition, more concretely without the free market, and free trade, and solid money, is a sham.

Unfortunately, what Jeremy Bentham called "sinister interests" tend to prevail at least in the short run. In a striking book, Leighton and Lopez (2019) recount what the theories of modern political economy have to say about the obstacles confronted by moves towards a free economy. However, the two authors do find rare instances when freedom wins over the *status quo*, such as in the US the dismantling of the FCC thanks to Ronald Coase and the deregulation of air travel due to the efforts of Alfred Kahn. We could add for the UK the opening to competition of the City by Margaret Thatcher. These examples show that technology and competition are powerful allies of economic freedom.

A combination of the defence of formal freedom with the untiring intellectual explanation of the benefits of the free market may convince public opinion that reactionary resistance against change brought by freedom harms the many for the benefit of the few.

A liberal society should be sustained by citizens and politicians playing clean about their intentions when calling on public intervention. They must refrain from systematically taking refuge in unfunded pay-as-you-go pensions, socialised medicine and education, public unemployment benefits, price controls, steeply progressive taxes. Private insurance and private generosity have been undermined by the growth and expansion of the welfare State. Despite those three hopeful instances, formal liberty, including equality before the law, a free market, and full respect for private property, is in danger.

I will end expressing my disappointment at the situation of liberty in post-Brexit Britain, now sliding down the slope to becoming a socialised Little England. This case among many others prompts me to ask some awkward questions. Do we need more than tolerance to ground our culture on a solid basis? Is a move in public opinion towards liberty possible? Are we not too obsessed with equality? Do we not show too much resistance against competition, especially in international trade? How can we make freedom compatible with democracy? All these questions can only be cleared by reinforcing the ethic of a free constitution with the moral virtues of decency and the honesty of an honourable person, among which the social virtue of refusing to countenance the corruption brought about by the selfishness of pressure groups and other abuses of legislative power.[4]

Notes

1 See Maskin and Sen (2004) for more details.
2 Read Drèze and Sen (2013) for a different point of view.
3 We must see economics as the science of exchange rather than as a much narrower science of the allocation of scarce resources, as a central planner would.
4 "Why is Finland such an honest country?", at BBC.com/travel/article/20200615-why-finnish-people-tell-the-truth.

References

Arrow, Kenneth (1950): "A Difficulty in the Concept of Social Welfare", *Journal of Political Economy*, vol. 58, nr. 4, pgs. 328–346.

Arrow, Kenneth (1963): *Social and Individual Values*. 2nd edition. John Wiley and Sons.

Becker, Gary (1976, 1995): "The Economic Approach to Human Behavior". Reprinted in Febrero, Ramon, and Schwartz, Pedro: *The Essence of Becker*. Hoover Institution.

Becker, Gary, and Stigler, George (1977, 1995): "De Gustibus non est Disputandum". Reprinted in Febrero, Ramon, and Schwartz, Pedro: *The Essence of Becker*. Hoover Institution.

Berlin, Isiah (1969): "Two Concepts of Liberty", in *Four Essays on Liberty*. Oxford University Press.
Bhagwati, Jagdish (2013): *Why Growth Matters. How Economic Growth in India Reduced Poverty and the Lessons for Other Developing Countries*. Public Affairs.
Buchanan, James, and Tullock, Gordon (1962): *The Calculus of Consent. Logical Foundations of Constitutional Democracy*. Vol. III of the Collected Works of James Buchanan. Liberty Fund. Indianapolis.
Drèze, Jean, and Sen, Amartya (2013): *An Uncertain Glory. India and Its Contradictions*. Princeton University Press.
Leighton, Wayne A., and Lopez, Edward J. (2019): *Madmen, Intellectuals, and Academic Scribblers*. Stanford University Economics and Finance.
MacIntyre, Alasdair (1981, 2007): *After Virtue*. Notre Dame University.
Maskin, Eric, and Sen, Amartya (2004), with Kenneth J. Arrow, Partha Dasgupta, Prasanta K. Pattanaik, and Joseph E. Stiglitz: *The Arrow Impossibility theorem (Kenneth J. Arrow lecture series)*. Columbia University Press.
Mill, John Stuart (1859): *On Liberty*. In *Essays on Politics and Society*. Vol. XVIII of the Collected Works of John Stuart Mill. University of Toronto.
Popper, Karl (1945, 1957): *The Open Society and Its Enemies*. Routledge & Kegan Paul.
Rasmussen, Douglas, and Uyl, Douglas den (1997): *Liberalism Defended. The Challenge of Post-Modernity Locke Institute*. Edward Elgar.
Sen, Amartya (1977): "Rational Fools. A Critique of the Behavioral Foundations of Economic Theory", *Philosophy and Public Affairs*, vol. 6, nr. 4, pgs. 317–344.
Sen, Amartya (2011): *The Idea of Justice*. Harvard University Press.
Sen, Amartya (2014): "Arrow and the Impossibility Theorem", in Maskin and Sen (2004): *The Arrow Impossibility theorem (Kenneth J. Arrow lecture series)*. Columbia University Press.
Smith, Adam (1759, 1790): *The Theory of Moral Sentiments*. The Glasgow Edition of the Works and Correspondence of Adam Smith.
Smith, Adam (1776): *An Inquiry into the Nature and Causes of the Wealth of Nations*. The Glasgow Edition of the Works and Correspondence of Adam Smith.
Thucydides, *History of the Peloponnesian War*. Various translations. [Pericles's Oration at the end of the first year of the Peloponnesian War.]

3 Economics versus the Classical Liberal Tradition in Political Economy

An Epistemological Divide

Martin Ricketts

3.1 Introduction

Edmund Burke, in his *Reflections on the Revolution in France*,[1] lamented that 'the age of chivalry is gone, – That of sophisters, oeconomists, and calculators, has succeeded'. It is not clear from this whether he saw the whole developing field of political economy as tainted by this new spirit. But it is revealing that, in the late eighteenth century, he had noticed an association between 'economists' and an excessive and misplaced rationalism that led its exponents to 'calculate' ideal social arrangements by means that ignored so much of the complexity of historically evolved institutions that it amounted to little more than 'sophistry'. These thoughts continue to resonate and can be discerned in far more recent criticisms of modern economic theory.

Indeed, in spite of Burke's early suspicion of what Friederich Hayek would later call 'constructivist rationalism', a doctrine which he traces to the work of René Descartes, the study of political economy did not (and does not) require acceptance of constructivism. David Hume, for example, was famously critical of the pure 'rationalist' position, while both Adam Smith and Adam Ferguson were concerned to investigate social arrangements that were 'the result of human action but not the execution of any human design'.[2] The formalisation of modern neoclassical economics around 1870, however, encouraged a naïve form of rationalism as models of 'utility maximisation' were perfected. These models were powerful tools of analysis and aids to consistent thought, but the problem of imperfect knowledge in Hayek's (1973, 12) words 'provisionally put aside' was ultimately 'conveniently forgotten'. The study of modern economics by the mid-twentieth century implicitly accepted that decision-making was, and ought to be, rational in the constructivist (fully informed) sense rather than rational in a broader 'evolutionary' or 'critical' sense[3] which accepts the inevitable limitations of conscious reason in the face of a world of pervasive change and uncertainty.

This tension between the emerging highly formalised and analytical discipline of 'economics' and its antecedent and more synthetic field of 'political economy' led, over the course of almost a century, to the effective disintegration of the latter into many component parts. When the 'unbounded rationality' of economic agents was recognised in certain contexts as potentially misleading

DOI: 10.4324/9781003504412-5

rather than merely a convenient assumption for limited purposes, whole 'alternative' schools of thought developed. 'Behavioural economics' introduced a richer account of the psychology of choice in situations where information was highly imperfect or difficult to interpret and where decision-making could sometimes be shown to be prone to systematic biases.[4] Imperfect knowledge and the role of property rights and differing forms of contractual relations in responding to this problem gave rise to the subject of 'the New Institutional Economics'.[5] Acceptance of radical uncertainty in the context of economic change led to methodological controversy and the development of 'Austrian Economics' as a separate field.[6] It also led to the incorporation of evolutionary thinking explicitly into economic analysis with conjectural (rather than fully rational) decisions subject to the test of the market and successful outcomes being reinforced and imitated.[7]

Epistemology is therefore at the heart of the distinction between 'Economics' and 'Political Economy'. It is not simply that the analysis of the process by which economic agents acquire knowledge is ignored in economic theory. Much effort has been put into treating this subject using formal techniques, and there is an enormous literature on 'the Economics of Information'. The problem is that the formal structure of neoclassical economics leads to a particular conception of the 'knowledge problem'. It is approached using the techniques of constrained maximisation, and this implies that knowledge must be treated in a way that is conformable with the constructivist rationalism underlying all models of choice in the standard literature. These models, however, are not suitable for addressing the problem of 'radical uncertainty'[8] or the importance of 'creativity' to the emergence of new knowledge. As a result, economics as a discipline has struggled to offer much insight into the foundations of economic development (as distinct from the mechanics of economic growth). The foundations of economic development are to a large degree cultural and institutional in nature, and the political economists of the nineteenth century considered these an integral part of their field of study.

The following sections consider the origins and nature of the divergence of economics from political economy in more detail. It is argued that the triumph of 'marginalism' did not, in itself, imply an inevitable fracture between political economy and economics. It was the formal mathematical treatment and the triumph of a mechanical as distinct from biological approach to economic processes (deriving from the differing approach to knowledge) that ultimately proved decisive – a triumph that was resisted by some of the founders such as Menger and Marshall. The consequences for the development of welfare economics and public policy are considered in Section 3.4 focussing on a critique by Rowley and Peacock (1975) while those for the theory of growth are reviewed in Sections 3.5–3.7. In both cases the limitations of pure 'economics' as a tool for understanding some of the more fundamental policy questions are highlighted. For these, a wider 'political economy' perspective is required. A re-absorption of economics into the broader and more integrated field of political economy would seem to be unlikely, however, given the methodological and epistemological differences.

3.2 The Gradual Divergence of 'Economics' from 'Political Economy'

The study of 'economics' only gradually came to be perceived as differing substantially from that of 'political economy'. In 1871 the seeds of this divergence were sown by the publication of the *Theory of Political Economy* by William Stanley Jevons and the *Principles of Economics – (the Grundsätze)* by Carl Menger. Around the same time (1874) there also appeared the *Elements of Theoretical Economics* by Léon Walras. These three major works are usually seen in the History of Economic Thought as having established the essential foundations of modern economics. The common threads that linked these publications were the focus on the microeconomics (as we would now say) of individual decision-making, and a theory of price determination linked to the *subjective* notion of 'marginal utility' rather than the older focus on a more *objective* (and long run) notion of 'value' related to the quantity of labour required in the production of a good.

The tendency towards more formal theorising and the emergence of conditions for static 'equilibrium' rapidly became apparent. Indeed in the preface of the first edition Jevons noted that 'The theory of economy … presents a close analogy to the science of statical mechanics'. Equilibrium requires that all people allocate their income so as to 'equalize the utility of the final increments of all commodities consumed'.[9] Jevons also states the normative conclusion that 'so far as is consistent with the inequality of wealth … all commodities are distributed by exchange so as to produce the maximum of benefit'.[10] He thus saw himself as developing a utilitarian theory, although it was understood early on that 'utility' in the new theory was 'ordinal' in nature and did not imply that inter-personal comparisons were possible. Making the most of given scarce resources became the main concern of the new approach and attention was diverted from the older classical interest in the 'magnificent dynamics'[11] of the growth and distribution of national wealth.

Although the movement towards the formal static theory of choice was implicit from the beginning it nevertheless gave rise to powerful resisting voices. This is particularly clear in the case of Alfred Marshall whose *Principles of Economics* was first published in 1890 and, over many editions, dominated the study of economics in England well into the twentieth century. Marshall showed a continuing regard for the classical tradition and did not accept that thorough incorporation of marginal analysis into economics would, or should, necessarily transform its character. The opening sentence, 'Political Economy or Economics is a study of mankind in the ordinary Business of life', suggests both a disinclination to make any important distinction between the two fields and a preference for a looser definition of the scope of economics compared with the tighter 'relationship between ends and scarce means' (Robbins 1935) which eventually prevailed.

At the root of Marshall's reservations about the drift towards static equilibrium concepts was his conviction that the 'central idea of economics … must be that of living force and movement'.[12] He continued, in other words, to think that the analysis of economic change and growth was at the heart of the discipline. Further, as Hodgson (2013) argues persuasively, Marshall was heavily influenced by the writing of Herbert Spencer on evolution. The latter saw 'progress' as a gradual path towards greater differentiation, complexity, and integration, and this is reflected clearly in Marshall's treatment of economic change. The general rule is that 'the development of the organism, whether social or physical, involves an increasing subdivision of functions … and a more intimate connection between them'.[13] Unlike Jevons, therefore, who, as we have noted, saw economics as analogous to 'statical mechanics', Marshall argued that 'the Mecca of the economist lies in economic biology'.[14]

This suspicion of 'statical equilibrium' methods is continually emphasised in the *Principles*. It is particularly clear when Marshall (1925, 461) is discussing economic organisation and long run supply under conditions of 'increasing return'. 'The statical theory of equilibrium', he writes, 'is only an introduction to economic studies; and it is barely even an introduction to the study of the progress and development of industries which show a tendency to increasing return'. The attention that he gives to the supply side of the market compared with the relatively limited space devoted to the marginal utility theory of consumer demand has been heavily criticised by more recent subjectivists,[15] but it was precisely this focus that was important in his suspicion of mathematical formalism. Improvements in knowledge, skill, and organisation were adopted gradually and diffused through an industry leading to 'declining long run supply price'. The 'supply curve' was therefore discussed in a way that implied it was not a truly 'static' analytical device. It represented a means of describing an evolutionary process over time and was not 'reversible'. If output fell, the industry would not move back along the same supply curve unlearning all the accumulated skills and knowledge that had led to productive improvements. Marshall devoted Appendix H to 'Limitations of the Use of Statical Assumptions in Regard to Increasing Return'. He was prepared to accept that pure theory was 'essential', and he was an accomplished mathematician, but he characterised much theory as 'elegant toying' and a 'very small part of economics proper'.[16]

By 'economics proper' Marshall seems to have meant the application of theory to the better understanding of 'the everyday business of life'. Theory required abstraction and simplification, but if it became too divorced from reality and was 'pushed to its more remote and intricate logical consequences it slips away from the conditions of real life'.[17] Mathematics was therefore confined to appendices and the economic interpretation was explained without its aid within the body of the text using practical examples suggested by historical experience. Indeed, unlike Menger who was highly critical of the 'Historical School' because it allegedly denied that any universal scientific principles were applicable and that everything was contingent upon the circumstances of the time, Marshall admired the work of economic historians such as Richard Jones (1790–1855) and Wilhelm Georg Friedrich Roscher (1817–94) and spent the winter of 1870–1 in Berlin. The early chapters of Marshall's *Principles* originally contained mainly historical material which, from the fifth edition onwards, was moved to appendix A, entitled

'The Growth of Free Industry and Enterprise'. This move of the historical material from the main text to an appendix symbolises the drift of the times and the ultimate triumph of formal analysis over historical context, instead of a full synthesis of the two to which Marshall apparently aspired in his earlier years.

The 'marginal revolution' therefore ultimately produced a schism between two diverging paths. By the mid-twentieth century, 'mainstream' thinking deriving from Jevons and Walras emphasised pure theory and the properties of a general competitive equilibrium as a benchmark of economic efficiency. This strand became increasingly mathematical, formal, and free from 'realistic' institutional and historical context. Critics of the mainstream, as noted in Section 3.1, questioned the existence of stable preference orderings on the part of consumers, their ability to calculate optimal choices in the face of complexity, and the unrealistic characterisation of 'perfect competition' that underpinned theorems of general equilibrium. But the common theme underlying these various attacks was a disagreement about how to treat the problem of information in economics.

3.3 The Epistemological Divide

In mainstream theory the inevitable uncertainty accompanying the passage of time is handled by imposing assumptions suitable for statistical analysis but incompatible with conditions of radical uncertainty.[18] Effectively people are assumed to choose not between known available outcomes but between known probability distributions of known outcomes which might occur at future points in time. The possible outcomes themselves (as distinct from the relative subjective values placed upon them) are also seen as objective pieces of information, understood in the same way by all people. People 'know' all the things that might happen as a result of making a particular decision. Perfect markets in time and state-contingent claims permit the analysis of competitive equilibria to be extended to allow for 'risk' and 'time'. A degree of Burke's complained of sophistry might be detected here. An analysis seemingly aimed at addressing the problem of 'uncertainty' requires an assumed degree of knowledge in some ways more remarkable than that associated with the standard theory under 'full information'.[19]

The precise 'modelling' of choice under risk is thus used in standard theory as a device to approach the problems of uncertainty and the passage of time. As Shackle (1972, 1979) objected, however, this subtly disguises the problems of choice by reducing them to mere calculation. Indeed the very word 'choice', he argues, suggests circumstances that are rendered impossible by the assumptions of static economic theory. 'The theoretician of value shows how men would choose, if there were no need for choice, if there were no possibility, no freedom, no meaning for choice'.[20] If a chooser 'knows' her subjective ranking of outcomes or probability distributions of outcomes, if she knows the various technical opportunities that the existing 'state of the arts' permit her to choose, if she is 'unboundedly rational', then the 'choice' is a foregone conclusion. Under such conditions it would be hard to explain why choice is such a burden. The act of choice itself is 'costless', and the process of choice, of continual adjustments to 'unexpected' events, cannot be handled without relaxing some of the assumptions. As Shackle (1972, 269) puts it, 'reason must compromise with time'.

It is a search for this compromise that characterises the study of political economy. The aim is not to depart from reason but to investigate the costs of choice which accompany realistic decision problems, whether individual or collective. Recognising these costs enables economists to make sense of many features in the institutional landscape, but in so doing they find themselves departing from the techniques of 'pure theory'. Taken to formal extremes the world of pure economics is drained of all institutional content. In political economy, institutions including the law governing the process of exchange itself, the existence of property rights and the use of money as an exchange medium are no longer simply assumed to exist but are seen as part of the subject matter. They are the means of coping with the hazards and uncertainties that accompany all attempts to coordinate activities for mutual advantage. In the world of political economy it is recognised that to study the *process of exchange* is wider than the study of *the price system*, important though the latter might be.

Hence the firm, which in neoclassical orthodoxy is little more than a production function and therefore entirely characterised by technology, becomes, in political economy, a social mechanism for handling transactions cost. The governance of firms varies according to the information and incentive problems that they confront in their differing fields of activity, and property rights are distributed so as to mitigate transactional hazards in a continual trial and error process. In this tradition, as represented by the work of Knight (1921), Coase (1937), Williamson (1985), and Ostrom (1990), there is an implicit (and sometimes explicit) acceptance of radical uncertainty and bounded rationality. Evolutionary ideas emerge from this tradition such as the accumulation of trust from 'continuous dealings', and the importance of durable 'relational contracts' in permitting non-codifiable (tacit) knowledge to be generated within firms. In other words, the New Institutional Economics, which starts from observing the mechanisms which are actually used by people in the 'ordinary business of life', is a continuation of the Marshallian tradition. Marshall (1925, 138) saw capital as consisting 'in a great part of knowledge and organisation' and he was reluctant to exclude from 'economics proper' methods of enquiry, such as historical research, that could cast light on the processes by which knowledge was acquired and economic coordination made more effective.

During the twentieth century attempts were therefore made to prevent economics from drifting away from its roots in political economy and becoming exclusively concerned with formal model building, which either diverted attention away from the knowledge problem or imposed a misleading method of approaching it. These attempts, however, have not succeeded in moving economics far from its constructivist and rationalist foundations. In the following section the epistemological foundations of the Rowley and Peacock (1975) critique of welfare economics are discussed. Later sections discuss the treatment of knowledge in the formal theory of economic growth and the resulting failure to address effectively the fundamental causes of economic development.

3.4 The Critique of 'Welfare Economics'

The normative theory of public finance and public policy was inevitably influenced by the increasing mathematical formalism of economic analysis following the marginal revolution. How to make the best use of scarce resources in collective choice was a question that could be considered using the same analytical tools as for private choice. There was, of course, the little matter of working out how a social ordering might be devised as an analogue to the private orderings assumed in the analysis of individual choice, especially if social choice was somehow to reflect the wishes of citizens and not be imposed by a dictator benevolent or otherwise.[21] The question of how social preferences might be revealed through various voting mechanisms did introduce some institutional context and reflected a literature in political economy going back to Nicolas de Condorcet. But the tendency to ignore the information problem in favour of establishing mathematical conditions for the 'efficient' allocation of resources in the public sector became apparent.

These conditions could, in principle, be addressed while remaining neutral on contentious questions such as the distribution of income and wealth which, at least in terms of distribution between social classes, was a major preoccupation of classical political economy. 'Economic efficiency', as defined by Vilfredo Pareto, could be perceived as a 'technical' matter. It simply required that no reallocation of resources could benefit one person in his or her own estimation without harming another. If there were potential unexploited gains from resource reallocation that would harm no one in their own estimation, and might therefore be universally approved, it would be wasteful not to take advantage of them. The ethical judgements required for Paretian Welfare Economics could be seen as quite weak, compatible with 'liberal individualism', and likely to be widely accepted.

By the middle of the twentieth century the role of public policy in correcting for economic inefficiency and the multifarious possible causes of 'market failure' had become the prevailing orthodoxy. Because policy was approached by reference to the conditions which were required for Pareto efficiency under perfect competition, this very demanding theoretical benchmark led to a virtually unlimited scope for government intervention. Realistic conditions almost everywhere departed in some degree from this ideal, either because competition was seen as 'imperfect' or because there were multifarious external effects that individual action in perfectly competitive markets could play no part in addressing. Indeed purposive action is not possible in a perfectly competitive environment where all transactors deal anonymously at prevailing prices. The alternative approach deriving from Coase (1960), which studied the ways that transactors might actively negotiate to achieve efficiency gains and the potential institutional mechanisms that might mitigate the inevitable transactions costs encountered, was much less widely understood. Coase's ideas required applied research and a comparison between available institutional responses to 'inefficiency'. The orthodox approach led to the danger of 'nirvana economics'[22] and a naïve assumption that public servants would have the knowledge and incentives to apply corrective policy instruments to 'failures' identified by abstract theorems.

Rowley and Peacock (1975) did not develop a specifically Coasean critique of Paretian Welfare Economics, but their objections to what they perceived as the latter's 'dangerous hegemony' (p. 1) were to a substantial extent based upon its fragile epistemic foundations. They proposed a 'liberal restatement' that emphasised 'the maintenance and extension of individual freedoms, defined by the absence of coercion …' a doctrine particularly associated with the work of J.S. Mill (1859). This, they argued, was quite distinct from the axiom of 'the primacy of individual preferences' that underlay Welfare Economics. The essential problem with Welfare Economics was that, in spite of the central place in the theory for individual preferences and an acceptance that individual utility was not inter-personally comparable, the theory was nevertheless compatible with authoritarian solutions to questions of economic policy.

The explanation for this apparent paradox had two strands. First Rowley and Peacock argued that the theory had itself been misunderstood by its practitioners and that any moves from economically inefficient to economically efficient resource allocations were interpreted as socially desirable, even when they made some people worse off. They criticised the Kaldor-Hicks compensation tests which underlay cost-benefit analysis (tests which required net gains to be achieved from a social change as evaluated by all the people affected but which did not require the actual compensation of losers) as being accorded an exaggerated respect by policy-makers. There had been a 'bold attempt to hoodwink the policy-makers into believing that the Pareto criteria were more powerful than in fact was the case' (p. 51).

The second and more fundamental strand to the critique was that the importance of the act of individual choice as a desirable thing in itself is not recognised in Paretian Welfare Economics. At a purely formal level, people will not distinguish between a decision taken by themselves or an identical decision taken by an outsider and 'imposed' upon them. In a world of public spirited and perfectly informed officials, therefore, it will not matter that an outside party is determining the allocation of resources providing that the result is as good as or better than would have otherwise occurred through private choice. Indeed, like the positive neoclassical pure theory from which it derives, normative economics is about rational calculation rather than choice and is therefore unable to address Rowley and Peacock's criticisms.

Choice is exercised in conditions of uncertainty where decisions require judgement rather than simple calculation. Uncertainty characterises almost any decision problem in the world as it actually exists, and it is this which demands the exercise of human faculties other than simple computation. 'He who chooses his plan for himself', writes J.S. Mill 'employs all his faculties'. These include 'observation', 'reasoning', 'foresight', 'discrimination', 'firmness', and 'self-control'.[23] Apart from 'reasoning', the other faculties would be redundant in a world of perfect information. Observation implies that there are still things to be discovered; foresight that people will have differing views of the future and that some will form better assessments than others; discrimination that it is possible to discern variations in apparently similar circumstances which might easily be overlooked; firmness and self-control that unexpected events will shake a person's confidence in their judgement. Ultimately therefore, the 'Liberal Restatement' offered by Rowley and Peacock was a re-assertion of 'classical political economy with modern trappings' (p. 3). However, it is less clear that their stated objective of attacking Paretian welfare economics 'on its own ground, using the standard weapons of modern economic analysis' was at the root of their critique. Rather their critique showed that these 'standard weapons' were applicable to situations in which the problem of knowledge had been 'put aside' and had unwittingly led to the abandonment of a rich inheritance of normative classical thinking about liberty and public policy.

3.5 Economics and the Theory of Growth

If the formal mathematical analysis of the optimal allocation of scarce resources diverted attention away from the information problem in normative welfare economics and public policy, it could not be ignored entirely in the theory of economic growth. Early models of economic growth such as Solow (1956) treated the advance of knowledge as exogenous and unexplained. Sustained increases in output per head over long periods of time, however, ultimately must depend upon advances in technology and the 'state of the arts'. Any theory of long run growth therefore requires a theory of the accumulation of knowledge, a theory that proved difficult to develop from a strictly rationalist foundation. On the one hand, the search for *new* knowledge could only be handled by assuming that research efforts could be represented by probability distributions of possible future outcomes. The radical uncertainty that inevitably attends technical or organisational innovation is therefore excluded as being beyond the reach of the analytical tools available. On the other hand, the incentive to invest in research effort is hard to understand if any new information is simply available to all contractors whether or not they contributed resources to its discovery. The assumption of static competitive theory that all economic agents have access to the same information effectively denies the possibility of growth from investment in research.

As a matter of positive economics the assumption that it was possible to 'produce' new knowledge by means of some 'meta production function' – a technology for producing new technology – was not to be dismissed simply because it carried the wrong metaphorical connections with mechanics rather than with evolutionary biology. For theorists of economic growth the use of probability theory to yield statistically 'expected' outcomes in the production of scientific knowledge was a natural extension of the established paradigm. Acemoglu (2009, 413) reflects this view when he writes that 'without such calculations we would have little hope of modelling the process of technical change'. The bigger challenge was to explain how growth could take place at all if new knowledge is a public good, a good that is non-rival and non-excludable. Papers by Nelson (1959) and Arrow (1962) made the public good attributes of knowledge a foundation for the economics of information, and this was accepted as a relatively uncontroversial starting point.

To generate growth endogenously it was necessary that 'free-riding' on newly discovered knowledge could be prevented and that the developers of new ideas could profit from them. This could take the form of exclusion devices, for example imposing costs on the dissemination of information through private efforts to enforce secrecy, or by introducing property rights (patents) that could be traded for a specified period of time. Romer (1990), for example, relied upon the existence of patents in his model of 'endogenous growth'. Knowledge could be made 'partially excludable' by distinguishing the applied 'designs' of artefacts in which new ideas are embedded, and on which patents are awarded, from the abstract knowledge itself which is made 'freely accessible' to all researchers.

As a matter of normative economics, these solutions were distinctly 'second-best'. To create a monopoly advantage, even one intended to reward innovation, would result in static 'efficiency losses' in standard theory. Further, even with patent protection for 'designs' the spillover benefits to other researchers of the newly discovered knowledge would imply that research effort is less than the socially 'efficient' level. With the exception of models of 'patent races' where a 'winner takes all' incentive structure might encourage 'overinvestment' in research, the general consensus amongst economists is that subsidising greater research effort is justified by economic reasoning. Indeed, Arrow (1962, 617) conjectured that a system that rewarded innovation and did not involve any charge to the users could be contrived and would permit social gains – as appeared to be the case in the Soviet Union at the time.

These conclusions reflect a very specific view of knowledge as a 'public good' along with a continuing impulse to use unrealisable ideally functioning perfectly competitive markets as a normative benchmark. From the perspective of political economy both of these features of the economic approach are invalid. Knowledge is a product of the competitive process itself and is misleadingly modelled in terms of production functions. The latter conception leads to the idea that governments might be in a position to 'produce' knowledge that is codifiable and freely available to all who would find little difficulty in understanding it and discerning its potential productive uses. In fact, as the theory of endogenous growth recognises, it is the search for competitive advantage (effectively transitory monopoly) that provides incentives and direction to research effort. Outside this 'classically competitive' environment, any research agency would struggle to determine where to direct their attention, and the results would simply reflect the interests of the researchers or politicians who exercised a modicum of control. There is agreement that perfectly competitive conditions would rule out innovation, but this is also the reason why it cannot therefore serve as a normative benchmark for an ideal market structure.

Of course, no serious economist actually believes that perfect competition is an ideal market structure. It is the quest for 'efficiency' that is driving the interest in what would happen in such a rarefied and idealised setting if information were 'freely' available. Perfect competition is merely an elegant theoretical toy for discussing the requirements for efficiency using static tools. But if we refocus our enquiry away from the ideal static role of prices in signalling the existing marginal social costs and benefits of goods and services (assuming that these are somehow computable) and away from the cynosure of Pareto efficiency, towards the *process* by which economic agents discover efficiency gains over time through agreement, voluntary cooperation and exchange, the importance of institutions in enabling scientific advance comes to the fore. This change of focus implies a move from pure economics to political economy.

3.6 Tacit versus Codified Knowledge and the Growth of Science

Historically the supposed 'public good' nature of scientific knowledge did not prevent the spectacular increases in income per head that have happened since the mid-eighteenth century. Nor is it obvious that the greater interest in governments in financing research since the mid-twentieth century has had a noticeable impact on the rate of growth. The industrial revolution was not initiated or supported by specific policies towards research but emerged spontaneously from the social, legal, and political conditions prevailing in particular countries by the late seventeenth century. Actual historical and institutional context therefore suggests that, whatever the difficulties of providing incentives to develop and spread new scientific information, they were not impossibly difficult to handle.

One significant element emphasised by Kealey and Ricketts (2014) is that the much-feared spillovers to free-riders, which are at the centre of the 'public goods' framework, are not a decisive impediment to scientific advance. This is because, although the external benefits of scientific work are, in themselves, very significant, they do not benefit those who are outside what is essentially a collaborative process. In other words, those who benefit from spillovers are those who are themselves contributors and who provide spillover benefits to others. Science is a 'contribution good' rather than a pure 'public good' and there are advantages to becoming part of a spillover-rich environment. These advantages of close association with other researchers led to the formation of increasing numbers of research societies and clubs across Europe. From the sixteenth to the eighteenth centuries a change from secrecy to much greater openness with respect to scientific discussion took place,[24] and Allen (1983) shows that by the nineteenth century there was, even in matters of technological innovation, a surprising (for economists) degree of information exchange between firms.

Cooperation is profitable for scientists because it is a condition of engaging continuously with the work of others. Attempting to understand new developments from outside would be a costly rather than a free ride. Scientific knowledge in endogenous growth theory is objective and codifiable. Further it can (and ideally should) be made 'freely available'. However, in the contribution good model, knowledge in new areas of science is 'tacit', only to be fully understood by those who are part of the scientific discussion. Polanyi (1967, 4) emphasised that tacit knowledge was difficult to impart to others ('we know more than we can tell') and could be acquired only by personal experience. Classic examples included knowledge of how to ride a bicycle, awareness of complex local idiosyncratic conditions, ability to coordinate with colleagues, and general 'know-how'. Hayek was particularly associated with the idea that decentralised markets were good at making use of dispersed sources of special knowledge that could not be transmitted to a central decision-maker. In the case of research, however, tacit knowledge is generated collectively rather than entirely by isolated experience. It inheres in those that are part of an extended community of researchers. To operate outside this community would be to experience higher costs and delays than to operate as a cooperative member.

This process of cooperative engagement in scientific research has affinities with the advantages of membership of a social 'club'. The purpose of the club is to facilitate the benefits from social interaction. An 'invisible college' is therefore a better metaphor for the source of new ideas than a 'meta production function'. Existing members of a 'college' will benefit from a larger club which will therefore be 'open' to newcomers. The scientific pool generated by the college as a whole is a form of 'commons', jointly accessible by all active scientists, but not a common resource that is depleted by use or easily exploited by non-contributors. Potts (2019) argues that this type of 'innovation commons' lies at the root of economic growth. It is a very different perspective from the public good model of knowledge which expects private research organisations to be mainly concerned with maintaining secrecy and maximising the value of their research output through the use of patent rights.

3.7 Institutions, Economic Growth, and Political Economy

Approaching the problem of growth from an institutional perspective implies far less reliance on maximising models of rational decision-making. As North (1991) emphasises, institutions are not 'constructed' rationally but are the outcome of path-dependent evolutionary processes. They include informal constraints (customs, conventions, and traditional rights) as well as formal ones (political constitutions, written legal codes, and defined property rights). If economic theory finds it hard to cope with the modelling of scientific advance, it faces even greater problems when it comes to the institutional framework supporting and protecting the freedom of action required for any economic development to occur. Theorists of economic growth, Acemoglu (2009, 140), therefore distinguish between 'proximate causes' of growth, such as physical and human capital accumulation and technological change, and 'fundamental causes' which are institutional and cultural in nature. Institutional factors are 'perhaps the most significant fundamental cause of economic growth', and Acemoglu considers them in part VIII of his textbook under the subtitle 'The Political Economy of Growth'. He refers to most of the topics covered in the book as concerning 'the mechanics of growth' which comprises models which represent 'the core of growth theory' but which 'leave unanswered some of the central questions raised' (p. 777). Again we see the association of Economics with 'mechanics' while for the investigation of 'fundamental causes' we require political economy.

For most of human history poverty rather than sustained development has been the norm, and this continues to be so for a large proportion of the present population of the world. As has often been observed, the power of continuous productivity growth to lift people out of poverty is capable of transforming the life chances of people to an extent undreamed of only a century ago. Compared with these potential gains, static economic efficiency pales into insignificance, although it might be conjectured that where efficiency gains are costly to negotiate economic growth would also be inhibited. The intrinsic fascination of the subject has led many economists to investigate it, and, in doing so, they begin to use more of the type of institutional and historical material that would have appealed to Marshall.

North (1981), for example, charts institutional changes over extensive periods of human history and concentrates on the emergence of differing forms of property and the problem of protecting it. The origins of the industrial revolution, he argues, can be found in 'a combination of better specified and enforced property rights and increasingly efficient and expanding markets' (p. 166). Baumol (2002, 2010) while highlighting the 'innovation arms race' and Schumpeterian competition between firms in oligopolistic markets is very aware that this mechanism depends upon cultural and institutional settings that permit entrepreneurship to flourish. In pointing to the historical rarity of these conditions he ranges over the history of imperial China and ancient Rome as well as medieval and early modern Europe. Mokyr (2017) emphasises culture as the critical element in kick-starting growth and considers the evolutionary forces that produced cultural change in Europe after the beginning of the sixteenth century. McCloskey (2016, 98) argues that institutions such as a tolerable legal framework cannot be sufficient conditions for technical progress since they have occasionally existed for significant periods of time in past ages. What distinguishes the enrichment brought by the industrial revolution was the rise of bourgeois values, social approval of wealth gained through enterprise, and greater appreciation of the more self-regarding virtues such as prudence. Acemoglu and Robinson (2013) concentrate on the more institutional side and compare the relative success and failure of countries often in close geographical proximity. Where 'extractive institutions' are prevalent, and power is concentrated in a small group who use it to distribute resources in their favour, development cannot be expected other than for relatively short periods of time. Sustained development requires 'inclusive political institutions', and the evolution of these institutions can be influenced by 'critical junctures', events such as the bubonic plague in fourteenth-century Europe, which had different consequences for the regions of Eastern compared with Western Europe.

All these contributions recognise that dynamic questions cannot be fully understood without historical and institutional context, and that some version of Marshall's Appendix A is necessary to enable pure theory to be interpreted and applied to practical circumstances, whether these concern the development potential of a whole country or the effectiveness of a particular type of organisation. Historical and institutional work, however, has tended to develop in parallel rather than in conjunction with formal theory. The source of this disjunction is ultimately the differing treatment of knowledge. For economic theory the problem of knowledge discovery and dispersal has to be approached in a way that can be handled by rationalist models of 'choice'. The assumptions underlying these models, especially with respect to the information available to economic agents, are often far removed from the practical circumstances of 'everyday life' in which conditions of radical uncertainty are pervasive. 'Political economy' studies the conditions in which such models are helpful in practice and when they might be seriously misleading. As Hutchison (1953, 91) remarks, when it came to questions of public policy Marshall paid little regard to 'social maximization formulae, but relied on detailed study of each case, illumined by a wide survey of the historical and contemporary facts, and by a trained cultivated judgement of human beings'. Coase's (1988, 19) distrust of 'blackboard economics' and determination to develop a research agenda around the transactions costs faced by actual economic agents fits easily within this tradition. But, notwithstanding Coase's optimism about the possibility of the objective measurement of transactions costs and the eventual incorporation of these costs into standard theory, in a world of radical uncertainty judgements about transactions costs will always be subjective. The tension between evolutionary trial and error processes of discovery and the calculating rationality of standard theory is one that may be made more creative, but is unlikely to be resolved.

Notes

1 Edmund Burke (1790, 170).
2 Adam Ferguson (1767) *An Essay on the History of Civil Society*, quoted in Hayek (1973, 150).
3 Hayek (1973, 29), in discussing what reason might tell us about the limits of reason, argues that the relevant distinction is not between 'rationalism' and 'anti-rationalism' but between 'a constructivist and an evolutionary, or, in Karl Popper's terms, a naïve and a critical rationalism'.
4 Cyert and March (1963) first presented a behavioural analysis in the context of the theory of the firm. More recently the psychological foundations have been developed by, inter alia, Tversky and Kahneman (1974), Kahneman (2011), Thaler (1991), and Thaler and Sunstein (2009).
5 As represented by scholars such as Coase (1937) and Williamson (1985) and summarised in (inter alia) Furubotn and Richter (1997) and Kasper and Streit (1998).
6 Certain foundational aspects associated with the Austrian School, deriving from the work of Carl Menger (1871), such as its thoroughgoing subjectivism, methodological individualism, and marginalism continue to underpin modern 'economics'. 'Austrian' thinkers, however, have resisted the formalism of economics which leads to an emphasis on 'equilibrium states'. The Austrian School has instead directed attention to radical uncertainty and the process of economic change. Hence, for example, Kirzner (1973), the entrepreneur, has a central role in Austrian economics which is absent from the mainstream.
7 Alchian (1950) and Boulding (1950) (1981) were early proponents of the use of evolutionary theory in economics. See also Nelson and Winter (1982).
8 See Knight (1921). A recent reflection on the dangers of ignoring conditions of radical uncertainty can be found in Kay and King (2020).
9 Jevons (1871) edited by Collison Black (1970, 170). A result already stated by Hermann Gossen (1854) though, not at that stage, known to Jevons.
10 Jevons (1871) edited by Collison Black (1970, 171).
11 A term coined by Baumol (1951).
12 Marshall (1925, Preface to 8th Edition).
13 Marshall (1925, Book IV Chapter VIII (241))
14 Marshall (1925, Preface to 8th Edition).
15 For example, Mitchell and Boettke (2017, 34–35).
16 In letters May 1900 and August 1902 reported in Hutchison (1953, 71).

17 Marshall (1925, 461).
18 The distinction between choice under conditions of 'risk' where probability distributions are known and 'uncertainty' where they are not was introduced by Frank Knight (1921).
19 Knight (1921, 20) makes this point when he writes that 'a *measurable* uncertainty, or "risk" proper … is so far different from an *unmeasurable* one that it is not in effect an uncertainty at all'.
20 Shackle (1979, 30).
21 Arrow (1951) famously demonstrated that it was impossible to devise a social ordering that satisfied a set of required conditions.
22 Demsetz (1969).
23 John Stuart Mill (1859), *On Liberty,* Lindsay (ed.) (1968), p. 117.
24 The development of research clubs and societies is described in Kealey and Ricketts (2021).

References

Acemoglu, D. (2009), *Introduction to Modern Economic Growth*, Princeton, Princeton University Press.

Acemoglu, D. and Robinson, J. A. (2013), *Why Nations Fail*, London, Profile Books.

Alchian, A. A. (1950), 'Uncertainty, Evolution and Economic Theory', *Journal of Political Economy*, 58, 211.

Allen, R. C. (1983), 'Collective Invention', *Journal of Economic Behavior and Organization*, 4, 1–24.

Arrow, K. J. (1951), *Social Choice and Individual Values*, New York, John Wiley.

Arrow, K. J. (1962), 'Economic Welfare and the Allocation of Resources for Invention', in *The Rate and Direction of Inventive Activity: Economic and Social Factors*, Princeton, Princeton University Press, 609–625.

Baumol, W. J. (2002), *The Free Market Innovation Machine: Analyzing the Capitalist Growth Miracle*, Princeton, Princeton University Press.

Baumol, W. J. (1951), *Economic Dynamics: An Introduction*, New York, Macmillan.

Baumol, W. J. (2010), *The Microtheory of Innovative Entrepreneurship*, Princeton, Princeton University Press.

Boulding, K. E. (1950), *A Reconstruction of Economics*, New York, Wiley & Sons.

Boulding, K. E. (1981), *Evolutionary Economics*, Beverly Hills, Sage Publications.

Burke, E. (1790) *Reflections on the Revolution in France and on the Proceedings in Certain Societies in London Relative to that Event*, London, J. Dodsley.

Coase, R. H. (1937), 'The Nature of the Firm', *Economica*, 4, 386.

Coase, R. H. (1960), 'The Problem of Social Cost', *Journal of Law and Economics*, 3, 1–44.

Coase, R. H. (1988), *The Firm, the Market, and the Law*, Chicago, University of Chicago Press.

Collison Black, R. D. (ed.). (1970), *Jevons: The Theory of Political Economy*, Harmondsworth, England, Penguin Books Ltd.

Cyert, R. M. and March, J. G. (1963), *A Behavioral Theory of the Firm*, New York, Prentice Hall.

Demsetz, H. (1969) 'Information and Efficiency: Another Viewpoint', *Journal of Law and Economics*, 2, 1.

Furubotn, E. and Richter, R. (1997), *Institutions and Economic Theory: The Contribution of the New Institutional Economics*, Ann Arbor, University of Michigan Press.

Gossen, H. H. (1854), translated by Blitz, Rudolph C. (1983), *The Laws of Human Relations, and the Rules of Human Action Derived Therefrom*, Cambridge and London, MIT Press.

Hayek, F. A. (1973), *Law, Legislation and Liberty*, Vol. 1, Rules and Order, London, Routledge and Kegan Pau.

Hodgson, G. M. (2013), 'Come Back Marshall, All Is Forgiven? Complexity, Evolution, Mathematics and Marshallian Exceptionalism', *European Journal of the History of Economic Thought*, 20(6), 957–981.

Hutchison, T. W. (1953), *A Review of Economic Doctrines 1870–1929*, Oxford, Clarendon Press.

Jevons, W. S. (1871), *The Theory of Political Economy*, London and New York, Macmillan and Co.

Kahneman, D. (2011), *Thinking, Fast and Slow*, New York, Penguin Random House.

Kasper, W. and Streit, M. E. (1998), *Institutional Economics: Social Order and Public Policy*, Cheltenham, The Locke Institute, Edward Elgar.

Kay, J. and King, M. (2020), *Radical Uncertainty: Decision Making for an Unknowable Future*, London, The Bridge Street Press.

Kealey, T. and Ricketts, M. (2014), 'Modelling Science as a Contribution Good', *Research Policy*, 43(6), 1014–1024.

Kealey, T. and Ricketts, M. (2021), 'The Contribution Good as the Foundation of the Industrial Revolution' in Dekker, E. and Kuchar, P. (eds.) *Governing Markets as Knowledge Commons*, Cambridge, Cambridge University Press.

Kirzner, I. M. (1973), *Competition and Entrepreneurship*, Chicago, University of Chicago Press.

Knight, F. H. (1921), *Risk, Uncertainty and Profit*, Boston, Houghton Mifflin.

Marshall, A. (1925), *Principles of Economics*, 8th Edition, London, Macmillan.

McCloskey, D. N. (2016), *Bourgeois Equality: How Ideas, Not Capital or Institutions, Enriched the World*, Chicago, University of Chicago Press.

Menger, Carl (1871) *Principles of Economics*, translated and edited by Dingwall, Jones, and Hoselitz, Bert. F., (1950), Glencoe, Free Press.

Mill, J. S. (1859), 'On Liberty', in Lindsay, A.D. (ed.) (1968), *Utilitarianism, Liberty and Representative Government*, Everyman's Library, No.482, London and New York, J.M. Dent & Sons.

Mitchell, M. D. and Boettke, P. J. (2017), *Applied Mainline Economics*, Arlington, Mercatus Center, George Mason University.

Mokyr, J. (2017), *A Culture of Growth: The Origins of the Modern Economy*, Princeton, Princeton University Press.

Nelson, R. (1959), 'The Simple Economics of Basic Scientific Research', *Journal of Political Economy*, 67, 297–306.

Nelson, R. R. and Winter, S. C. (1982), *An Evolutionary Theory of Economic Change*, Cambridge, Harvard University Press.

North, D. (1981), *Structure and Change in Economic History*, New York, Norton.

North, D. (1991), 'Institutions', *Journal of Economic Perspectives*, 5(1), 97–112.

Ostrom, E. (1990), *Governing the Commons*, Cambridge, University Press, Cambridge.

Polanyi, M. (1967), *The Tacit Dimension*, Garden City, Doubleday Anchor.

Potts, J. (2019), *Innovation Commons: The Origin of Economic Growth*, Oxford, Oxford University Press.

Robbins, L. (1935), *An Essay on the Nature and Significance of Economic Science*, London, Macmillan.

Romer, P. M. (1990), 'Endogenous Technical Change', *Journal of Political Economy*, 98(5), S71–S102.

Rowley, C. K. and Peacock, A. T. (1975), *Welfare Economics: A Liberal Restatement*, York Studies in Economics, London, Martin Robertson.

Shackle, G. L. S. (1972), *Epistemics and Economics: A Critique of Economic Doctrines*, Cambridge, Cambridge University Press.

Shackle, G. L. S. (1979), 'Imagination, Formalism and Choice', in Rizzo, M.J. (ed.), *Time, Uncertainty and Disequilibrium*, Lanham, Lexington Books, D.C. Heath, 19–31
Solow, R. M. (1956), 'A Contribution to the Theory of Economic Growth', *Quarterly Journal of Economics*, 70, 65–94.
Thaler, R. H. (1991), *Quasi-Rational Economics*, New York, Russell Sage.
Thaler, R. H. and Sunstein, C. R. (2009), *Nudge: Improving Decisions About Health, Wealth and Happiness*, London, Penguin Books.
Tversky, A. and Kahneman, D. (1974), 'Judgement under Uncertainty: Heuristics and Biases', *Science*, 185, 1124–1131.
Walras, L. (1874), Éléments d'Économie Politique Pure, L Corbaz, Lausanne.
Williamson, O. E. (1985), *The Economic Institutions of Capitalism: Firms, Markets, Relational Contracting*, London, Collier Macmillan.

Part II

State-Sponsored Capitalism

A Critique

4 On Industrial Policy

Back to Bananas[1]

Alberto Mingardi

4.1 Introduction

"Industrial policy" is now the centre of public policy in the West. The cultural hegemony of the so-called "neo-liberalism",[2] if it ever existed, has been swept away by a powerful effort to have governments conducting the orchestra of industrial production.

The involvement of governments in the economy is hardly news. Indeed, the last century saw public spending on a trajectory towards ever greater values as a percentage of GDP. While full-fledged government ownership of companies is no longer a political goal in many countries, such high levels of spending end up with having a pronounced influence on the allocation of factors of production.

Juhász, Lane and Rodrik (2023) wisely point out that governments made abundant use of industrial policy, "even when they seem ideologically hostile to it", mentioning that Reagan "protected U.S. steel, auto, and motorcycle industries from import competition to encourage them to invest in technological upgrading" and that Thatcher "actively courted Japanese auto makers and promoted their UK investments with financial incentives". A realistic understanding of politics would suggest that decisions to selectively intervene in favour of a particular market player were not free of political considerations. That is, it is hard to assume that whatever public good justification is offered for specific subsidies or spending schemes should be taken at face value. It does not take a particular commitment to ideological libertarianism to understand that spending decisions that will *explicitly* affect some citizens more than others are going to be influenced by the pressures of interest groups and will be planned not to alienate but rather to please a certain constituency. It is uncontroversial that their ambition for re-election affects the time horizon of a politician's decisions, once in government.

Yet advocates of industrial policy seem to believe that government is an economic agent free from the anxiety of producing returns on its investment in a given period of time and thus free from the short-sighted constraints that hobble the actions of private actors. The ability to command greater resources than private investors and this liberty from short-term accounting make government the ideal backer of ambitious projects, with the potential to eventually transform an economy. The need for such a "transformation" has been strengthened, in the last few years, by

DOI: 10.4324/9781003504412-7

the need to design public policies intended to cope with climate change and by what many have called "the return of geopolitics" – which we may better call the attempt to scale globalisation down.

While international trade has been so far less affected by political disputes than expected (see Hogan & Hufbauer 2023), it is hard to deny that perhaps some of the most relevant political acts, by the US government and the European Commission in the last few years, have been moved by the logic of designing and implementing a more stringent industrial policy.

This implies more discretion on the part of governments in their intervention in the economy. These discretionary interventions may not sound upfront outrageous, like Emilio Vargas Molina who, as soon as he is raised to absolute power, declares the official language of San Marcos – the fictional state in Woody Allen's "Bananas" – to be Swedish and requires citizen to change their underwear every half hour, wearing it on the outside to enable the authorities to check the citizens' compliance with the new rule. But a closer scrutiny may reveal that they are nonetheless weakening the rule of law. The industrial policy advocates promise us Utopia. But they may lead us, if not to Woody Allen's *Bananas*, to look more like a Banana Republic nonetheless.

4.2 Take the Money and Run

"Industrial policy" is hardly a new notion. As John Burton remarked in a 1983 Institute of Economic Affairs (IEA) pamphlet, "government intervention in the process of economic evolution" has a very long history but modern industrial policy injects "taxpayers finance into *selected* firms or industries" (Burton 1983, 28, emphasis added). More recent definitions are likewise fairly broad: as an example, the International Monetary Fund considers as part of industrial policy "any targeted government intervention aimed at developing or supporting specific domestic firms, industries, or economic activities to achieve national economic or noneconomic (e.g., security, social, or environmental) objectives" (Evenett, Jakubik, Martin & Ruta 2024, 6)

Back in the early 1980s, Burton distinguished between industrial policies "which are designed to accelerate the rate of (successful) business experimentation" and those "aimed at thwarting, decelerating, or reversing the process of 'economic selection'" (Burton 1983, 29). The set of instruments that can be seen as the industrial policy toolbox (ranging from tariffs to subsidies) is wide enough to be applied for the pursue of two, apparently dissonant, goals.

In our days, industrial policies are advocated to speed up industrial developments and fostering new technologies (particularly in the areas of so-called green and digital transitions) but also to sustain the manufacturing base of a given country. "Reshoring" or, more recently, "friendshoring" has been part of the industrial policy rhetoric for the last decade. Industrial policy seems to pivot around an idea of *how* an economy should look like, *what* should be part of the economic landscape, and then add it if it is missing. While the latter points may be consequent on the first, that anybody can really have such a straightforward panoramic view of the economic landscape is questionable.

It is often argued that industrial policy recently made a "comeback" (see, just as examples of a wider bodies of journalistic comments, Feingold 2023; Shihi 2023), which assumes that it went away at some point in the past. Discretionary government interventions have always been part of the menu. But politics being a matter of words and symbols, how the government advertises what it does is perhaps as important as what it actually does.

In recent years, particularly since the outbreak of the Global Financial Crisis in 2007/2008 but even more so since the COVID-19 pandemic, governments have stopped pretending discretionary interventions in the economy – *selective* support to this or that company or industry – were either marginal or compatible with a broader rule-based policy framework. If we can agree that "ideas have consequences", how the transmission chain between political and economic ideas and facts work is hardly a set matter. During the alleged hegemony of neoliberalism (roughly speaking, from the Reagan to the Obama years), public opinion was apparently leery of interventions which were openly targeted to "pick the winners" of the competitive game. That attitude has changed.

Simon Evenett and his coauthors document, in year 2023, "a total of over 2,500 NIPs [new industrial policies] worldwide, out of which 71 percent are trade distorting" (Evenett et al. 2024, 7).

> Recent data for China, the European Union, and the United States, shows [sic] that on average there is a 73.8 percent probability a subsidy for a given product by one major economy is met with a subsidy for the same product by another within one year.
>
> (Evenett et al. 2024, 5)

In Europe, the element of novelty is perhaps the fact that industrial policy is nowadays a matter that EU institutions are taking into their own hands. This seems to reflect a change, at least in the Union's rhetoric. The European Union has been, right from its beginning, oscillating between "an Adam Smith baseline and a Colbertist one" (Jasay 2002). These different sensibilities imply a certain tension between those favouring political investment in a common market fostered by liberalisations and those seeing the EU as an "economic bloc" and hence in need of an industrial policy.

The first approach met perhaps the line of least resistance, as post-war Europe needed to restore trade and because of a general lack of interest, by European states, in having an autonomous competition policy. Indeed, the European Union has long been focused in policies aimed at levelling the playing field among member states. Article 107 of the Treaty on the Functioning of the European Union (TFEU) disciplines state aids, with the goal of making it the least distortionary and therefore preserving market discipline in the European single market. Indeed, "beyond the customs union and the unique Community competence in trade policy, a key feature of the Treaty of Rome—perhaps surprisingly—was the creation of a robust framework for a unique Community competence in competition policy. That included not only anti-cartel policy, but also a bar against state aids (government subsidies to individual firms)" (Portes 2021, 44). But the history of the European project can hardly account for as an exclusively pro-market adventure. One can easily remember that in 1950 the European Coal and Steel Community was "a narrowly conceived sectoral institution for the public regulation of only a single branch of production, the traditionally cartelized heavy industry of Western Europe" (Gillingham 2021, 82). Recent accounts of the history of industrial policy in the EU have accordingly stressed how its beginnings date to very debut of the European Community, when "the focus was notably on the strategic industries of coal, steel, electricity and railway" (Tagliapietra & Veugelers 2023, 14).

It has been observed that "from the year 2000 onwards, both the Member States and the EU began to be increasingly involved in developing industrial policy more actively, with a stronger focus on horizontal measures" (Szczepański & Zachariadis 2019, 6). The "Europe 2020" strategy already included among its "flagship initiatives" an "industrial policy for the globalization era" – but the document prepared by the Barroso commission seems to use the word to mean a series of different policy initiatives, aiming at both "supporting the development of a strong and sustainable industrial base able to compete globally" (so-called European champions) and "improving the business environment, notably for SMEs" (European Commission 2016).

The tone of the 2021 "State of the Union" address by Ursula von Der Leyen was distinctly different. The President of the European Commission announced "unprecedented" investments "in 5G and fibre … in digital skills" (and semiconductors and climate policy) and of the need to provide "a clear direction to markets and investors alike" (Von der Leyen 2021). State aid rules had been relaxed, to deal with the pandemic situation. Von der Leyen's baseline is the following: the world has problems, these problems can be solved with R&D, such R&D should be financed and "directed" by the EU institutions.

In the United States, the rhetorical turn is even sharper. With his anti-Chinese agenda, President Trump made "clear that he will take an active role in shaping industrial policy – one business at a time" (Bajaj 2016). But Trump's approach was hardly consistent and included a mixture of subsidies, tax cuts, deregulation initiatives and tariffs – all for the sake of making America great again vis-à-vis China. His economic activism was intertwined with his interpretation of foreign and trade policy. He considers it as an exercise in deal-making more than any kind of system. The most decisive act of the Trump administration – Operation Warp-Speed, which helped a faster development of COVID-19 vaccines – was a peculiar attempt at industrial policy: the government essentially entered in a procurement deal to only buy finished, FDA-approved doses of vaccines, regardless of their country of origin, and put together a deregulation package. One of the most successful vaccines, the BioNTech/Pfizer, was developed by a company which did not enter the deal but signed an advance-purchase contract. Operation Warp-Speed was not inspired by economic nationalism (one of its beneficiaries was to be French Sanofi, that however never developed a successful vaccine) and was neutral regarding the choice of technologies.

President Biden has brought to industrial policy a way more systematic approach. On April 27, 2023, the President's National Security Advisor, Jake Sullivan, gave a speech of paramount importance, defining the Administration's approach to foreign and industrial policy, the one being the logical consequence of the other. A foreign policy emphasis is very much part of contemporary industrial policy *rationale*.

Sullivan acknowledged the success of the United States, post-WWII reliance on multilateral trade agreements and (relatively) free enterprise:

> the United States led a fragmented world to build a new international economic order. It lifted hundreds of millions of people out of poverty. It sustained thrilling technological revolutions. And it helped the United States and many other nations around the world achieve new levels of prosperity.
>
> (Sullivan 2023)

The United States, starting with GATT (General Agreement on Tariffs and Trade) in 1947, have been the driving force nudging the world towards a freer and more integrated international economy. The United States' reliance on the openness of markets is recognised as key in reducing world poverty levels (in 1990, more than 30% of the world population lived under the poverty threshold, in 2018 it was 10%, in spite of a population 2 billion people bigger) and in fostering technological development too.

But for these successes, Sullivan argued that a relatively free market economy has weakened the American industrial base. It was based on the idea "that markets always allocate capital productively and efficiently – no matter what our competitors did, no matter how big our shared challenges grew, and no matter how many guardrails we took down".

Still, the core of its speech was the ambition to pursue not necessarily a more *efficient* allocation of resources, but one independent of exclusively economic criteria. In particular, the new Biden Administration "industrial and innovation strategy" is not meant to exclusively pursue a strengthening of the US "industrial base" (meaning: manufacturing in sectors deemed as "essential") but also to foster an adaptation to "a new environment defined by geopolitical and security competition"; "face an accelerating climate crisis" and "the challenge of inequality".

This is all to be accomplished by "building our domestic capacity" and moving the aim of trade policy from "tariff reduction" to an instrument to "build the world that we want". In the wake of the Russia-Ukraine conflict, globalisation as we knew it is considered a failure: the metric of success is no longer lifting people from poverty nor strengthening trade nor enlarging the boundaries of consumer choice, but democratic transition. Free trade (assumed, in this case, to be the only variable which mattered) failed because China and Russia did not become more "like" the United States or, as a cynical may say, more subservient to the United States. The economy did not serve a political imperative, hence it should change.

The crown jewel of the Biden strategy is the "CHIPS and Science Act", to which one should add the "Inflation Reduction Act" (IRA). The IRA's declared aim is to curb inflation, yet it purports to achieve this goal by "withdrawing excess purchasing power from the economy by way of increased taxation" (European

Parliament 2023). Many observed that "President Biden and a Democratic Congress were eager 'not to let a good crisis go to waste', and so used it to justify big increases in public spending and investment to achieve economic, social and environmental justice" (Pearlstein 2022). The fiscal cost is estimated to be as high as $1,000 billion (Gros, Mengel & Presidente 2023).

The priority of coping with climate change brought the Biden Administration to subsidise different industries. In June 2022, President Biden also called on the power of the Defense Production Act (DPA) to accelerate the domestic production of clean energy technologies. While these are complex normative acts, full of handouts and disguised provisions, the implications thereof are yet to fully emerge and mostly intertwined with the protection of special, national interests (see, for example, Lancaster 2023), the direction taken is one of more thorough intervention by Washington in the allocation of the factors or production: saying yes or no to different technologies and suppliers, partly with geopolitical motivation, partly for the sake of fostering a greener economy sooner.

The European Commission has responded by aiming at a more active involvement in industrial policy, so far through the use of a temporary financial instrument, the Recovery and Resilience Facility which was set up by the so-called Next Generation EU programme to cope with the economic distress caused by the pandemic and lockdown and then morphed into something different. While the United States' IRA influences and subsidies production through tax breaks, the EU does so by putting debt-financed funds on the table.

The ends (curbing global warming and adjusting to what governments have themselves labelled a geopolitical shock, as if they had nothing to do with it) justify the means. But the choice of means has consequences too. Consider the idea that transitioning to electric vehicles is necessary to achieve carbon neutrality. Some car-makers, for example former Toyota President Akio Toyoda (Davis 2023), have long expressed scepticism. Electric vehicles have certainly some advantages over fossil fuel-powered cars, but the coin is inevitably two-sided. Electric vehicles tend to be more expensive, they need an extensive network of EV charges to be convenient, they are still unsuited for long-distance travel. Ironically, thinking of the protectionist undertones of industrial policy, the use of lithium batteries makes Western countries more dependent on China (Backhaus 2021). It is also telling that subsidies to electric vehicles manufacturers were disbursed lavishly, until the European Commission figured out that Chinese manufacturers mastered that production in an apparently more efficient way than European competitors. The swift change of emphasis on electric cars by government authorities and the media, in late 2023, makes one wonders how much of the "Green deal" industrial policy was actually a cover-up for old style protectionism: once foreign car-makers proved to profit out of it, the insistence over net zero commitments faded out.

The jury, of course, is still out, but transitioning to electric vehicles seems to be far less of a smooth path than official documents acknowledge. Picking a technology as a winner is not as easy as it seems. And it can well be a badly disguised attempt to benefit some special interests, at the cost of others. All such attempts, as production is not as easily planned as political leaders maintain, can always fail.

4.3 Mariana and Her Sisters

Few economists have affected this new fashion of industrial policy more than Mariana Mazzucato, author of *The Entrepreneurial State*, a book which was originally a monograph published by the think tank Demos in England and later turned, in the 2013 edition, into an international bestseller.

In editing a comprehensive collection on applications on her ideas, Karl Wennberg and Christian Sandström (2022, 4) have argued that a succession of crises – the Global Financial Crisis in 2007–2008, the Euro crisis in 2011–2013 and the pandemic in 2020 – prepared the scene for "the renaissance of industrial interventionism". Since Mazzucato's work has been so influential in reshaping the contemporary discourse, I will focus on it as the paramount example of advocacy of industrial policy.

Of course, she is hardly alone. Certainly left-of-centre economists have been engaged in refashioning an economic role for the state for quite some times. The "Washington Consensus" and "Neo-liberalism" have long been a target of advocates of greater state intervention. Yet Mazzucato, though academically less prestigious than many others (consider Paul Krugman, Dani Rodrik, and Joseph Stiglitz to name only the best known), has boldly added something which was perhaps missing in the public debate.

In an interview, some 50 years ago, Milton Friedman observed that "It's fortunate that the capitalist society is more productive, because if it were not it would never be tolerated. The bias against it is so great that, as it is, it's got to have a five-to-one advantage in order to survive" (Machan, Cobb & Raico 1974). Particularly after 1989, capitalism was seen as perhaps less *equitable* than the alternative, but more efficient. The left, for example, in the 1990s, after the fall of the Berlin Wall, made peace with the market economy apparently realising that, in order for wealth to be redistributed, it needed to be created first. And a market economy was generally considered good at that. In particular, it was seen as capable to produce those technological novelties, from washing machines to cell phones, which have so dramatically changed our daily lives.

Mazzucato's work is superbly suited to confirm the biases of those who do not like a capitalist society, but it also insinuates that capitalism is actually not more productive, as they were mistakenly brought to believe by free market propagandists. Why then not go for more public involvement in the economy, if it also proved to be the thing which is really behind our cornucopia of innovative goods?

Her argument persuaded many because it was perfectly attuned to a very intuitive understanding of how the development of new technology, and ultimately wealth creation, works.

Biochemist Terence Kealey call it "the linear model": Government money → science → technology → economic growth. The model starts with recognition that advances in knowledge are what accounts for growth and progress.[3] New knowledge benefits way more people than those who were actively involved in a discovery or an invention. From this obviously true fact, the linear model infers that no individual researcher or company would ever spend the effort and resources needed for Research and Development (R&D), since his reward is bound to be a small share of the overall benefits. "Ever since Francis Bacon", writes Kealey, people have agreed that science should not be a matter of trade secrets, not "monopolized but … be used largely by others, including competitors, enemies, and the unborn" (Kealey 2008, 17). As science was labelled a public good, it was easy to infer that government should finance it. In the model, technology and its applications are a necessary consequence of some prior "pure" science, which is in turn the consequence of some prior government investment.

While science and technology are obviously interconnected, such connection is far from linear. Economic historian Joel Mokyr, who stressed – more than any other scholar – the importance of scientific advancement for economic growth, has shown how tinkerers, producing better instruments for their own needs, have in fact yielded scientific insights, rather than the other way around.

In Mazzucato's scheme, private businesses are basically living off what the government presciently achieved before. On their own, at best, they reach for the low-hanging fruits, after the government grew the tree. If this is right, if the linear model – which Mazzucato endorses – is correct, the capitalist society, to use Friedman's word, will not be tolerated any longer. What was seen as its redeeming virtue – its capacity to create growth and foster innovation – is actually due to the *noncapitalist* element in it: government, an economic actor which is not constrained by those factors that limit all the others.

For Mazzucato, if this is not properly recognised, it is largely because errors in our accounts of how innovation works. Such errors are due to economists, who endorsed "Market Failure Theory". Such a perspective is equated with the idea that government intervention can be accepted largely as a corrective to instances of market failure. Mazzucato stresses the substantial influence, in that regard, of free market economists,[4] who stand for a double test before accepting new interventions:

> market failure is only a necessary but not sufficient condition for governmental intervention. The sufficiency results from an assessment that the gains from the intervention outweigh the associated costs due to 'government failures' (…). Thus, there would be a trade-off between two inefficient outcomes, one generated by free markets (market failure) and the other by governmental intervention (government failure).
>
> (Mazzucato and Penna 2015, 7)

The narrative that emphasises government failures aims, in Mazzucato's eyes, to make us disregard the essential contribution of government investing in technologies that later were turned into consumer goods. For "different types of public actors have been responsible for actively shaping and creating markets and systems, not just fixing them" (Mazzucato 2017, 15).

Mazzucato hence sees herself, in her own words, as engaged in a "discursive battle", to restore the credibility of the state as an economic actor (Mazzucato 2013, 9). This is a radical effort: though sometimes Mazzucato seems to accept that governments can be inefficient or wasteful, she is not assuming a high likelihood of such possibility. Therefore, even when she deals with very concrete examples of government investments, she is very parsimonious with details of how a particular set of rules and institutions works – and how they may be offsetting issues, such as the time horizon of politicians being set on political cycles, the political actors' opportunistic behaviour, the need of preventing political priorities and interests to hijack investments that have ostensible different goals, et cetera. In short, Mazzucato deems market agents to be short-sighted and selfish, but tends to disregard the possibility that political decision-makers may be just like that. Scepticism towards politics being always loyal to its stated goals is dismissed as government bad-mouthing.

To solve this "Public Relations problem" of industrial policy and governments, Mazzucato did not choose to revisit the evidence on its record in countries that openly and proudly engaged in it, such as Italy. With a brilliant move, she decided to claim that industrial policy mattered the most where you did least expect it: in the United States.

The most popular of her claims are that the Internet is nothing but a contrivance of the public sector and that the iPhone, the signature product of the smartphone age, is in itself more a consequence of smart planning by public agencies in R&D than of Steve Jobs's genius.

After World War II, basic research in the United States was largely nationalised, in a manner consistent with the " permanent war efforts" that absorbed the country's attention during the Cold War. Vannevar Bush, the director of the Office of Scientific Research and Development, the agency set up by President Franklin Delano Roosevelt to coordinate scientific research for military purposes, famously argued for keeping the same model alive in peacetime – hence the birth of the National Science Foundation and other government agencies. V. Bush was a believer in what Kealey defined as the "linear model".

Mazzucato focuses her attention on DARPA (Defense Advanced Research Projects Agency), considering it a "dynamic and flexible structure" that "increased the flow of knowledge across competing research groups" (Mazzucato 2013, 77). On the *institutional* reasons for such flexibility and apparent success, Mazzucato tends to be parsimonious, lest she becomes entangled with institutional structure and organisational details. She credits DARPA for nothing less than the creation of the Internet.

It cannot be denied that the federal government supported universities to develop the concepts and the hardware which turned out to be the building blocks of the Internet, such as FTP (file transfer protocol) and TCP/IP (transmission control protocol/Internet protocol) standards. The fundamental idea behind the Internet is that of "packet switching", a digital networking communications method in which data are transmitted in suitably sized blocks, called packets. This concept was developed by two MIT researchers, Joseph Carl Robnett Licklider and Leonard Kleinrock, who eventually worked on ARPANET, the network that became the basis for the Internet. With the benefit of hindsight, perhaps DARPA just picked the right guys for the job (Chandler 2005, 170).

Yet we should likewise remember that the TCI/IP router was developed (for ARPANET) by a private business, Cisco (Chandler 2005, 172), while the optical fibre that made it possible for Internet to reach millions of houses was developed by Corning Glass Works, another private enterprise. Two further points should not be overlooked: the government grants that allegedly led to the invention of the Internet were essentially military spending, and those grants were channelled through the US university system.

The Internet is more of an ecosystem of inventions and instruments than anything that could be considered a "device" or a "tool". By singling out ARPANET's contributions – packet switching and the forerunners of modern e-mails – Mazzucato assumes that they are the key ingredients in the internet recipe, key in the sense of irreplaceable and necessary. Symmetrically, she implicitly deems all the *commercial* development of the Internet, which happened in the 1990s, with a tumultuous series of innovation ranging from https secure protocols to the development of private Internet Service Providers, to be irrelevant.

Price Fishback (2007: 516) admits that "no one can deny the vast repercussions of militarily motivated activities" in the development of the Internet. He goes on to say, "The military's role was clearly sufficient to develop the early technologies, but arguably it was not necessary. The credit for these technologies should go to the actual people performing the research" (Fishback 2007, 521).

It is one thing to write that a few key building blocks of the Internet were developed by researchers that happened to be on the military's payroll, a totally different one is to assume that the Internet makes the case for government unambiguously envisioning the *creation* of a new market or product.

It is important to notice that Mazzucato does not simply maintain that public investment (either in the military or in base research) ultimately can have spillover effects that reach and benefit consumers. That would be an uncontentious claim, though one could always wonder about the opportunity cost of such investment (or believe that military investment is dangerous per se, regardless of the fact that former military technologies mutated into daily appliances for most of us). Mazzucato proposes us a radically different view: that bureaucracies exercise "mission-directed directionality". They should be considered *directly* responsible for consumer goods that ended up carrying technologies which were developed for other purposes. In other words, civil applications of military technology, for example, should not be considered indirect consequences of the development of the latter: but an example in which government foresight *shaped* a future consumer goods market.

Mazzucato captivated the imagination of her readers by arguing that government is also responsible for the invention of the iPhone. To show how touch-screen devices are something we owe to industrial policy, Mazzucato argues that it was government funding that allowed a young PhD student at the University of Delaware, Wayne Westerman, to complete his degree and go on to cofound FingerWorks, which "revolutionized the multi-billion-dollar mobile electronic devices industry" (Mazzucato 2013, 103). Can we really argue that if somebody at a certain point transforms his own doctoral thesis into an entrepreneurial idea, the latter is the product of industrial policy? Is this really the case just because his university was government-funded and his PhD was partially funded by a scholarship from the National Science Foundation, like some 2,000 others every year?

Mazzucato credits economist Richard Nelson as a major influence for the notion of a "direction" of economic growth. Nelson was one of the first arguing for the rationale of government financing of research (Nelson 1959) and then became a critic of "standard" Neo-classical understanding of growth and innovation (see, inter alia, Nelson 1995, 1998). His view of institutions and government, in particular in the process of technical advancement, is distinctly more nuanced than Mazzucato's. Her understanding of how a direction may be given to production is perhaps best expressed by this apparently matter-of-fact proposition: "The ambition to achieve a particular type of economic growth (smart, inclusive, sustainable) is a direct admission that economic growth has not only a rate but also a *direction*" (Mazzucato 2017, 5). What is rational is real and what is real is rational: if governments pretend they can *direct* growth in a certain way, it means growth is always *directed* one way or another.

Even though when she speaks she tends to be more nuanced and moderate, in print Mazzucato presents a rather bleak diagnosis of the free market economy. Market actors are hopelessly short-sighted and such short-sightedness reduces the rate of innovation in society. Private investors, in particular, are blinded by their "emphasis on short-term results" (Mazzucato 2019, 61).

Though businessmen are certainly imperfect, and would formulate and act on many value judgment which prove to be wrong at the market test, one may find it surprising that allocations of resources by other human beings, who instead work as government agent, proved unequivocally superior. Yet Mazzucato's view of the private sector as short-termist and egotistical (two things that it may well be, and yet they won't necessarily make government better at any investment) is such that for her it is well-nigh impossible not to believe that, behind any genuine innovation, we must find the benevolent, visible hand of the State.

She sees the scarcity of capital standing in the way of many discoveries and innovations, as some research programmes are not pursued for as long as they should, because of the apparent lack of (immediate) results. Private investors, who "have skin in the game", tend to be highly discriminating, thus forfeiting some investments in favour of others. But this is, if not the human condition altogether, the essence of economic activity: resources are scarce, human desires are not, ideas possibly are not either, but we need to allocate the first to serve the latter two. Private property and a market economy are means to ration resources, selecting between human desires which need to be pursued, on the one hand, and the ideas to more effectively pursue them, on another. Of course, in the process many roads end up not to be taken – but we cannot know where they would lead. How long has the idea of an electric car been ignored, because of short-termist, fossil-fuel hungry private businesses?

Rejecting Mazzucato's argument does not mean endorsing the idea that only what is immediately useful or expedient or profitable ought to be *studied.* Academic institutions traditionally pursued research programmes that are none of these things. But neither the research they pursue has to be understood as conductive to productive innovations per se, nor *directed* towards that goal.

Mazzucato sees government investment as necessary to unleash human creativity. If we did away with the scarcity of capital altogether, and research programmes could be pursued whatever their immediate shortcomings, we will end up having far more innovations. The closest thing that we have to an investor for whom capital is not scarce is the government, and thus it should be in charge of innovation.

This line of reasoning[5] thus tends to present private businesses as standing in the way of greater innovation, because they are tyrannised by short-sightedness and selfishness, that are ultimately the consequence of scarcity. Plentifulness makes perfection: it is the potential lack of budget constraints on the government's part, more than any specific institutional device, that makes it the ideal backer of new projects. Unsurprisingly, this seems to be a way of thinking which political decision-makers tend to appreciate.

4.4 Shadows and Fog

Mazzucato's work provided the main justification for the trends I have tried to survey, albeit impressionistically, in the first part of this chapter. Her own website chronicles her own accomplishments, both in terms of honours and of prestigious advising positions. Her voice has certainly been heard in Brussels as well as in Washington, DC. The ideas that she championed, and the style and words she used to champion them, have acquired currency. Their popularity grew even within the economic profession. To the point that very strong assumptions became considered like truisms by many, including very serious scholars.

For example, in a recent symposium on industrial policy, Nobel Laureate Michael Spence has written that "the objective of industrial policies is to alter market outcomes in ways that align them better with a country's broader economic and social objectives" (Spence 2023). The sentence is a chilling reminder of the simple-mindedness of the contemporary public debate, all the more frightening as it comes from such a distinguished source. Does a country really have "objectives", social and economic? Is it fair to equate them with whatever line of action a government is at a certain moment in time pursuing? Such a line of action is not perhaps more appropriately seen as reflecting the objectives of a political party or coalition, which is at best just a section of a country? If so, are we sure that such objectives are innocent of any specific interest group's meddling?

The strong reliance on industrial policy should alarm us, for two different, though intertwined, reasons. The first one concerns the understanding of the economy, or better to say: of *production*. The second one should concern us, in terms of individual liberty.

One rather staggering common feature of Jake Sullivan's speech and other similar approaches is the fact they consider the idea that market allocates resources efficiently "an oversimplified assumption". In fact, they do not challenge it: they would simply see resources allocated for the sake of goals other than efficiency. But for justifying this turn, they deploy the most oversimplified of assumptions, that is, they seem to imply that production can easily and simply be trimmed to accommodate political goals, at no cost in terms of efficiency. Production is far more complicated than it is typically accounted for. Even the smallest entrepreneurial venture sees the entrepreneur, or the managers, and the workers, facing a multitude of daily problems and learning by doing.

The linear model, as refashioned by Mazzucato, assumes not only *directionality* but an incredible smoothness in such directionality.

The first of these assumptions is historically questionable. As we have briefly outlined, it does not seem very plausible that the commercial development of the Internet or of mobile telephony was "envisioned" in any sense by those who proposed or financed a particular innovation for totally different reasons. Mazzucato adopts an argument akin to the idea that something may always happen, so to say, "downstream", to justify some "upstream" investment. This is, however, a dangerous way or arguing: literally *any* investment or *any* policy can be justified, in this way. But even defence and military spending, perhaps one may say: especially defence and military spending, should be considered and undertaken on the basis of a concrete cost-benefit analysis, given the declared goal. The declared goal of any military scientific programme is no less specific to the circumstances it is undertaken in, than anything else.

The second (the smoothness in such directionality) is just unrealistic. Markets are often criticised for the abruptness and severity of the adjustments they go through: when circumstances change, adaptability is paramount. But adaptation to new circumstances is in itself a process of change and learning, which requires difficult choices taken in conditions of uncertainty. Even if the "direction" of technological development was clear – if, for instance, compact nuclear fusion reactors were seen by virtually all credentialed observers as the answer to our energetic needs, and being compatible with bettering environmental conditions, this would hardly answer all the questions their producers need to ask themselves. Moving from a project to its realisation – assuming such realisation needs to be economical, that is: to allocate scarce resources in the most cost-effective way – is not a trivial detail. The bulk of economic activity concerns petty details, incremental improvements, continuous switching from one supplier to another, from one raw material to another, in short from a set of factors of production to another. If innovation is a recipe, it is an ever changing one.

Breakthrough innovation does not happen in a vacuum and is seldom achieved just because of brilliant ideas and new technological achievements. "Gadgets" alone are not the be-all and end-all of innovation. What made the gasoline-powered car such a phenomenal invention was not merely the technical achievement of the automotive industry: it was it meeting a *demand*.

What private business does, in a market economy, is ordering factors of production in a way consistent with its attempt to meet and anticipate consumer demand. Production is not like playing with Lego: it does not imply piling one little brick upon another, up to the point in which our construction looks like the picture on the box. There is, in fact, no picture. Consumption is the ultimate end of production – and this is perhaps where liberty enters the picture. Whatever its faults, the market economy organises production to serve the consumers' freely expressed desires. It is based upon attempts (not always successful) to imagine what they may want, not to *forcing* them to go with this product or, for that matter, with this technology.

The profit motive constrains suppliers: it forces them to work to the benefit of others, and to consider the latter's needs and wants, rather than their own.

Top-down industrial policy tends to forget about what we, following F.A. Hayek, call the "knowledge problem" (Hayek 1945): information of the kind which is needed to produce goods and services, and goods and services which match real consumer demand, is dispersed in society and is hardly available to economic planners. Whatever their wisdom, they will not have the knowledge of the circumstances of time and place where production happens, which are the domain of the man on the spot.

But of course, the way in which contemporary industrial policy enthusiasts argue altogether dismisses the knowledge problem. To echo Spence, what are a country's "broader economic and social objectives?" The reasonable answer would seem to be: who knows. A "country" does not speak nor write, but individuals do. But of course, if we assume its objectives to be simply those that the pro tempore decision-makers fashion, then the riddle is easily solved.

To understand the force of Hayek's argument about dispersed information, you need at first to assume that production ought to serve demand. Yet, if the drive of policy becomes the need to have consumers swallow things they do not necessarily care for, the picture understandably changes. In the comments by Jake Sullivan, we see exactly that: the candid assumption that the US administration is so powerful as to reshape the world, and if the world to be reshaped is the whole economy, so be it. Everything becomes simple, once you substitute the virtually endless needs and desires of flesh-and-blood human beings with some overarching values.

4.5 The Front

This should be enough to see why this new wave of industrial policy puts individual liberty in jeopardy. For one, the people's concrete needs are substituted for by some higher value, popular among decision-makers. The fact that the policy impacts the organisation of production and not the stocks of available goods and services directly is only a charade: when you control supply, you control demand. Industrial policy will limit the ends individuals can pursue, by restraining the access to attend to them.

Such an activist State in the realm of production is not compatible with the rule of law – no matter how it tries to hide this fact. The rule of law is a contentious and complex concept, but it would be relatively uncontentious to claim it basically consists of a series of rules uniformly applicable and endorsed regardless of the identity of the actors involved. Industrial policy is about cherry picking and discretionary power. It aims to selective prize one or another, for extra-economic features of this or that particular producer (being State-owned, being involved in this or that kind of production, being national, et cetera).

Limiting political discretion is the Sisyphean task of classical liberalism – which often failed at it. But a public opinion totally intrigued by industrial policy convinced that discretionary choices by government today "creates" markets tomorrow, believing that economic growth is for us to be planned at the conditions set by temporary decision-makers, makes the task simply impossible to accomplish.

It is ironic, but the rhetoric of entrusting the State to pursue innovation will make our legal systems looking more and more akin to those of States that we used to dismiss as "Banana Republics". The road to Bananas is paved with great ambitions.

Notes

1 I am grateful to Juan E. Castañeda and David Perazzoni, for having read and commented upon a previous version of this paper. It is very unlikely this book will ever end up in his hands, still I feel the need to apologise to Woody Allen, too.
2 The word serves little more than the purpose of labelling intellectual views that the labellers don't like, blaming upon them whatever inequities that come with the status quo. Perhaps for this reason enjoys wide popularity.
3 This is "Schumpeterian growth", based upon technical advancement and innovation, rather than "Smithies growth", which comes out of enlarging the division of labour. Though scholars like to distinguish them analytically, they are often intertwined.
4 Mazzucato tends to quote, as a standard example of free market economists, a primer in public choice (Tullock et al. 2002), first published by the IEA in London and then by the Cato Institute. It is worth noting that that work is not specifically concerned with the way in which market economies produce innovation or build on dispersed knowledge – but on government failure. This concept can be seen as the true *bete noire* of Mazzucato.
5 With a distinguished co-author, I tried to deal with it at length in McCloskey and Mingardi (2020).

References

Backhaus, Richard. 2021. "Battery Raw Materials – Where from and Where to?" *ATZ Worldwide*, Vol. 123, No. 9, pp. 8–13. Available at https://www.ncbi.nlm.nih.gov/pmc/articles/PMC8390110/

Bajaj, Vikas. 2016. "Donald Trump's Company-by-Company Industrial Policy". *The New York Times*, December 8. Available at https://www.nytimes.com/2016/12/08/opinion/donald-trumps-company-by-company-industrial-policy.html

Burton, John. 1983. *Picking Losers...? The Political Economy of Industrial Policy*. London: Institute of Economic Affairs.

Chandler, Arthur. D. Jr. 2005. *Inventing the Electronic Century: The Epic Story of the Consumer Electronics and Computer Industries*. Cambridge, MA: Harvard University Press.

Davis, River. 2023. "Toyota Chairman Says People Are Finally Seeing the Reality About EVs Akio Toyoda's Comments Come Amid Cooling U.S. Demand and a Price War with China". wsj.com, October 25. Available at https://www.wsj.com/business/autos/toyota-chairman-says-people-are-finally-seeing-the-reality-about-evs-31f1669c

European Commission. 2016. EUROPE 2020. A strategy for smart, sustainable and inclusive growth. Available at https://op.europa.eu/en/publication-detail/-/publication/6a915e39-0aab-491c-8881-147ec91fe88a/language-hr

European Parliament. 2023. EU's response to the US Inflation Reduction Act (IRA). Available at https://www.europarl.europa.eu/RegData/etudes/IDAN/2023/740087/IPOL_IDA(2023)740087_EN.pdf

Evenett, Simon, Adam Jakubik, Fernando Martin & Michele Ruta. 2024. *The Return of Industrial Policy in Data*. WP/24/1. International Monetary Fund.

Feingold, Spencer. 2023. "Industrial policy has officially made a comeback, chief economists say". *Davos Agenda. World Economic Forum*, May 2. Available at https://www.weforum.org/agenda/2023/05/growth-summit-industrial-policy-officially-comeback-chief-economists/

Fishback, Price V. 2007. "Seeking Security in the Postwar Era" in Price V. Fishback et al. (eds.) *Government and the American Economy: A New History*, pp. 507–556. Chicago, The University of Chicago Press.

Gillingham, John R. III. 2021. "The Monnet Method and the Obsolescence of the EU" in Giavazzi, Francesco, Lefebrve D'Ovidio Francesco & Alberto Mingardi (eds). *The Liberal Heart of Europe. Essays in Memory of Alberto Giovannini*, Cham, Palgrave Macmillan., pp. 81–90. Available at https://link.springer.com/chapter/10.1007/978-3-030-60368-7_7

Gros, Daniel, Philipp-Leo Mengel & Giorgio Presidente. 2023. *The EU and the US Inflation Reduction Act. No Rose without Thorns*, IEP Working Paper. Available at https://iep.unibocconi.eu/sites/default/files/media/attach/IEP@BU_WP01_0_NoRoseWithoutThorns_correct.pdf

Hayek, F.A. 1945. "The Use of Knowledge in Society", *The American Economic Review*, Vol. 35, No. 4, pp. 519–530.

Hogan, Morgan & Gary Clyde Hufbauer. 2023. *Despite Disruptions, US-China Trade Is Likely to Grow*, October. Washington, DC: Peter Institute for International Economics. Available at https://www.piie.com/publications/policy-briefs/despite-disruptions-us-china-trade-likely-grow

Jasay, Anthony de. 2002. "Between Colbert and Adam Smith)", *Cato Journal*, Vol. 21, No. 3, Winter. 359–367.

Juhász, R., N Lane & D. Rodrik. 2023. *The New Economics of Industrial Policy*. Available at http://tinyurl.com/2ckdgn4z

Kealey, Terence. 2008. *Sex, Science and Profits*, London, Heinemann.

Lancaster, Joc. 2023. "The Inflation Reduction Act Is Screwing Up the Market for Electric Vehicles", *Reason.com*, March 24, Available at https://reason.com/2023/03/24/the-inflation-reduction-act-is-screwing-up-the-market-for-electric-vehicles/

Machan, Tibor, Joe Cobb & Ralph Raico. 1974. "An Interview with Milton Friedman", *Reason*, December. Available at https://reason.com/1974/12/01/an-interview-with-milton-fried/

Mazzucato, Mariana. 2013. *The Entrepreneurial State: Debunking Public vs. Private Sector Myths*, London: Anthem Press.

Mazzucato, Mariana. 2017. *Mission-Oriented Innovation Policy. Challenges and Opportunities*, London: UCL Institute for Innovation and Public Purpose.

Mazzucato, Mariana. 2019. *The Value of Everything. Making and Taking in the Global Economy*. London: Penguin.

Mazzucato, Mariana & Caetano Penna. 2015. "Beyond Market Failures: The Market Creating and Shaping Roles of State Investment Banks", Institute for New Economic Thinking Working Paper Series No. 7. Available at https://papers.ssrn.com/sol3/papers.cfm?abstract_id=2586246

McCloskey, Deirdre N. & Alberto Mingardi. 2020. *The Myth of the Entrepreneurial State*. Great Barrington, MA: AIER.

Nelson, Richard. 1959. "The Simple Economics of Basic Scientific Research", *Journal of Political Economy* 67, pp. 297–306.

Nelson, Richard. 1995. "Recent Evolutionary Theorizing about Economic Change", *Journal of Economic Literature*, Vol. 33, No. 1, pp. 48–90.

Nelson, Richard. 1998. "The Agenda for Growth Theory: A Different Point of View", *Cambridge Journal of Economics*, Vol. 22, No. 4, pp. 497–520.

Pearlstein, Steven. 2022. "Why the 'Inflation Reduction Act' is no such thing", *The Washington Post*, August 7. Available at https://www.washingtonpost.com/us-policy/2022/08/07/inflation-reduction-act-false/

Portes, Richard. 2021. "The European "Postwar Consensus" and the Birth of the EEC", in Giavazzi, Francesco, Lefebrve D'Ovidio Francesco & Alberto Mingardi (eds). *The Liberal Heart of Europe. Essays in Memory of Alberto Giovannini*, Cham, Palgrave Macmillan., pp. 41–46.

Shihi, Will. C. 2023. "The New Era of Industrial Policy Is Here", *Harvard Business Review*, September–October. Available at https://hbr.org/2023/09/the-new-era-of-industrial-policy-is-here

Spence, Michael. 2023. In Defense of Industrial Policy. Project Syndicate, May 5. Available at https://www.project-syndicate.org/commentary/industrial-policy-us-chips-and-science-act-debate-by-michael-spence-2023-05.

Sullivan, Jake. 2023. Remarks by National Security Advisor Jake Sullivan on Renewing American Economic Leadership at the Brookings Institution, April 27, Available at https://www.whitehouse.gov/briefing-room/speeches-remarks/2023/04/27/remarks-by-national-security-advisor-jake-sullivan-on-renewing-american-economic-leadership-at-the-brookings-institution/

Szczepański, Marcin & Ioannis Zachariadis. 2019. *EU Industrial Policy at the Crossroads. Current State of Affairs, Challenges and Way Forward*, Brussels, European Parliamentary Research Service.

Tagliapietra, Simone & Reinhilde Veugelers. 2023. "Industrial policy in Europe: past and future" in Tagliapietra, Simone & Reinhilde Veugelers (eds). *Sparking Europe's New Industrial Revolution. A Policy for Net Zero, Growth and Resilience*, Brussels, Bruegel, pp. 13–28.

Tullock, Gordon, Arhur Seldon & Gordon Brady. 2002. *Government Failure: A Primer in Public Choice*, Washington, DC, Cato Institute.

Von der Leyen, Ursula. 2021. State of the Union Address, September 15. Available at https://ec.europa.eu/commission/presscorner/detail/en/SPEECH_21_4701

Wennberg, Karl & Christian Sandström (eds). 2022. *Questioning the Entrepreneurial State. Status-quo, Pitfalls, and the Need for Credible Innovation Policy*, Cham, Springer.

5 State-Sponsored Capitalism and the Erosion of Liberal Democracy

Aris Trantidis

5.1 Introduction

Democratic backsliding, autocratisation or de-democratisation are terms that describe the process by which the governing party starts building what Robert Dahl described as an 'inclusive hegemony' (1971: 8, 34), a system with a formally open structure of political participation but low levels of political contestability. Starting with a political playing field that favours the government against the opposition (Diamond, 2002: 28), this process can get to a degree that democratic politics will be 'guided' or 'managed' by the government (Colton and McFaul, 2003; McFaul, 2005; Konitzer and Wegren, 2007). A victory for the opposition, while not impossible, would require a level of opposition mobilisation, unity, skill and heroism far beyond what would normally be required for victory in a genuine democracy (Diamond, 2002: 24). This political system can slide further down into 'competitive authoritarianism' and 'electoral authoritarianism' (Schedler, 2006; Levitsky and Way, 2010), ultimately, to a situation in which the political force in government never loses an election and all other parties are 'without hope of being in government' (Ware, 1996: 159 and 165).

A strategy of autocratisation requires making fundamental changes in the properties of a democratic system. These changes do not merely depend on how the government acts. Autocratisation is about interactions between the government and its social, economic, political and institutional environment. On the one hand, liberal democracy is bolstered by the capacity of socioeconomic actors to openly oppose state policies, criticise the government, express their differentiated views publicly and disseminate information that exposes what some may think as government mistakes or abuses of power. On the other hand, the preferences and capacity of these actors, including any bargaining power they have versus the government, are defined by the kind of relationships they develop with state power, the position they occupy within the spectrum of state regulations and distributions, the economic resources they can use, the sources from which they get these resources and, ultimately, the kind of state power exercised upon them.

How government exercises state power in the economy and society has profound political implications. In *The Road to Serfdom*, Hayek (1944) argued that a planned economy could progressively and stealthily lead to political authoritarianism.

DOI: 10.4324/9781003504412-8

Planners will not know what should be produced and in which quantities and will thus fail to produce satisfactory and desirable distributive outcomes. As a result, there will be mounting grievances in society as well as demands from the public for stronger powers to be granted to the government to get these planning decisions right. This will be creating a political and economic landscape governed by authoritative decisions and can eventually come to resemble a dictatorship. Hayek's projection was never tested in liberal democracies (Trantidis and Cowen, 2020). Post-war social democratic parties in Western Europe abandoned the idea of socialist planning and opted for a mixed economy with market forces as the main producers of goods and services under state regulations, a level of taxation and several transfers of resources in the form of welfare benefits and industrial subsidies.

The mixed economy includes government policies that sponsor certain types of economic activity and can benefit specific economic actors and exclude others by selection. Policies to support or create business opportunities, build infrastructure, tackle crises with emergency actions, transfers and rules, support nascent industries, promote exports and protect domestic production from imports involve taking discretionary and often *ad hoc* and personalised decisions. State sponsorship of social and economic activity also extends to the media through state licenses and advertisement, and to people working in the broader public sector through appointments, promotions and terms of employment. State sponsorship creates a nexus of expectations and demands linking the government with social and economic actors that build up civil society: firms, charities, Non-Governmental Organisations (NGOs), professional associations, etc. These relationships diminish the overall autonomy of civil society from what the state does. The state's role in sponsoring activities in economy and society sets up a structure of incentives and disincentives that impacts on the decisions of individuals and their organisations or firms. What is more, the people in charge of government can use state power to pursue their own goals, but, in a democracy, they must still negotiate with the social stakeholders.

With this chapter, I explore the political implications of state sponsorship for liberal democracies and associate them with the current concern with democratic backsliding as a possible trajectory for consolidated democracies. In Section 5.2, I argue that increasing levels of political polarisation and factionalism, typically seen as a negative feature of populist tactics and contentious politics, are unavoidable consequences of the state's distributive and regulatory power. Political divisions and clashes reflect diverse and often conflicting interests and preferences in society that can hardly be accommodated by a single political organisation. This inevitably fuels political contestation but also builds up democracy's resilience to efforts by a single political group to dominate politics and society. The point is that competition between relatively autonomous socioeconomic actors with sufficient resources to gain some bargaining power versus the government and exert some influence on the political sphere, even for rent-seeking purposes, is what actually sustains a relatively pluralist structure of collective action and prevents one-party domination. However, how the government shapes this network of interactions, including how much negotiating power social actors have, depends on the model and reach of state sponsorship in the economy.

In Section 5.3, I explain how state-sponsored capitalism is sowing the seeds of democracy's decline. An economic structure in which the government can discretionarily sponsor economic activities and choose winners and losers is likely to develop into a clientelist system. State sponsorship becomes the subject of clientelist exchange between the political organisation in government and the socioeconomic actors competing for access to the opportunities and benefits by which the recipients, such as firms or individuals, receive privileges in return for their support and loyalty to the distributing political organisation. Reciprocation can come in the form of campaign donations, party membership, open expressions of support and criticism of the opposition, positive media coverage and their own political campaign inside their workplace. This way, clientelism serves as a mechanism for political parties and individual politicians to build a network of loyal supporters that plays a crucial role in the mobilisation and consolidation of broader electoral support. Political organisations have a strong incentive to turn state sponsorship into the predominant method of allocating resources while economic actors a strong incentive to adjust their behaviour accordingly to receive government-granted privileges. Ultimately, clientelism becomes the prevalent mode of interest accommodation and takes precedence over considerations of public interest on behalf of patrons in government and over the valuing of autonomy from the part of actual or prospective clients.

In Section 5.4, I show how the practice of clientelism in a state-sponsored economy can generate social conditions that greatly support the political organisation in government in its effort to reduce its exposure to political competition. In a state-dominated economy, few socioeconomic actors can thrive or survive without government-granted privilege. Monopoly control over clientelist distributions of socioeconomic privilege enables a political organisation to threaten those who wish to express dissent or criticism with exclusion from these privileges. The same practice disciplines the behaviour of its supporters. Without alternative clientelist networks, socioeconomic actors must adjust their political behaviour, sometimes even by taking a public stance against their own preferences. This structure preempts the formation of collective action that will step up to defend political liberties against government abuses and institutional reforms. It becomes a structure of co-optation, affecting the decisions and behaviour of business and organisations such as unions, NGOs, and professional associations in a coercive way. By preventing the rise of autonomous political contenders, the political organisation can proceed with rising the level of political repression with electoral impunity.

5.2 De-democratisation and Democratic Resilience: The Autocrat's Dilemma

Whether a transition from democracy to hybrid forms of authoritarianism can occur in consolidated democracies is a difficult question to answer given the dearth of actual cases. We can only imagine how aspiring autocrats can succeed in prevailing over long-standing democratic institutions, a competitive party system and a vibrant civil society. Yet in recent years, many have been alarmed with the success of populist forces whose political conduct has been disrespectful of core pillars of liberal democracy, such as the rule of law, parliamentary scrutiny, the independence of the judiciary the role of institutional checks and balances, political and social diversity, minority rights and the free press, often pitting the 'people', which populists claim to represent against the 'elites' and their institutions (cf. Canovan, 1999: 3; Mudde, 2004: 543; Taggart and Rovira Kaltwasser, 2016; Aslanidis, 2016).

Some authors try to understand how these populist politics can undermine a consolidated democracy, including the United States, and can open a path to authoritarianism (Bermeo, 2016; Snyder, 2017; Galston, 2018; Sunstein, 2018; Runciman, 2018; Weyland and Madrid, 2019).[1] Most arguments were framed as predictions based on observations of historical cases in which competitive political systems experienced pressures for autocratisation, either succumbing to them or surviving them. The key question is whether there are conditions today similar to those that enabled authoritarian leaders to destabilise democracy elsewhere. This a form of political prognosis based on a diagnosis of what has happened in dissimilar cases in the past. However, these countries exhibit notable dissimilarities from consolidated democracies. We cannot solely rely on 'lessons from the past', but we must complement our findings with an argument that is coherent and sensible.

Drawing on the study of autocratisation from Latin America in the 1970s and Europe in the 1930s, Levitsky and Ziblatt (2018) argued that democratic backsliding could start in a polarising political landscape from political leaders whose behaviour breaks away from norms of mutual toleration and political forbearance. These political actors can seek to undermine or even suspend democratic institutions, particularly during a political or economic crisis where emergency powers can be justified. Weyland and Madrid (2019) noted that institutions, political parties and civil society organisations in consolidated democracies can offset this prospect if they act as countervailing forces against the anti-liberal and anti-democratic force.

Broadly speaking, opposition forces, the free press, civil society and rule-of-law institutions such as the judiciary form the countervailing forces that are crucial for its resilience against an authoritarian agenda in a democracy. Aspiring autocrats will confront an environment hostile to their plans. They can deploy a polarising populist rhetoric, but they will find it harder to galvanise support amidst a population with heterogeneous ideas, preferences and explanations (Halikiopoulou, 2019). Democratic resilience is built up by opposition parties, social organisations and democratic institutions that counter strategies of autocratisation with their own activism, criticism, alternative ideas and proposals for better government. A populist rhetoric and the ensuing climate of polarisation are likely to activate and animate these sources of resistance and this situation will most probably increase, rather than decrease, the risk of electoral defeat for the populist government.

Autocratisation is a strategy paved with obstacles. Gerschewski identified three 'pillars' of authoritarian stability: legitimacy, co-option and repression. Stable authoritarian regimes establish a strong claim of legitimacy by gaining and maintaining high levels of popularity; they also engage in mass-scale co-option to create strong links between themselves and major social and economic actors and groups in society and the economy, such as businesses, the media, labour unions, civil society organisations and academic institutions; finally, they rule by adjusting the level of political repression to prevent the opposition from threatening their incumbency (Gerschewski, 2013, pp. 18–23: cf. Ghandi and Przeworski, 2006, 2007; Murtazashvili, 2012; Maerz, 2018: 18). The challenge for aspiring autocrats in a democracy is that they must work towards building these three pillars from scratch while trying to neutralise democratic resistance. Operating in a system of institutional checks and balances, they cannot resort to outright tactics of repression to suddenly and openly restrict political freedoms with actions such as prohibitions of political activities, mass-scale electoral fraud and political violence.

It can be argued that, in a competitive political system, aspiring autocrats find themselves in front of a difficult terrain to navigate themselves through. Exposed to political competition and the prospect of electoral defeat, they must maintain popularity scores unusually high for a competitive system and win elections by a comfortable margin (Levitsky and Loxton, 2013; Saikkonen, 2015) while, meanwhile, they must also start reforming the democratic institutions that stand on their way by introducing new rules to enable them to carefully escalate repression. However, at an early stage, their anti-liberal and anti-democratic actions will most likely trigger political opposition and protests. This type of reactions could jeopardise their goal to win the next election. Their actions will be confronted by forces in society too and will be vetoed and blocked by formal institutional checks. They must find legitimate opportunities for institutional reform, but they need sizeable public approval if these reform proposals must be submitted to processes of constitutional revision such as a referendum. All these actions seem like a herculean task.

The question 'how can it happen here?' is about how aspiring autocrats will find a way to counteract democratic resistance by weakening the political opposition and eroding the autonomy of civil society, thereby reducing their exposure to political competition, keeping their popularity scores high and reforming democratic institutions with public support. To understand how aspiring autocrats can succeed in undermining democratic resistance, we must identify how processes already unfolding in democracies could take forms that will facilitate a transition to authoritarianism along these dimensions. Existing political practices may have possible reformulations that generate structures of government-society relations more susceptible to democratic backsliding.

5.3 Clientelism and the State-Sponsored Economy

Political systems are complex ecologies consisting of entangled economic social and political activities that undergo evolution through ongoing interactions among socioeconomic and political actors, groups and organisations (Wagner, 2012: 73). A peculiar characteristic of this system is that, throughout human history, these interactions include efforts by some actors to gain control of the state's coercive power to obtain the socioeconomic privileges it distributes, as well as efforts by other groups to resist this outcome or offset it. In that regard, the political sphere is a structure of competition characterised by dynamic asymmetries of power that are always very relevant for how the economy and society evolves. These interactions are hosting both competition and co-operation among organisations and amidst shifting networks of active agents that come to shape economic and social life. In that political ecology, the state imposes a formal hierarchical order of governance in the form of binding rules, coercive institutions and formal avenues for access to decision-making processes, but this order intersects with ongoing interactions between government authorities, political organisations and the rest of society. Governments are formally in control of most of the state's hierarchical order, but the social ecology is shaped by all actors who take part in these interactions, though asymmetrically. Government is by far the most powerful force shaping socioeconomic activities and defining their terms and conditions, and, as a result, it becomes the target of competition by actors who want to gain control over it or influence its decisions. Harold Laswell described politics as the art and science of 'who gets what' in society (1936). This phrase epitomises the nature of politics as a competitive process for influencing or capturing the power of government to allocate socioeconomic resources and opportunities within its jurisdiction.

What needs to be stressed is that political competition is shaped by two key competitive processes, on the one hand, economic actors and social groups competing for goods and services distributed by the government and, on the other hand, political actors competing for political office. Most government allocations involve resources that are excludable and rivalrous, much like private or 'club goods'.[2] Multiple social actors and groups compete with one another for access to political power and the resources it distributes, but, unlike the market process, those with political power are ultimately the only side that decide how these resources are to be allocated – who wins and who loses. This generates a parallel sphere of competition among political actors who wish to obtain this power.

Governments become recipients of claims and demands by socioeconomic actors with multiple differentiations of interests, preferences and socioeconomic status in terms of income employment, location, ethnic origin, gender and education. These differentiations offer the grounds for social actors to form several organised groups to promote their claims and demands with collective action. Social diversity and collective action generate political contestability that reflects, more or less, the wide spectrum of these differentiations and the ensuing conflicts. Moreover, this interplay between political power and interest groups creates a dynamic and evolving landscape of political activity, social mobility and political loyalties, dissatisfaction and protest.

Democracy is a form of political system that aims at regulating political competition with open and transparent rules for public participation and government decision-making. The etymology of democracy entails a command that this system of governance is about making the *demos*, the body of citizens, control government power (*kratos*), or at least, realistically, about granting citizens a degree of influence on state power. Really existing democracies exhibit more nuanced state-society relations. Citizens are divided by antagonisms and compete through collective organisations. These organisations are allowed to engage in non-violent forms of activity as they seek to influence government decisions. To the extent that a political system allows these actors to freely approach, challenge, contest and inform government power in a peaceful way, this system is democratic. Robert Dahl's conceived of democracy as a system of public contestation open to public participation (Dahl, 1971: 4, 8, 34). Dahl's definition of democracy creates two axes along which all political systems can be positioned based on how open they are to the participation of citizens and their organisations, as well as on how contestable the political arena becomes as the result of this participation (Dahl, 1971: 8, 34). Political systems scoring high on both dimensions are classified as democracies, or in Dahl's words as *polyarchies.* In that regard, a formal structure for political participation is a necessary but not sufficient condition for a system to be called a democracy. There must also be a contestable political arena because contestation is the inevitable result of the activities of the social and political forces promoting their substantive issues, and the main way of challenging the government and seeking to influence its decisions (Trantidis, 2016b). Political parties as well as within-party factions articulate differentiated political agendas in the public debate or behind closed doors. These groups try to attract supporters and gather the necessary means to disseminate their message and build some bargaining power.[3]

Democracy thus creates two political 'markets', one for politically granted privileges and one for votes. In the paper 'Entry Barriers in Politics' (1965), Gordon Tullock described the democratic process resembling an auction mechanism in which politicians bid for the right to a natural monopoly, the government. This 'right to monopoly' means that political power decides over the provision of goods and services by government decision-making in the form of a monopoly that rules out competition by any other entry. Because, in democratic systems, the right to run this 'monopoly' is decided competitively in elections, there is a competition for votes to determine who is elected in a position to control the distribution mechanism. While, in democracies, open elections decide who will control political power, running for election requires political actors to gather campaign-related resources, mainly money donations and the active engagement of core supporters, to be able to appeal to the electorate. A secondary market for resources emerges between political actors looking for campaign contributions and socioeconomic actors endowed with enough resources that seek access to political privileges. Campaign resources define the ability of a political organisation to perform a number of tasks necessary for its survival and growth: activating political support by appealing to existing social divisions and diverse preferences, capitalising on policy disagreements, shedding light on the inconsistencies and policy failures of its opponents and projecting an alternative vision of government.

In a competitive system, this secondary market for resources is likely to host a system of clientelist exchanges. Clientelism describes 'the distribution of resources by political power through an agreement in which politicians – the patrons – make this allocation dependent on the political support of the beneficiaries – their clients' (Trantidis, 2016a: 12). Clientelist exchanges emerge at the intersection of political power with social and economic activities. Political actors competing to gain political power negotiate with socioeconomic actors for an agreement that will satisfy the demands and claims of both sides. Access to government-granted resources is negotiated between government authorities and potential beneficiaries in the form of exchange: 'did you (will you) support me?' (Stokes, 2007: 604–605). Clientelism is an actual 'market' for political support because these exchanges have a specific bidding 'price' for the rents and other privileges the government distributes. Patrons give preference to those who will make the highest valued contribution to their campaign infrastructure and support network: donors, activists, prominent figures and journalists.

The potential for clientelist exchange is present in all areas of regulation of state sponsorship of economic activity, such as protectionism and industrial subsidies, state contracts, favourable regulations for business activities and the actual enforcement of rules. Clientelist discrimination transforms government-granted resources into clientelist privileges, namely special benefits that a group or a person enjoy through loyalty and support for a political authority.

What is more, clientelism affects the terms of the other competitive field: how political actors compete for power and who is more likely to win. By gathering campaign resources through clientelist exchange, politicians and political organisations strengthen their capacity for electoral mobilisation. These resources allow parties to systematically send political images and messages, creating a recognisable 'name-brand' for the general voters (cf. Aldrich, 1995). Voters form and change loyalties following information about party agendas and policies (Klingemann and Wattenberg, 1992). Political parties need loyal supporters and campaign resources to be able to appeal to voters, and, for that purpose, they must find a way to prevent a free-riding problem regarding how the beneficiaries of their policies will behave. Clientelism is an effective way by which patrons can recruit loyal supporters and gather sizeable campaign resources. Not engaging in clientelism negatively affects the capacity of a party or a politician to gather financial resources, party membership, campaign activists, favourable media coverage and endorsements by prominent public figures. This way, clientelism can greatly skew the distribution of campaign resources and largely boost the capacity of the clientelist political parties to perform a number of tasks necessary for their electoral success, such as appealing to the electorate by making their political proposals and ideological differences visible on the political agenda. For a political system to be competitive, at least two parties must engage in clientelist practices to build their political campaigns in some comparable sizes and levels of strength. A sharp asymmetry in the organisational capacities between the government and the opposition is expected to have an impact on their relative mobilisation capacity.

It is important to stress that the terms under which clientelist exchange takes place differ substantially from market transactions primarily in terms of bargaining power, the enforcement mechanism, externalities and selection process. The government's power to allocate resources – which is what fuels the competition for access to power and competition for access to resources – also provides the capacity for *discrimination* in terms of who gets what, when and how. This capacity can be deployed by a political organisation to elicit and monitor the beneficiary's loyalty. Although the typical view of rent-seeking is that groups or corporate interests lobby the government to enact policies that will serve their interests, clientelism is primarily embedded into power structures and this power structure affects the bargaining power of the prospective and actual clients. There are networked relationships connecting political organisations with rent-extracting actors, such as big donors, individual politicians and political leaders. This type of connection can be a highly asymmetrical relationship in which one party of the exchange is much stronger than the other in terms of negotiating power, or a relationship between equals in which all parties retain more or less a strong negotiating position. Depending on what resources each side possesses and is willing to trade in a clientelist relationship, few clients may have a stronger bargaining position than others. In addition, few patrons occupy the supply side of clientelism while myriads of candidate clients inhabit the demand side. Hence, a clientelist network can take different shapes, with some nodes being more powerful and better connected than others. These differentiations in terms of negotiating power within a clientelist network can help us answer an important question: how clientelism can sustain a process of autocratisation.

When clientelism is provided through a system of top-down controls operated by a political organisation, its leadership can detect and punish the clients who behave differently from what it was agreed or even defect to the other side by excluding them from the clientelist benefits. Actual sanctions act as general disincentives for those who may wish to behave similarly in the future. From the point of view of political organisations, clientelism is about building a network of stable and active loyal supporters, which is important for their cohesion and stability (Piven and Cloward, 1992). Because clientelism is a conditional form of distribution of excludable resources by political power to beneficiaries, clientelism offers patrons a disciplinary power over socioeconomic actors. Clientelism becomes the way by which politicians and political organisations overcome their own 'problem of collective action' (Olson, 1965), which includes preventing and tackling within-party factionalism and defections (Boucek, 2010).

Finally, the practice of clientelism has an important impact on for the structure of the economy and society. Political organisations have a strong reason to keep increasing the number of special benefits they distribute through clientelist exchange by expanding the areas in which state sponsorship applies. Political competition favours a preference for clientelism (Trantidis, 2016a), which challenges the assertion that in a democracy the provision of public goods will outweigh the provision of private goods because of the larger size of the winning coalition for a leader to consider (cf. the 'selectorate theory' of Bruce Bueno de Mesquita et al., 2003). In clientelism, the winning coalition is the clientelist network first. Because campaign resources are vital for one's political campaign, political organisations may go as far as making policy pre-commitments to the most important of their clients, pledging that their preferences will take precedence in the design of public policies and even override electoral pledges. Broadly speaking, these privileged networks form what I called a 'preselectorate', namely, groups whose interests are granted priority by political actors and organisations in return for the special support and funding they provide. Clientelism can thus become a key mode of interest accommodation that is crucial for the electoral success of political organisations. In a two-party system, clientelism becomes a Nash equilibrium.[4] No political organisation has an incentive to unilaterally restrict its own engagement in clientelism, as this will favour its opponents and will trigger defections of supporters from its ranks (Trantidis, 2016a).

Further expansion of the clientelist system is consequently affecting the autonomy and strength of civil society. Social associations, including unions and other professional organisations, including rent-seeking businesses, will no longer fit the typical image of actors with organisational autonomy and preferences independent from the government (Buchanan, 1972). Instead, they are integrated into *a clientelist mode of interest intermediation* that creates strong dependencies on political sponsorship and favours the building of longer-lasting political loyalties (Trantidis, 2015b). In other words, rent seekers are not independent bidders for power and resources, as in Tullock's bidding process, but clients who are invited to be insiders and whose behaviour is monitored by the patrons. Their privileges come with the price of having their political autonomy diminished.

The established approach in economics is to view rent-seeking as a distortion of market competition due to the externalities it imposes on all other non-participating actors. What is missing from this approach is a focus on the political implications of rent-seeking and its variegated forms, particularly, whether the networked structure of rent-seeking can be differentiated in terms of: (a) how far state sponsorship is extended in an economy (the structure of the economy), (b) the relative bargaining power of the socioeconomic actors involved and (c) the ensuing degree of political competition that this system of interactions will generate. As the next section explains, the structure of the economy (a) determines what happens with (b) and (c).

5.4 Economic Structure and Limited Contestability

If de-democratisation is the process by which a political organisation succeeds in undermining the capacity of opposition groups and dissenting organisations to resist its authoritarian agenda, this process requires a way by which this organisation can accommodate society's diverse and often conflicting claims to political power. It is very unlikely for governments to satisfy all claims simultaneously or consistently. Instead, clientelism can fuel further competition and generate new animosities from those excluded or dissatisfied. These grievances can only be handled and managed by a political organisation by forms of disciplinary power which involves the flip side of clientelism: retaliation in the form of exclusion from clientelist benefits threating those who free-ride, defect or think about doing just that. The patron's disciplinary power is effective to the extent that its clientelist network is a structure of power asymmetries, and, as mentioned earlier, this depends on how many clientelist networks there are for prospective and actual clients to choose from. For political leaders, rather than negotiating with rent-seeking actors as equals, their preference is becoming the central nodes of the clientelist network. Reducing the negotiating power of their clients requires reducing the scope of exit they have to activities that do not fall within the reach of the leader's network. If clients can choose amidst multiple clientelist organisations, this enables them to retain an autonomous standing and use defection as a bargaining chip. Reducing the range of economic activities that allow socioeconomic actors to thrive autonomously from clientelism is the first step political leaders must take to strengthen the disciplinary potential of clientelism.

When a political party obtains monopoly control over the supply of clientelism, and most economic opportunities depend on discretionary state actions, clients have no alternative options for switching alliances or for moving their activities outside the reach of clientelist rewards and sanctions (Trantidis, 2015a). In that case, the room for 'exit' and autonomous 'voice' is significantly reduced. Mass-scale and largely unmitigated applications of clientelist sanctions on society can sustain a process of autocratisation by skewing the terms in which political competition takes place in favour of the incumbent. In a socioeconomic structure in which the political organisation in government can determine winners and losers in society and the economy, favouring its supporters, punishing its opponents and threatening its dissenters, to elicit, leaves little room for the opposition forces to recruit supporters and gather adequate resources to effectively challenge the government actions. Unrivalled and uncontested by any other political force, the regime can move on to passing institutional reforms further restricting political freedoms and escalating political repression (Figure 5.1).

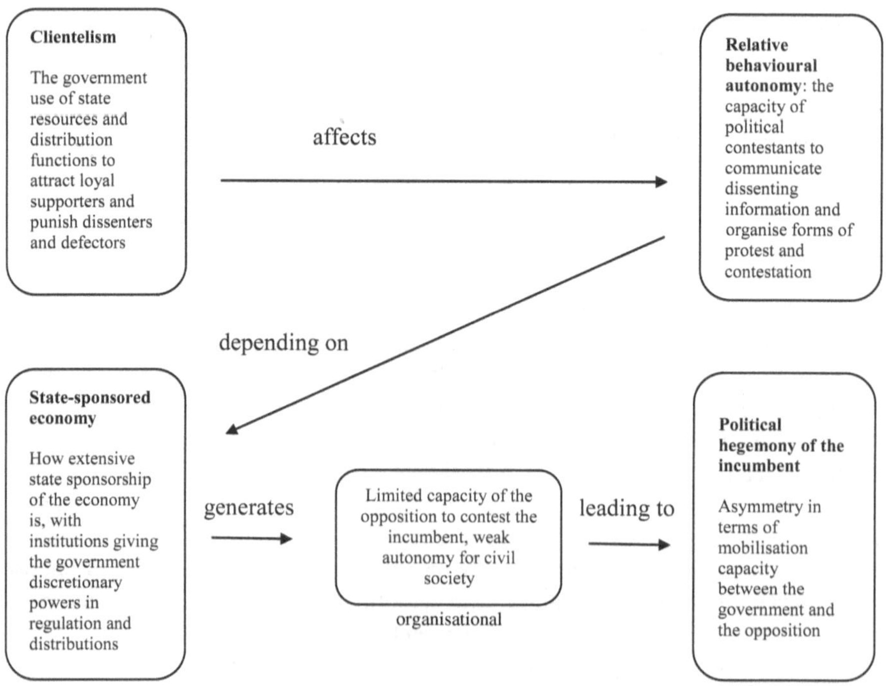

Figure 5.1 Clientelism, state sponsorship and political hegemony.

How extensive state sponsorship is determines whether socioeconomic actors have some scope to remain indifferent to clientelism. For state-sponsored activities, the disciplinary effect of clientelism has a more overwhelming effect on political behaviour, when there is no room for exit to alternative clientelist networks. How much of the economic activity is subjected to state sponsoring defines the *structural boundaries* to political manipulation by clientelism. The larger the extent of state sponsorship becomes, the larger the number of economic actors exposed to government discretion. In addition, if the political organisation controls the government, there are forms of retaliation that are unmitigated, such as tax inspections conducted to find or even fabricate irregularities, refusal to grant access to funding schemes or exclusion from government procurement. Private entrepreneurs can be threatened with the loss of licenses and subsidies or the termination of a public procurement contract. Employees working for the government, or a state-controlled company, can be threatened with unfavourable placement or even loss of employment. Other forms of *material retaliation*, for instance, result from the state's direct or indirect control over the decisions of major suppliers when they are owned by the state, or when they operate under mixed ownership schemes, or when they are clients themselves and must align their decisions with the patron's strategy.

The process connecting clientelism and political behaviour is a probable hypothesis, not a deterministic relationship. There is an association between (a) the practice of clientelism with the gathering of political support and campaign resources and (b) advantages in terms of campaign organisation and political communication with the capacity for electoral mobilisation. This connection is based on the assumption that most socioeconomic actors make rational choices with information signalled to them about prospective costs and benefits attached to different behavioural options. Based on the same assumptions of rational behaviour, it is expected that clientelism affects the cost and benefit assessments of key socioeconomic actors, whose risk calculations are sensitive to the character and range of clientelist incentives and disincentives. Exposed to clientelism, they are expected to adjust their behaviour and be careful in forming connections with others that avoid the communication of dissent and support of protest.

Under these conditions, this form of clientelism becomes an authoritarian practice. An overarching system of rewards and sanctions generates an effect on political behaviour similar to what typical threats of repression do, because discrimination by exclusion from these allocations and retaliation through sanctions are unavoidable and unmitigated. In the absence of exit options, clientelism generates essentially involuntary adjustments of political behaviour by those vulnerable to a system of clientelist rewards and sanctions operated by a single political organisation. Clientelism becomes a system of controls over political behaviour that is coercive in the Hayekian sense, meaning there is manipulation of one's options by way of threatening or imposing actual sanctions on behavioural choices that will defy the coercer's preferences (Hayek, 2011: 199). It stifles the expression of genuine political preferences.

The model works depending on how dominant the state is in the structure of economy, how extensive the range of discretionary distributions of socioeconomic privilege is (state sponsorship) and the degree to which the institutions in place allow or prohibit clientelist exchange. The larger the state-sponsored sector becomes, the more it reduces the possibility of economic actors to exit to non-politicised areas of economic activity (Trantidis, 2015). The dominant party's monopoly over the supply of clientelism in a large political sector of the economy reduces the political autonomy of most socioeconomic actors. In that case, autocratisation is the process by which a clientelist political system is established in a predominantly state-sponsored economy. The aspiring autocrat is then free to develop two complementary 'pillars' of autocracy: legitimation through elections with a populist discourse, which a weak opposition cannot challenge, and repression that no longer animates public reaction.

5.5 Final Remarks

In consolidated democracies, autocratisation – the transition from democracy to hybrid forms of authoritarianism – is possible only if aspiring autocrats find an effective way to offset resistance from opposition parties, society and institutions. Aspiring autocrats must reduce their exposure to political contestation and overcome democratic resistance. They cannot use typical tactics of repression such as electoral violence, fraud or the banning of candidates not at an early stage. This chapter stresses that autocratisation is a conceivable development for consolidated democracies to the extent that the socioeconomic structure allows the government to build a comprehensive system of clientelist rewards and sanctions. The same analysis indicates why there are grounds to believe that democratic backsliding and ensuing autocratisation are less likely to occur in an economy that retains its autonomy from state sponsorship and clientelism.

This analysis is revealing about what societies can do to prevent such a development. A synergy of institutional and structural conditions determines the autonomy of socioeconomic activity from partisan control. As Figure 5.2 shows, that institutions that govern the economy can allow or obstruct autocratisation by way of political clientelism, by establishing constitutional rules that protect and promote a sufficient space of socioeconomic autonomy from government, particularly for the key actors that build up its very immune system against authoritarian politics: civil society, the media and political parties. First, economic institutions must contain and/or regulate the expansion of state sponsorship in the economy and society, particularly preventing it from becoming too large and engulfing most socioeconomic activities. This means prohibiting forms of distribution and regulation that give the distributing authority highly discretionary powers to choose beneficiaries in a discriminatory way. For instance, general rules for regulation or rules for selection whereby the criteria for being qualified and eligible for government are general and impersonal allow for less discretion on behalf of the officials and reduce the scope for clientelism (Trantidis and Cowen, 2020). Second, to the extent that a degree of state sponsorship of economic activities is inevitable, for instance in government contracts for infrastructure projects and defence, institutional reforms must constrain the potential for partial-discriminatory treatment of economic actors at will, outside of general specifications of who is entitled and how policy implementation takes place, and, subsequently, reduce the potential for clientelism.

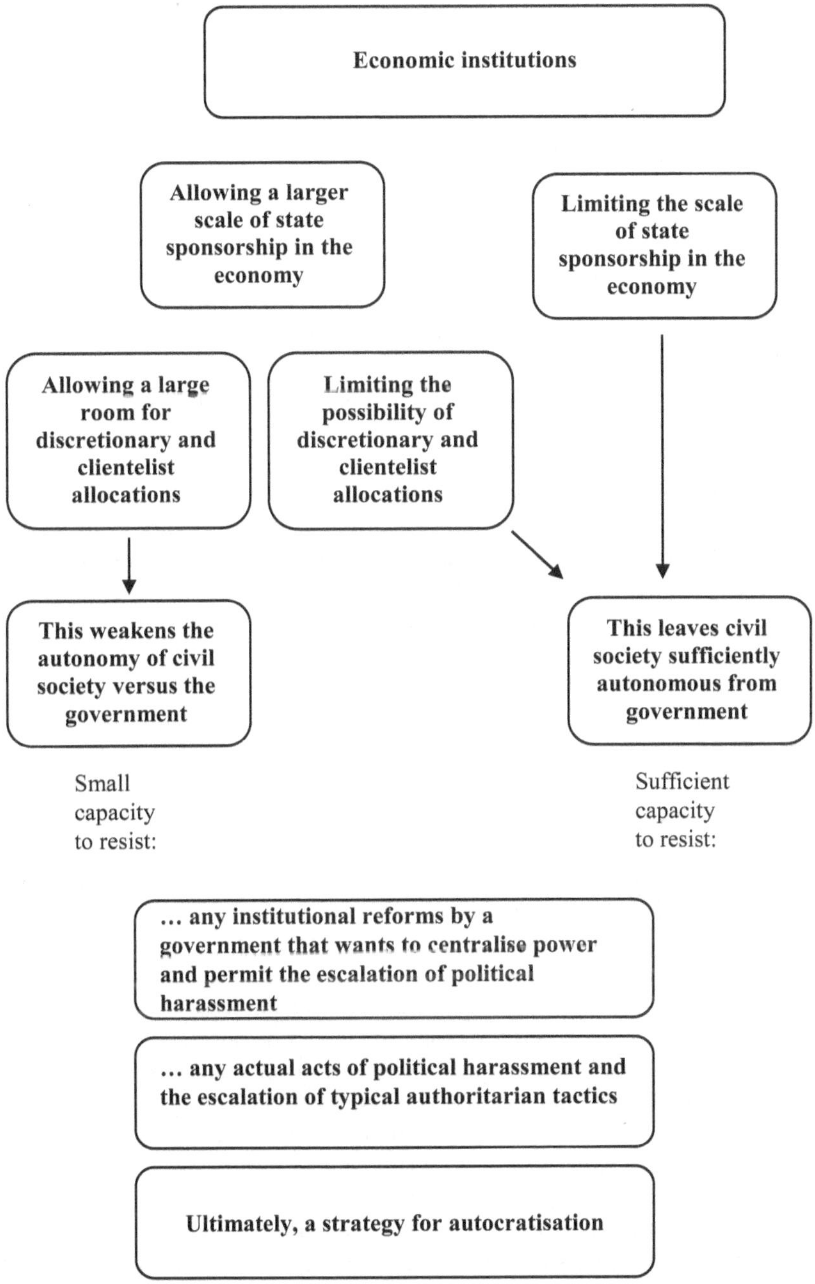

Figure 5.2 Institutions and democratic resilience.

State-sponsored capitalism is, to some extent, inextricably present in most forms of state intervention in the economy, such as government procurement contracts, subsidies, regulatory allowances, tariffs and other protectionist or developmental policies that can be designed to benefit not only specific economic activities but also specific firms or people. Most regulatory and distributive policies leave room for allocations of privilege by clientelist exchange. Some policies are more amenable to clientelism than others because the authority can identify beneficiaries at the individual or firm level in advance of their design. For instance, economic protectionist policies can benefit specific firms while welfare-state provisions tend to be entitlements offered on general criteria. This does not preclude the possibility that welfare state policies will be enacted or implemented in a clientelist manner, but it is easier to devise rules that will preclude discrimination in the allocation of these services. Democracies already ban discriminatory treatment in terms of access to public healthcare and education – the government cannot pick and choose the specific individuals who would be allowed to attend a school, enter a state pension scheme or have access to Medicaid in the United States, for instance. Broadly speaking, as Lowi (1964) argued, policies differ with regard to whether their impact can be differentiated at smaller units, such as people and firms. Policies that are more amenable to this 'disaggregation' are more prone to becoming the object of clientelist exchange. In general, when prospective beneficiaries are identifiable, this invites clientelist exchange. For example, an external tariff may be justified as part of an industrial policy to protect a large number of beneficiaries, but the government can adjust the tariff to favour specific industries. Finally, circumstances such as a crisis or an emergency can be invoked by a government to justify policies designed to have impact at the firm level, opening the way for clientelist exchange.

In trying to assess the broader political implications of a policy and, consequently, in seeking to understand the implications of an economic reform, it is important to keep in mind that clientelist motives consistently shape political decisions and come to affect society and the economy in several and rather profound ways. State-sponsored capitalism fosters the practice of clientelism while clientelism reinforces the political incentives for the expansion of an economic model of state sponsorship. Discrimination is then a central aspect of politics in action when allocating resources and opportunities. Rather than a pathology of modern democracies, this discriminatory approach to state regulations and allocations can become an existential threat to their very nature of liberal democracy. Unfortunately, while the existential risk liberal democracies currently face comes from the development of a clientelistic state-sponsored society, much of the discussion about democratic backsliding focuses on populism broadly speaking and has neglected the problem of clientelism. In my view, if we want to prevent democratic backsliding, our focus should be on clientelism. Civil society must be aware of that risk and must become active in protesting and challenging reforms that allow for discriminatory treatment by governments under the guise of serving the public interest in view of some exigencies and emergencies. In addition, constitutional reforms must be enacted to prohibit rules and policies with high scope for discrimination or at least involve judicial scrutiny of government decisions based on general principles of generality and non-discrimination.

Notes

1 The term 'consolidated democracy' refers to the criteria for democratic consolidation presented by Juan Linz and Alfred Stepan (1996). The definition does not preclude a reversion to authoritarianism. In general, the term unequivocally includes the United States, Canada, Western Europe, Southern Europe, Australia, New Zealand and Japan.

2 In economics, a 'club good' is a type of good that has some characteristics of both public and private goods. It is excludable but non-rivalrous in consumption, meaning that it is possible to choose the individuals who would have access to it (for example, based on their contribution or payment), but their consumption does not reduce the availability of the good to others, including new users, usually up to a certain point or limit. Think of a subscription to a TV channel or a film screening website. Likewise, clientelism involves state distributions where the selection of some beneficiaries and the exclusion of others are possible, but these distributions include a large pool of available resources and allocations, including favours, with no set limit and therefore ample scope to provide them to new users (clients).

3 John Plamenatz paid attention to the opportunities for political contestation beyond those derived by the formal set of rights each citizen enjoys. A political system is a democracy when 'citizens are free to criticize their rulers and to come together to make demands on them and to win support for their policies they favour and the beliefs they hold; and where the supreme makers of law and policy are elected to their offices at free and periodic elections' (Plamenatz, 1978: 184–188). In similar vein, Schattschneider understood democracy as a *competitive* political system 'in which competing leaders and organizations define the alternatives of public policy in such a way that the public can participate in the decision-making process' (1960: 141). Similarly, Morlino pointed to

> … a set of institutions and rules that allow competition and participation for all citizens considered as equals. Such a political arrangement is characterized by free, fair, and recurring elections; male and female universal suffrage; multiple organizations of interests; different and alternative sources of information; and elections to fill the most relevant offices
>
> (Morlino, 1987: 54)

4 A Nash equilibrium is a situation where each participant optimally selects their strategy, considering the strategies chosen by others, assuming these strategies remain unchanged. In this equilibrium, no player has an incentive to alter their strategy independently, as doing so would not lead to a more favourable outcome given the strategies of the other players. It signifies a stable state wherein each player's strategy is deemed optimal in light of the strategies of their counterparts.

References

Aldrich, John, 1995, *Why Parties? The Origins and Transformation of Party Politics in America*. Chicago, IL: Chicago University Press.

Aslanidis, Paris. 2016. 'Is Populism an Ideology? A Refutation and a New Perspective'. *Political Studies* 64(1): 88–104.

Bermeo, Nancy. 2016. 'On Democratic Backsliding'. *Journal of Democracy* 27(January): 5–18.

Boucek, Francoise. 2010. 'The Factional Politics of Dominant Parties'. In Maththijs Bogaards and Francoise Boucek (eds.) *Dominant Political Parties and Democracy*. London: Routledge, pp. 117–139.

Buchanan, James, M. 1972. *Theory of Public Choice: Political Applications of Economics*. Ann Arbor, MI: University of Michigan Press.
Bueno de Mesquita, Bruce, Smith, Alastair, Siverson, Randolph M. and Morrow James D. (2003) *The Logic of Political Survival*. Cambridge, Massachusetts: MIT Press.
Canovan, Margaret. 1999. 'Trust the People! Populism and the Two Faces of Democracy'. *Political Studies* 47(1): 2–16.
Colton, Timothy J. and McFaul, Michael. 2003. *Popular Choice and Managed Democracy: The Russian Elections of 1999 and 2000*. Washington, DC: Brookings Institution Press.
Dahl, Robert. 1971. *Polyarchy: Participation and Opposition*. New Haven, CT: Yale University.
Diamond, Larry. 2002. 'Elections without Democracy: Thinking about Hybrid Regimes'. *Journal of Democracy* 13(2): 21–35.
Galston, William A. 2018. *Anti-Pluralism: The Populist Threat to Liberal Democracy*. New Haven, CT: Yale University Press.
Gerschewski, Johannes. 2013. 'The Three Pillars of Stability: Legitimation, Repression, and Co-optation in Autocratic Regimes'. *Democratization* 20(1): 13–38.
Ghandi, Jennifer and Przeworski, Adam 2006. 'Cooperation, Cooptation and Rebellion under Dictatorship'. *Economics and Politics* 18: 1–26.
Ghandi, Jennifer and Przeworski, Adam. 2007. 'Authoritarian Institutions and the Survival of Autocrats'. *Comparative Political Studies* 40(11): 1279–1301.
Halikiopoulou, Daphne. 2019. 'Right-wing Populism as a Nationalist Vision of Legitimating Collective Choice: A Supply-side Perspective'. *The International Spectator 54*(2): 35–49. https://doi.org/10.1080/03932729.2019.1588544
Hayek, Friedrich A. 1944/2007. *The Road to Serfdom*. Chicago, IL: University of Chicago Press.
Hayek, Friedrich A. 2011. The Constitution of Liberty: The Definitive Edition. In Ronald Hamowy (ed.) *The Collected Works of F. A. Hayek*, v. 17, pp. 37–54. Chicago, IL: University of Chicago Press.
Klingemann, Hans-Dieter and Wattenberg, Martin. 1992. 'Decaying versus Developing Party Systems: A Comparison of Party Images in the United States and West Germany'. *British Journal of Political Science* 22(2): 131–149.
Konitzer, Andrew and Wegren, Stephen. 2007. 'Federalism and Political Recentralization in the Russian Federation: United Russia as the Party of Power'. *Publius* 36(4): 503–522.
Laswell, Harold. 1936. *Politics: Who Gets What, When, How*. New York: Whittlesey House.
Levitsky, Steven and Loxton, James. 2013. 'Populism and Competitive Authoritarianism in the Andes'. *Democratization* 20(1): 107–136.
Levitsky, Steven and Way Lucan, A. 2010. *Competitive Authoritarianism: Hybrid Regimes After the Cold War*. Cambridge: Cambridge University Press.
Levitsky, Steven and Ziblatt, David. 2018. *How Democracies Die*. London: Viking.
Linz, Juan and Stepan, Alfred. 1996. *Problems of Democratic Transition and Consolidation: Southern Europe, South America, and PostCommunist Europe*. Baltimore, MD: Johns Hopkins University Press.
Lowi, Theodore J. 1964. 'American Business, Public Policy, Case Studies and Political Theory'. *World Politics* 16(4): 677–715.
Maerz, Seraphine. 2018. 'The Many Faces of Authoritarian Persistence: A Set-Theory Perspective on the Survival of Authoritarian Regimes'. *Government and Opposition* 55(1): 64–87.
McFaul, Michael. 2005. 'Transitions from Postcommunism'. *Journal of Democracy* 16(3): 5–19.
Morlino, Leonardo. 1987. Democratic Establishments: A Dimensional Analysis. In Enrique A. Baloyra (ed.) *Comparing New Democracies : Transition and Consolidation in Mediterranean Europe and the Southern Cone*. Boulder Colorado: Westview Press.
Mudde, Cas. 2004. 'The Populist Zeitgeist'. *Government and Opposition* 39(4): 542–563.
Murtazashvili, Jennifer. 2012. 'Coloured by Revolution: The Political Economy of Autocratic Stability in Uzbekistan'. *Democratization* 19(1): 78–97.

Olson, Mancur. 1965. *The Logic of Collective Action: Public Goods and the Theory of Groups*. Cambridge, MA: Harvard University Press.
Piven, Frances F. and Cloward, Richard. 1992. 'Normalizing Collective Protest'. In A. Morris and C. McClurg Mueller (eds) *Frontiers in Social Movement Theory*, pp. 301–325. New Haven, CT: Yale University Press.
Plamenatz, John. 1978. *Democracy and Illusion: An Examination of Certain Aspects of Modern Democratic Theory*. London: Longman.
Runciman, David. 2018. *How Democracy Ends*. London: Profile Books.
Saikkonen, Inga A. L. 2015. 'Electoral Mobilization and Authoritarian Elections: Evidence from Post-Soviet Russia'. *Government and Opposition* 52(1): 51–74.
Schattschneider, Elmer. E. 1960. *The Semisovereign People: A Realist's View of Democracy in America*. New York: Holt, Rinehart and Winston.
Schedler, Andreas. 2006. 'The Logic of Electoral Authoritarianism'. In Andreas Schedler (ed.), *Electoral Authoritarianism: The Dynamics of Unfree Competition*. Boulder, CO: Lynne Rienner Publishers, 1–26.
Snyder, Timothy. 2017. *On Tyranny: Twenty Lessons from the Twentieth Century*. London: Bodley Head.
Stokes, Susan C. 2007. 'Political Clientelism'. In Carles Boix and Susan C. Stokes (eds.) *The Oxford Handbook of Comparative Politics*. New York: Oxford University Press.
Sunstein, Cass R. (ed.) 2018. *Can It Happen Here? Authoritarianism in America*. New York: Dey Street.
Taggart, Paul and Rovira Kaltwasser, Cristóbal. 2016. 'Dealing with Populists in Government: Some Comparative Conclusions'. *Democratization* 23(2): 345–365.
Trantidis, Aris. 2015a. 'Clientelism and the Classification of Dominant Party Systems'. *Democratization* 22(1): 113–133.
Trantidis, Aris. 2015b. 'Clientelism and Economic Policy: Hybrid Characteristics of Collective Action in Greece'. *Journal of European Public Policy* 23(10): 1460–1480.
Trantidis, Aris. 2016a. 'Is Government Contestability and Integral Part of the Definition of Democracy?' *Politics* 37(1): 67–81.
Trantidis, Aris. 2016b. *Clientelism and Economic Policy: Greece and the Crisis*: London and New York: Routledge.
Trantidis, Aris and Cowen, Nick. 2020. 'Hayek versus Trump: The Radical Right's Road to Serfdom'. *Polity* 52(2): 159–188.
Tullock, Gordon. 1965. 'Entry Barriers in Politics'. *American Economic Review* 55(1/2): 458–466.
Wagner, Richard. 2012. 'A Macro Economy as an Ecology of Plans'. *Journal of Economic Behaviour and Organization* 82(2): 433–444.
Ware, Alan. 1996. *Political Parties and Party Systems*. Oxford: Oxford University Press.
Weyland, Kurt and Madrid, Raul (eds.) 2019. *When Democracy Trumps Populism: European and Latin American Lessons for the United States*. Cambridge: Cambridge University Press.

6 The Missionary Theory of Industrial Policy

Lessons from the COVID-19 Pandemic Response

Mark Pennington

6.1 Introduction

The response to the COVID-19 pandemic seems to have prompted an important cultural-economic shift. In many countries governments are now being urged to be 'brave enough' to act on multiple fronts and to act 'big and bold' to address challenges that are presented as similar in form to those of COVID-19. This rhetoric was apparent during the pandemic itself and its presence is felt today in calls for grand and visionary strategies to address climate change through green 'new deals', measures to reduce inequality, and more generally in the case for new forms of industrial policy. Though these trends were perhaps accelerated by the pandemic they were already evident prior to those events in the rise of what I will refer to in this chapter as the 'Missionary Theory of Government' – or to narrow this down somewhat to the 'Missionary Theory of Industrial Policy'.

I will suggest that what we saw throughout the COVID-19 pandemic is an example of 'mission-oriented policy' in action – an experience which indicates not only the economic problems associated with such an orientation but also the threats it poses to human freedom. I begin my remarks by sketching out the argument for government to assume what we might perhaps call the 'missionary position'. Having outlined what I see as the core theoretical problems with this stance, I then examine some important similarities that might allow us to understand the pandemic response as an example of this missionary position. I proceed finally to argue that many of the problems witnessed in the pandemic response and of the threats to freedom it has revealed are likely to be replicated *on a near permanent basis* were we to follow the advice of those advocating the missionary theory of industrial policy.

6.2 What Is Mission-Oriented Industrial Policy?

So, what is mission-oriented industrial policy and who advocates for it? Perhaps the most influential protagonist for this policy stance is Mariana Mazzucato.[1] Mazzucato claims that problems of relative economic stagnation in some of the major economies in recent years reflect a lack of mission-commitment

DOI: 10.4324/9781003504412-9

from governments – which she associates with predominantly market-led or 'neo-liberal' theories that she considers have been dominant over recent decades. The latter suggest that outside relatively small-scale interventions to 'fix' gaps within specific markets, governments should not be involved in the process of innovation or of picking winners. In essence, what she argues, and she is surely right in this regard, is that the neo-liberal market model is a *mission-less* theory of government. For Mazzucato, however, this is its greatest failure. Lacking such a mission from their governments' citizens, entrepreneurs and investors alike occupy an atomistic world where chronic uncertainty about the plans of others leads to a pervasive short-termism undermining the willingness to engage in bold and longer-term innovations. On this view, having a government with the willingness to make bold and strategic investments that goes beyond tinkering at the edges of existing markets is the key to reducing uncertainty and to giving entrepreneurs and investors the confidence to act. Government should be responsible for creating the conditions within which markets can be allowed to operate by lowering uncertainty. Instead of seeing the state as intervening in and potentially distorting pre-functioning markets we should see the state as *creating the conditions within which market creativity can be operative* – 'creating the conditions' here however does not mean following the classical liberal prescription of a state securing property rights and contracts – but of a state committed to *leading the market through missionary government.*

There is it should be noted nothing especially new about this theory – one can trace its origins to Keynes's view that problems of radical uncertainty in markets and of forecasting an unknowable future which he saw as depressing the animal spirits of capitalist entrepreneurs can be addressed through a 'somewhat comprehensive socialisation of investment'.[2] For Keynes, if the state acts big and bold, this will increase confidence for private investors and entrepreneurs to follow in its visionary wake. On this view, only the state can transcend concerns with private self-interest and build a sense of 'mission' around the pursuit of common goods – and it is precisely when people have a sense that others in their society are pursuing such goods that they may start to have the confidence required to make the necessary investments. If government *narrows the options* that people face, then they will have more confidence to act.

Essentially, Mazzucato adopts Keynes 'comprehensive socialisation of investment' idea and applies it to the realm of innovation. On her view, we need a bold new view of industrial policy with states focussed on delivering missionary commitments aimed at common goods such as the fight against climate change. Bold government investments in these areas will she suggests trigger a wave of innovation in cleaner, greener technologies that would not be forthcoming if government action was limited to mundane and unambitious schemes such as carbon taxes and other 'small scale' market 'fixes'. If the state spends large volumes of public money on such programmes, this will stimulate a series of positive spill-over effects with all manner of unforeseeable market possibilities generated.

6.3 Theoretical Problems of the Missionary Position

There are numerous problems with adopting this missionary position in economic affairs,[3] but I would like to focus here on the following:

The first is that having government agencies pursue missions does not contra Keynes or Mazzucato, overcome or ameliorate the problem of uncertainty. As anyone with the slightest familiarity with Hayek's arguments would recognise, wherever we are dealing with 'complex phenomena' there is *ineradicable uncertainty* about whether those concerned have in fact chosen the right mission to pursue, uncertainty about what kind of missions might have been pursued if the funds in question were allocated differently, and what benefits they might have produced in comparison. Such knowledge cannot be accessed or produced by missionary governments because by definition, adopting the missionary position precludes other missions from being implemented. If the chosen policy stance allows 'too many' other visions to see the light-of-day, then it can no longer be considered as being sufficiently missionary. Missionary government seeks to eliminate competition on many dimensions, but it is precisely competition that allows the opportunity costs of different missions and their relative contribution to improving peoples' lives and welfare to be revealed.[4] The missionary position ignores the role of competition as fundamentally a contestation between rival ideas and of the role of market prices, and of profit and loss signals in continually summarising the outcome of that contestation. Insofar as internal competition between missions is eliminated or constrained, the primary source for evaluating them will be limited to observing what happens outside ones' borders – but in such contexts the pool of ideas will be unduly constrained. Moreover, in the absence of feedback as direct as that provided by profit and loss accounting it will also be much harder to discern which particular bits of the mission should be retained from those that should be discarded.

Second for a missionary commitment to count as such those concerned must refuse to recognise the possibility that they might have chosen the wrong vision – they must exhibit a single-minded determination to stick with the mission because according to the underlying theory it is that very sense of certainty that engenders confidence in others. If the possibility is entertained that the mission might be the wrong one or that it might need to be revised, then this may reveal the underlying uncertainties and lead to a loss of confidence both in the mission and its purveyors.

Third, it follows from this that suppression of dissent is a likely concomitant of the missionary position. To maintain the integrity of their visions and for people to keep faith with them at very best those assuming a missionary stance must ignore contrary voices and at worst they must actively suppress such voices lest they undermine faith in the chosen direction. This dynamic is likely to produce something akin to a permanent 'war footing' in public 'debate' – where to sustain the mission dissenters must be treated as morally deficient or corrupt. Walter Lippman summarised this aspect of what he described as the 'planning mentality' very well in 1936, when he wrote:

> …the war spirit (read missionary spirit) identifies dissent with treason, the pursuit of private happiness with slackerism and sabotage, and on the other side obedience with discipline, conformity with patriotism. Thus, at one

> stroke war extinguishes the difficulties of planning, cutting out from any individual any moral ground on which he might resist the execution of the official plan.[5]

Now, of course Mazzucato and other supporters of missionary government would never couch their proposals in this way. On the contrary, they are shot through with references to the role of public participation and of the creation of public-private partnerships – you might say corporatism – in building and sustaining support for mission commitment. Yet none of this window-dressing disguises the suppression strategies that will inevitably be involved. Those who will be consulted in formulating the mission commitment will of necessity be those who have expressed support or sympathy with it – or who have some private interest in supporting it. Otherwise the alleged uncertainty constraining effects from having a coherent and single-minded public goal would be void.

6.4 The Missionary Theory and Pandemic Response

What I would like to suggest now is that the problems I have identified above were very clearly evidenced in the COVID-19 pandemic response. To be clear, if there is going to be a missionary role for government an event like a pandemic is probably the time when this stance *should* be adopted. There is a strong case for thinking that a market-led or bottom-up approach may be inadequate for public goods reasons and that governments must do something to stabilise expectations when faced with the spread of an infectious disease – and especially perhaps a new one. The argument here is very similar to what might hold in a state of war. Put simply, you cannot afford to try out multiple competing military strategies and tactics when facing an enemy at the door – someone must take a decision, and fast. Nonetheless, there are serious problems arising from such settings that must also be recognised, and I want to suggest that these were evidenced in the case of COVID-19 response.[6]

First, mission commitments do not eradicate uncertainty. In their COVID-19 responses, many governments did indeed adopt single-minded mission commitments, but this was in a context where it was unclear what the mission should be. Should it have been protecting people from the health risks from the virus or from the economic consequences of those policies? If the focus should have been on health, how might the missionaries discover and weigh the health effects of measures to combat the virus compared with the effect of those measures on other dimensions of health? If the focus should have been more on protecting the economy, how would policymakers know what the effect on the economy of the pandemic would be relative to the effect of economic policies to offset those effects? And of course, all these questions multiply when it is recognised that health and economic dimensions are inextricably linked.

Two further points need to be made. On the one hand, even today, there is no clear evidence to suggest whether lockdown policies or those that were more relaxed produced better outcomes[7] – either on health dimensions – number of deaths from covid versus deaths from other conditions – or on economic dimensions such as speed of post-pandemic recovery. Countries with or without lockdowns and with different political traditions and institutions have performed both relatively well and relatively badly. And, even where certain policies have coincided with an apparently successful outcome – it is not clear whether the policy itself generated the apparent success or a contextual factor of culture, geography or institutions, which may have produced the outcomes in question. Sweden, for example, though heavily criticised for not 'locking down' at the time, now looks to have emerged from the pandemic with one of the lowest levels of 'excess deaths' in Europe. It does not follow, however, that the Swedish response would have delivered similar results if it had been adopted in the United Kingdom or France.

Note, I am not saying which COVID-19 policies were a success or failure, but that insofar as any policies were successful this may largely have been down to fortuitous accident rather than to the wisdom of any directional intelligence or missionary focus. I am also suggesting that there is and has been no systemic mechanism for policymakers to discern what the best response might have been. In a future pandemic, therefore, it will be far from obvious what has been learned from the experience we lived through between 2020 and late 2022.

Second, throughout the pandemic and in true missionary style, there was often minimal willingness from public health bureaucrats and from politicians to concede the possibility that they may be making mistakes or of the need to revise or to change course. The attitude appeared to be that any concession of ground to those pointing to contrary evidence or suggesting an alternative course would undermine support for the policy and ultimately lead citizens to behave in ways contrary to it.

Third, not only were politicians and public health experts reluctant to concede ground on their chosen strategies but there were significant and concerted attempts by public health officials and politicians – alongside supportive portions of the media and private enterprise to suppress dissent.[8] This attempted suppression occurred not only within nation states and governmental jurisdictions but was directed at whole countries and regions and especially those that did not follow a 'lock-down' strategy. This was one of the most disturbing aspects associated with the missionary character of pandemic response. The threat to freedom of expression and the related challenges to scientific and academic freedom on which the growth of knowledge ultimately depends were profound and their effects may be very long lasting.

6.5 The Experience of Missionary Industrial Policies

While these downsides associated with pandemic response were perhaps unavoidable, given the difficulties of relying on a 'mission-less' or market-based approach, problems of this type are likely to become a near permanent feature of the political economic landscape were we to replace predominantly market-led processes for guiding investment and resource allocation and to assume the missionary position instead. Now of course, a key difference between pandemic response and industrial policy is that the former takes place in the context of a potential emergency-situation, whereas the latter may be adopted and adapted over a much longer timescale. Nonetheless, the problems I have identified as arising in evaluating pandemic response policies, and of the suppression of dissent that has often accompanied them, would simply be played out over such a timescale were missionary industrial policies pursued.

First, there is no systemic mechanism to reveal whether missionary industrial policies will contribute to, or detract from, economic growth. Strong economic growth has occurred with and without industrial policies, so the evidence on whether it is necessary for governments to have a missionary focus to secure growth is anything but clear. In the case of the industrial revolution in Britain, Mokyr notes that industrial take-off took place in a context where the state had little or no economic vision and consumed only around 5% of GDP.[9] Equally, there have been numerous examples of missionary strategies that have been disastrous failures – many post-colonial regimes in Africa and the Indian experience pre-1991 epitomised such an approach. Nonetheless, there have also been some apparent and notable success stories – China which is cited favourably by Mazzucato and many others, being an important example in point. Yet even here, it is not clear that it was the strategy itself that was responsible for the growth – or whether the growth was achieved *despite the strategy* in question.

In his excellent book *Capitalism with Chinese Characteristics*, Jasheng Huang[10] has noted two phases of Chinese economic growth. The first phase between 1978 and 1990 arose out of the chaos after the cultural revolution and was led by predominantly bottom-up and market-led development focussed on agriculture and small-scale manufacturing that emerged without any overarching strategy or mission commitment. The second post-1990 'missionary phase' was an urban focussed approach based predominantly on attracting foreign direct investment. Huang notes no significant difference in growth performance between these bottom-up and top-down phases. What he does suggest, however, is that the second phase was introduced as part of a deliberate strategy from Beijing to crush dissent following the attempted student revolution in 1989, by limiting the potential development of alternative centres of economic and political power in the countryside.

Also of relevance to this argument is the experience of the United States. Mazzucato maintains that many of the technological innovations we benefit from today in the digital arena had their origins in large-scale public spending projects and notably in massive cold war military spending where the US state committed its directional intelligence wholeheartedly to secure a common good – a commitment responsible for triggering subsequent waves of innovation and growth. The problem here, however, is that while some of this military spending may have generated benefits, Mazzucato offers no analysis of the multiple acts of such spending that failed to generate beneficial spin-offs – opportunity costs simply do not concern her – arguably a common trait of the 'missionary' or what Hayek refers to in *The Road to Serfdom* as 'the single-minded idealist'.[11]

Mazzucato also fails to recognise that far from reflecting the value of directive intelligence the innovations she identifies seem to have been unintended or accidental consequences emerging from the sheer volume of spending in the defence sector – unintended consequences that were seized upon by entrepreneurs operating in competitive markets guided by profit and loss signals. Put differently, Mazzucato's case for missionary policy seems to be that if a government commits to spending enough public money on a favoured mission it would be remarkable if none of this spending did any good. Yet this position hardly amounts to a ringing endorsement of the state's supposed capacity to exercise 'directional intelligence'.

Note, in drawing on these examples I am not suggesting that mission-oriented policies can never have net beneficial consequences – but that as with the COVID-19 pandemic response, there is no systemic mechanism to discern in which contexts such benefits might be secured. And, if certain policies have 'worked', there is as much if not more reason to believe that the successes are attributable to fortuitous accident rather than to the foresight of a directive intelligence pursuing a coordinated 'mission' or 'plan'.

Finally, what missionary oriented industrial policies whether successful or otherwise have had in common is that they have tended to occur either in authoritarian or semi-authoritarian regimes that routinely seek to narrow debate and to suppress dissent. This is most evident in the Chinese case. It is also apparent in the US military-industrial complex where the highly militarised setting if not explicitly authoritarian is not exactly open to contestation and to challenge from the wider public through the open processes of public participation Mazzucato claims would accompany her preferred version of a missionary state.[12]

This tendency to suppress dissent is I would suggest potentially the most disturbing feature of the socio-political environment required to sustain missionary policies and is one shared with the COVID-19 pandemic response. The missionary position generates a dynamic where governments and their supporters must do what they can to prevent people from seeing the possible currency or value of alternative visions. It requires the population to be on a permanent war or emergency footing – with a concomitant tendency to demonise those unwilling to toe the line. This is a feature, and not a bug, of the missionary approach.

Nowhere do we see this feature more clearly today than in the policy space surrounding climate change, which Mazzucato and others want to be the focus of a new missionary zeal. The net zero agenda is clearly a mission committed strategy in this regard– and it is also one accompanied by increasingly illiberal attempts to suppress dissent. By dissent here, I do not mean the freedom to question the phenomena of anthropogenic climate change itself – important though that may be – I for one have never challenged the anthropogenic climate change theory. What I am suggesting is that we are now in a political environment where it is becoming difficult to challenge or to question the proposed policy responses to climate change. This is so not only with respect to whether adaptation rather than mitigation should be pursued but also how the net zero agenda should itself be delivered. Whatever its faults, the virtue of a carbon tax is that it leaves scope for significant pluralism within the energy sector in terms of how individuals and firms respond to what is a centrally imposed price by allowing them to experiment with substitutes for fossil fuels or continuing to use these fuels if they are willing to pay the necessary compensation. Under a missionary environment, however, there is now increasing pressure to specify which substitutes should be favoured – with renewables such as solar and wind power the subject of the relevant zeal.

As happened during the COVID-19 pandemic, many of those questioning these missionary policy positions are liable to be labelled as 'deniers'. Even those supporting net zero but who question the timescale for its delivery or dissent from the focus on solar and wind are presented as at best insufficiently progressive or at worst as corrupted by special interests (a charge never levied at the vast array of actors in universities, finance and banking and in the wind and solar sectors whose interests may profit from the missionary regime).

6.6 Conclusion

We live in challenging times and understandably perhaps people may be prone to seek inspiring and confident visions such as those offered today by the proponents of missionary government. I have suggested in this chapter that the economic case for missionary industrial policies is unproven – that insofar as they have successes these are attributable to accident rather than to design or to the alleged powers of any directive intelligence. I have also argued that the logic advanced by those who support these policies – and the practical experience of them – suggests a direct threat to individual freedom through the suppression of dissent. For that reason alone, the liberals of all parties should reject them.

Notes

1 See, for example, Mazzucato, M. (2021) *Mission Economy: A Moonshot Guide to Changing Capitalism*, London: Allen Lane. This work builds on the ideas previously expressed in Mazzucato, M. (2011) *The Entrepreneurial State*, London: Allen Lane.
2 Keynes, J.M. (1936: chapter 24) *The General Theory of Employment, Interest and Money*, London: Palgrave Macmillan.
3 For a comprehensive analysis of these, see, for example, Wennberg, K., Sandstrom, C. (2022) *Questioning the Entrepreneurial State*, Springer.
4 In my view, the best enunciation of these problems continues to be Lavoie, D. (1985) *National Economic Planning: What is Left?* Cambridge, MA: Ballinger.
5 Lippman, W. (1936: 67) *The Good Society*, New York: Grosset and Dunlap.
6 For a more detailed discussion of the arguments summarised here, see Pennington, M. (2021) Hayek on Complexity, Uncertainty and Pandemic Response, *Review of Austrian Economics*, 34: 203–220, https://link.springer.com/article/10.1007/s11138-020-00522-9?wt_mc=Internal.Event.1.SEM.ArticleAuthorOnlineFirst.
7 A recent study published by the Institute of Economic Affairs suggests little evidence that 'lockdowns' were more effective than more voluntaristic approaches – though arguably these results are highly sensitive to the classifications of the relevant variables adopted by the authors. See Herby, J., Jonung, L., Hanke, S. (2023) *Did Lockdowns Work?* London: Institute of Economic Affairs.
8 For a more detailed discussion of this, see Pennington, M. (2023) Foucault and Hayek on Public Health and the Road to Serfdom, *Public Choice,* 195: 125–143, https://link.springer.com/article/10.1007/s11127-021-00926-6.
9 Mokyr, J. (1999) Editors Introduction: The New Economic History and the Industrial Revolution, in *The British Industrial Revolution: An Economics Perspective*, Boulder,

CO: Westview Press. See also McCloskey, D. (2016) *Bourgeois Equality*, Chicago: University of Chicago Press.

10 Huang, J. (2008) *Capitalism with Chinese Characteristics*, Cambridge: Cambridge University Press

11 Hayek, F.A. (1944: 61) *The Road to Serfdom*, London: Routledge

12 Two other examples that suggest a relationship between missionary government and illiberalism in this regard which are often held up as exemplars of missionary success are South Korea and Singapore. The former was a semi-dictatorship under Park Chung Hee in its 'missionary' period and the move towards more liberal economic policies coincided with a move to democratic rule (Juang, 2008 *op cit.*). Singapore remains a semi-authoritarian political regime with limited access to elite policy networks by the public at large. As in the case of the United States and China – the economic successes of South Korea and Singapore are hard to attribute to their industrial policy stance. South Korea's success may equally be explained by its highly outward orientation on trade, while in Singapore policies that have been targeted at expanding the domestic entrepreneurial base appear for example to have disproportionately benefited large corporations from outside of Singapore – for a recent critique of Singaporean policy on these lines see Cheang, B. (2022) *Economic Liberalism and the Developmental State: Hong Kong and Singapore's Post War Development*, London: Palgrave.

References

Cheang, B. (2022): *Economic Liberalism and the Developmental State: Hong Kong and Singapore's Post War Development*. London: Palgrave.

Hayek, F. A. (1944): *The Road to Serfdom*. London: Routledge.

Herby, J., Jonung, L., Hanke, S. (2023): *Did Lockdowns Work?* London: Institute of Economic Affairs.

Huang, J. (2008): *Capitalism with Chinese Characteristics*. Cambridge: Cambridge University Press.

Keynes, J. M. (1936): *The General Theory of Employment, Interest and Money*. London: Palgrave Macmillan.

Lavoie, D. (1985): *National Economic Planning: What Is Left?* Cambridge, MA: Ballinger.

Lippman, W. (1936): *The Good Society*. New York: Grosset and Dunlap.

Mazzucato, M. (2011): *The Entrepreneurial State*. London: Allen Lane.

Mazzucato, M. (2021): *Mission Economy: A Moonshot Guide to Changing Capitalism*. London: Allen Lane.

McCloskey, D. (2016): *Bourgeois Equality*. Chicago, IL: University of Chicago Press.

Mokyr, J. (1999): Editors Introduction: The New Economic History and the Industrial Revolution, in *The British Industrial Revolution: An Economics Perspective*. Boulder, CO: Westview Press.

Pennington, M. (2021): Hayek on Complexity, Uncertainty and Pandemic Response. *Review of Austrian Economics*, 34, 203–220.

Pennington, M. (2023): Foucault and Hayek on Public Health and the Road to Serfdom. *Public Choice*, 195, 125–143.

Wennberg, K., Sandstrom, C. (2022): *Questioning the Entrepreneurial State*. Berlin: Springer.

7 "Misinformation" as Censorship Stratagem

Daniel B. Klein[1]

Friedrich Hayek explained in *The Road to Serfdom*, written in the United Kingdom in 1944, that anti-liberal regimes rely on propaganda and that propaganda relies on censorship. Propaganda and censorship travel together. The book's lesson is that the National Socialists, with whom "we" in 1944 Britain are at war, are not so different from what socialist tendencies, if not stayed and reversed, will lead to. The book's dedication reads: "To THE SOCIALISTS OF ALL PARTIES."

Hayek (1944, 159–60) explains the need of censorship in the chapter "The End of Truth": "Public criticism or even expressions of doubt must be suppressed." Propaganda from the government is not sufficient: "[T]he minority who will retain an inclination to criticize must also be silenced." "[T]he plan itself in every detail … must become sacrosanct and exempt from criticism." Consider the following sentence in light of recent years: "The basis of unfavorable comparison, the knowledge of possible alternatives to the course actually taken, information which might suggest failure on the part of the government—all will be suppressed."

Down the road to serfdom, in the sciences themselves, Hayek says, the "search for truth cannot be allowed … and vindication of the official views becomes the sole object." In totalitarian countries, scientific disciplines "become the most fertile factories of the official myths which the rulers use to guide the minds and wills of their subjects." In scholarly disciplines, "the pretense that they search for truth is abandoned and … the authorities decide what doctrines ought to be taught and published" (Ib., 161).

Hayek had seen how things unfolded on the European continent and was alarmed by what he saw in United Kingdom: "[C]ontempt for intellectual liberty is not a thing which arises only once the totalitarian system is established but one which can be found everywhere among intellectuals who have embraced a collectivist faith" (Ib., 163). The farther we go down the road to serfdom, the more fragile and vulnerable are official narratives to criticism. As a result, Hayek (p. 164) says, "intolerance … is openly extolled" by the mindguards and minions of official narratives.

Nowadays, the anti-liberal censors invoke "misinformation." That word adds the prefix *mis-* to the word *information*. Accordingly, *misinformation* invokes the presuppositions invoked by *information*.

DOI: 10.4324/9781003504412-10

In using "information" as a censorship stratagem, anti-liberals commit a category error. It is a folly to speak of differences in interpretation and judgment as differences in information. Consider statements censored as "misinformation," such as whether COVID-19 virus came from a lab, or concerning the value of Ivermectin, or the incidence of myocarditis. The censors have often invoked the opinions of certain organizations, such as the World Health Organization (WHO). But the matter of what sources are trustworthy is a matter of interpretation and judgment, not information. It would be a matter of information only if the censored voice had said, "The WHO said X" when the WHO had not said X. *That is not what the censored voice is censored for.* Rather, the censored voice is censored for rejecting the judgment that what WHO says should be taken as presumptive truth.

If the anti-liberals who are behind the censorship projects were to take one step toward truth, they would admit that the statements they censor are matters of interpretation and judgment. They would say: "We censor statements and voices we don't like." Or, as Martin Gurri (2023) puts it: "Disinformation Is the Word I Use When I Want You to Shut Up." They would describe their projects as waging war on miscreancy, not misinformation. Then, the nature and character of their designs would then be clear.

Rather than platforming the testing and comparing of differing interpretations, anti-liberals stomp on that process to protect their own opinions, interests, and agendas. One may say that they themselves are the greatest purveyors of misinformation and practitioners of disinformation. But there is a traditional term for disinformation: Lying. And there is a traditional term for programmatic lying: Propaganda. Propaganda is big lies, told programmatically.

Without censorship, the big lies would be torn to shreds. Thus, big lying begets more falseness: To protect the big lies, they engage in stratagems against the critics of the big lies. This chapter is about the second sort of falseness, the category error used to rationalize censorship of contestation of the big lies.

Enormous censorship projects are afoot, from governments and allies in the private and non-governmental organizations. It is not hard to discern the political bent of such projectors. That bent is plain from their selection of statements to censor, from the dissenting character of the platforms they wage war on, and from everything else known about those projectors (Glennon 2024; Gutentag 2023c; Select Subcommittee on Weaponization 2023; Taibbi 2023). The bent is also plain from where we find resistance to censorship. Connecting the dots takes virtue, not cleverness.

In this chapter I explore why the "misinformation" verbalism has been used. I do so in order that we may better repel it and reject the anti-liberalism it represents. As anti-liberals wield the term "misinformation," the false presupposition in "misinformation" is in "information." The prefix "mis-" is predicated on a concept involving the sort of accurateness in things where such accurateness is potentially operative. Because the tacit presupposing of accurateness is false, the ploy involves a category error: A proper category is capacious—interpretation, judgment, understanding, opinion—but they pretend it is information.

7.1 What This Chapter Is Not About

This chapter is not about the big lies guarded by censorship. I am circumspect in identifying big lies.

Second, this chapter is not about the nature, structure, network, and apparatus of the anti-liberal censors. It is not about the projects in censorship now afoot—in the United States, Canada, the United Kingdom, the European Union, and elsewhere—and rationalized as combatting "misinformation" and "disinformation." The array of such operations is hard to delineate and describe, not least because they are cloaked and morally confused. The array has been called the censorship-industrial complex (Shellenberger 2023). At the core, the array has government throwing its weight around and its initiation of coercion. And, besides government coercion, there are allies. These allies often enjoy monopolistic positions, stemming from government handouts, privileges, and sweetheart deals, as with broadcasters, universities, NGOs, and pharmaceutical companies, or from having cornered certain network externalities, as with certain huge media platforms such as Facebook. They do the bidding of the anti-liberals in a variety of ways, from deplatforming, smearing, and waging lawfare. Banks and other large organizations often are themselves threatened and intimidated into doing the bidding of the anti-liberals.

The best way to learn about the array of nefarious operations is to read those who combat them. I am aware of some of the leading organs based in the United States, including *Racket News* (Matt Taibbi and colleagues) and *Public* (Michael Shellenberger, Alex Gutentag, and colleagues), and Lee Fang, and, in video on Rumble, X, and other platforms, Glenn Greenwald, Redacted (Clayton Morris), and Tucker Carlson. I am not endorsing things they say, but if one wants to learn about the nefarious projects afoot, they report on developments, offering their own interpretations and judgments.

Before moving on to what this chapter is about, let me say two more things about what it is not about. First, to support governmental policing against miscreancy is to flaunt one's anti-liberalism and illiberality. The motive sometimes is to signal commitment to anti-liberalism, in a manner parallel to how religious cults sets up rituals and practices for signaling commitments (Iannaccone 1992). Vice signals vice, the ticket in some spheres to promotion and advancement. And acting viciously spurs the evildoer to act viciously again, to defend against exposé and accountability for their own earlier viciousness. In protecting their rackets, they verge upon a downward spiral. Second, methods that have been used by government actors to manipulate affairs in other countries are now aggressively used to manipulate affairs within the domestic polity. Government actors are warring on their domestic adversaries using methods they use on foreign adversaries (Gutentag 2023a, 2023b; Malone 2023). They protect democracy, they say, abroad and at home.

7.2 What This Chapter Is About

Let's say that one of the censors is named Mr. Green and a person he censors is Mr. Orange. Mr. Green reads and dislikes a piece of discourse by Mr. Orange, and labels it "misinformation" or "disinformation." This chapter is about the folly that inheres in Mr. Green's verbalism. We might say that Mr. Green regards Mr. Orange's discourse as miscreancy. This chapter is a conceptual investigation of Mr. Green's treating a matter of supposed miscreancy as a matter of information. I argue that Mr. Green engages in intellectual folly in doing so.

I say "miscreancy" to ascribe to the anti-liberals a quasi-religion and then ironically call "miscreancy" what they regard to be miscreancy. I use "miscreancy" as a truthful parody of their character. The medieval fanatics who persecuted and censored supposed miscreants likewise pretended to a false accurateness to their religious creed, an accurateness implied by the prefix "mis-."

"Misinformation" is not the only verbal device or stratagem used by anti-liberal projectors. They deploy a panoply of bad verbalisms, such as "fact-checker." A verbal falsehood often involves a false presupposition. The presupposition is left unsaid. Victims are then burdened with articulating the presupposition. They attempt to articulate those presuppositions as they scramble to defend themselves. Only by articulating the presupposition can they expose its falseness. For the anti-liberals, the confusion is a feature, not a bug.

7.3 Knowledge's Richness

In Klein (2012) I say that knowledge involves three chief facets. Those facets help us see why "misinformation" and "disinformation" (as used in censorious verbalisms) involve a category error. Later in the paper, a fourth facet—*fact*—is incorporated into the theory of knowledge offered here.

The three chief facets are information, interpretation, and judgment:

- *Information:* The word comes from the Latin *forma* for "form." A piece of information is *in form*, or in the pertinent format. A bit or element of information implies a format, a set, an array, of possible elements, a format within which the actual element is realized. If I tell the group: "The dinner will be at P.J. Skidoos," it is apt to call the communication information because that particular location is a realization within the array of possible local venues for the dinner.

  The "format" within which a bit or element of information exists can be thought of as *a working interpretation*, natural to the context of the matter under discussion ("Where will we meet for dinner?"). A working interpretation has been *working*, by definition. The definitional features suggest a certain precision and accuracy, a cut-and-driedness. (The word *precise* from Latin suggests pre-cut.) The cut-and-driedness stems partly from the nature of the working interpretation itself (e.g., locations in our locale). In my youth, we pick up the phone and called up "Information" to be informed of someone's phone number. And the cut-and-driedness stems partly from the fact that it is an established *working* interpretation, so practices and expectations have settled over time on certain conventions and rules. Adam Smith likened a system of relatively precise and accurate rules to grammar, whereas the rules of aesthetics, like those of the pursuit of happiness, and virtue, are "loose, vague, and indeterminate" (Smith [1790], 175, 327).

I should add that a communication of any kind might be said to have an informational aspect in the actuality of the event of communicating. That is, if Kent tweets "God exists!," we might say that the cosmos metaphorically informs us: *Kent tweeted "God exists!"* In this sense, when it rains the cosmos metaphorically informs us: *It rains*. But the information (or *fact*, if you prefer, in this case) *Kent tweeted "God exists!"* is different from saying that "God exists" is itself information. There is, after all, only one cosmos, and that aspect of the cosmos, God's existence, calls upon one to interpret and judge understandings of the cosmos; God's existence is not a matter of mere information. The same can be said of other aspects of our singular cosmos, such as whether Ivermectin can prevent hospitalization and death, whether Covid came from a lab, and other claims that the "misinformation" stratagem is deployed against.

- *Interpretation*: This facet of knowledge takes us beyond the working interpretation. It creatively presents other formulations—wholly distinct "forms"—within which facts are interpreted. It opens things up to the generation and multiplying of interpretations; you now face a portfolio or menu of interpretations, and it is a portfolio that can always grow yet another interpretation.
- *Judgment* is the action facet of knowledge. It involves the estimating of interpretations and taking stock in interpretations estimated highly. Judgment involves a degree of commitment—belief, creed, credence—which propels you to act on the interpretations you take stock in. If you do not actually act on the interpretation you purport to take stock in, you are a hypocrite and a quack. If you are aware of your hypocrisy, you are a liar of sorts; if you are not aware of it, you are in denial, self-deluded. Lying, denialism, self-delusion, and cynicism are features of moral baseness.

When anti-liberals label opposition "misinformation" or "disinformation" they invoke presuppositions built into the word *information*, presuppositions that are false. When anti-liberals label opposition "mis-" or "disinformation," they are, at best, objecting in the interpretation and judgment dimensions of knowledge, or, at worst, they are speaking in a way that has abandoned civil engagement, using words as instruments of wickedness. Proceeding upon a false presupposition, they commit a category error.

Usually, what people argue fervently over is not information, but interpretations and judgments as to which interpretations to act on. What is being labeled and attacked as "misinformation" is not a matter of true or false information, but of true or false *knowledge*.

The question of whether a movie is in black-and-white or in color can almost always be readily decided, because we basically share an interpretation of "black-and-white" and "in color," making the question a matter of information. Within the information dimension of knowledge, variance is resolved in a straightforward manner. Very little interpretative engagement and dialogue are called for.

If interpretative effort is called for, the matter is no longer within the information dimension. Films that depart from the usual standards, such as *Pleasantville*, in which certain characters come to see "in-color," make us reconsider or refine our interpretation of a film being "in black-and-white" or "in-color."

More broadly, the interpretative dimension is where we roam when we ask whether *Citizen Kane* is a better movie than *Roman Holiday*. Only to be ironic would someone say: Dad misinforms you when he says that *Citizen Kane* is better than *Roman Holiday*. The irony there would be in the implied high self-estimation, as the speaker sets up his own aesthetic sensibilities in judging movies as a standard so precise and accurate as to warrant "misinform" when Dad deviates from that standard.

The anti-liberals are without irony. They dodge interpretive engagement by labeling dissenting statements "mis-" or "disinformation." They are bullying and intimidating their opponents.

We notice that sometimes, as in an announcement of BBC Verify, the anti-liberals use the novel term "mistruth," which was scarcely ever used prior to a several decades ago. The "mis-" prefix does not well fit on the word *truth*, which pervades knowledge river-deep, mountain-high. Think of *mistake, misspeak, misremember, misplace, mislay, misquote, misdirect*, and so on. The prefix "mis-" is proper when the betterness of a readily identifiable alternative—the accurate quotation, for example—is hardly a matter of dispute. I doubt that much time will be spent by BBC Verify on correcting misquotations.

7.4 Misinformed by the Supermarket Clerk

I enter a supermarket and ask a clerk where the peanut butter is, and he responds, "Aisle 6." I go to Aisle 6 but don't find it there. I wander around the store and find the peanut butter in Aisle 9.

The clerk was mistaken. He gave me false or bad information. The idea *Peanut butter is in Aisle 6* is a matter of information, an idea sitting within a set of working interpretations. The working interpretations include those of ordinary human purpose and of ordinary trust and common decency. The clerk and I were *not* playing a game, nor was it April Fools' Day. Importantly, the working interpretations include those of plain English—the semantic conventions of "peanut butter" and "6," the syntactical conventions of English, and so on.

On April Fools' Day, working interpretations are what we depart from when we play tricks on one another. The tricks create an unexpected asymmetry between the interpretation of the targeted person—who wishes to add a dash of salt to his soup—and the trickster—who unscrewed the top of the saltshaker. The target interpreted the world as presenting a saltshaker with top screwed on as usual (the working interpretation). The trickster relished her anticipation of the target's shock and surprise in discovering the faultiness of his interpretation of the world.

Asymmetric interpretation is essential to humor. Another form of humor is the put-on, as when the trickster feigns his own frustrations, and we enter into the asymmetric interpretations of the amused target of the trick, as in Buster Keaton put-ons from *Candid Camera*.

Likewise, humor often plays upon departures from semantic conventions, as in punning "Knock, knock" jokes and "Who's on First" by Abbot and Costello. A precondition of humor is a certain trust and joint interest in the truths that humor gets at. Without those preconditions, there is no humor.

Despotism conceals its designs. It conceals its true beliefs and intentions. By its nature, it abuses working interpretations. Despotism is untrustworthy. Its relationship with ordinary organic interpretation is never playful. That is why despotism is incapable of being humorous. It cannot make a joke, and it cannot take a joke. Adam Smith wrote:

> Reserve and concealment … call forth diffidence. We are afraid to follow the man who is going we do not know where.
>
> (Smith 1790, 337)

Afraid, we attend the despot with diffidence. Despotism is grim.

While despotism is humorless, it can be the butt of humor. In 1625, Hugo Grotius noted: "Stratocles was laughed at in Athens for proposing a law that whatever was thought good by Demetrius, should be reckoned right and pious" (Grotius 1625, 290). Today, humorists such as J.P. Sears, Greg Gutfeld, Jesse Watters, Gad Saad, and Alex Christoforou help us chuckle at despots.

I take my peanut butter to the check-out line where the same clerk is working, and say, "I found it—but in Aisle 9!," trying to be humorous as though a joke had been played on me. The clerk responds, "Ah?! Sorry about that!" Being a mere matter of information, the mistake *is readily accepted*. That ready acceptance is the hallmark of the information dimension of knowledge. Mistakes happen, but, provided we keep within that dimension, the mistakes are readily accepted. "Sorry about that!" is the hallmark of informational slip-ups.

7.5 Kids Jumping Out of Windows

The aisle for peanut butter is a matter of information. Now let's turn to an example that is not. During oral arguments in *Murthy v. Missouri*, 2024, Supreme Court Justice Ketanji Brown Jackson posited a "hypothetical":

> Suppose someone started posting about a new teen challenge that involved teens jumping out of windows at increasing elevations … And kids all over the country start doing this. There is an epidemic. Children are seriously injuring or even killing themselves in situations. Is it your view that government authorities could not declare those circumstances a public emergency and encourage social media platforms to take down *the information* that is instigating this problem? … Can the government call the platforms and say?: '*This information* that you are putting up on your platform is creating a serious public health emergency. We are encouraging you to take it down.'
>
> (Jackson as transcribed by the present author, Forbes 2024 (video); italics added)

Justice Jackson would have spoken more justly if she had talked about the platforms being advised to take down the content, the material, the videos, the postings, or the communications. Instead, she says "the information." Let's continue with the hypothetical aired in this historic case. Suppose a nefarious video valorizes someone jumping out of a third-floor window: "This dude WALKS OFF CALMLY after a third-floor jump!" What is the informational nature of the posting?

Whether government authorities should alert the platform of such videos is an important question. But to address that question we should not treat the issue in terms of misinformation or disinformation. We do not discuss such disturbing videos in terms of misinformation. The same goes for good content. To return to the example of *Citizen Kane* versus *Rear Window*, it would be absurd to suggest that *Citizen Kane* is the lesser movie because it contains more misinformation and that is maker, Orson Welles, engaged in disinformation.

When I told the supermarket clerk that the peanut butter was in Aisle 9, he readily accepted the correction. For the window-jumping material, the actual cause for concern is swaying kids to jump out of windows. What would be correct information? If we rendered the video as a statement susceptible to true-or-false assessment, it would be something like: *It is cool to jump out of third-floor windows*. The statement is foolish, wrongheaded, false. But "misinformation"? That is a category error.

The matter of what it is that confused kids, in their personal situations, find cool is not one of sufficient accuracy or concreteness to warrant couching a discussion of it in terms of "information." What kids find cool is very much a matter of interpretation and judgment. The governmental activities that are on trial in *Missouri v. Murthy*, however, *are* defended in terms of combatting misinformation and disinformation. By using "misinformation," the defendants—and their censorious allies—are pretending that they are merely protecting the public from cut-and-dried falsehoods. In doing so, they misrepresent their doings and slip responsibility for arrogating to themselves decision as to what is safe and sound for people to see or hear. Furthermore, the free-speech advocates are then portrayed as proponents of speaking cut-and-dried falsehoods. The stratagem kneecaps them by trapping their objections in the limited dimension of information, forcing them to epistemologize so as to fight off censorship. The "misinformation" stratagem is attractive to the censorious because it flatters their vanity, chicanes so as to slip responsibility, and kneecaps their opponents. Hubris built the Tower of Babel and the result was semantic chaos. Today we see both hubris and semantic chaos in censorship operations that assert themselves as combatting misinformation.

7.6 Unintentional and Intentional

When one person, Bob, misinforms another, Jim, without realizing that the information is false, the mistake is amendable to ready correction, without fuss, assuming the falseness is realized by Jim or Bob. Such misinformation events are trifling; we don't debate them or dwell on them. Misinformation is rather like a typo, corrected by a proofreader.

Scarcely ever do we speak of the mistake with the five-syllable Latinate word *misinformation*. Heavy usage of the word *misinformation* often occurs in connection with "anti-misinformation" projects, usage by the perpetrators and cheerleaders or by those who fend off threats from the perps.

When Bob misinforms Jim intentionally, however, information mistakes are dishonest. They are lies. We dwell on them as lies, not as matters of misinformation. The misinformer is a liar. Some now promulgate the word *disinformation*.

In distinguishing *misinformation* from *disinformation*, Dictionary.com explains "the critical distinction between these confusable words: intent". Wikipedia says the same. Its entry on Disinformation begins: "Disinformation is false information deliberately spread to deceive people" (https://en.wikipedia.org/wiki/Disinformation). According to those sources, then, disinformation is lying. It is false information spread by those who know that it is false information. To disinform is to lie.

The distinction based on intent is not sharp. Is the following misinformer a *dis*-informer?: He does *not* know that the information he spreads is false but he fails in performing basic due diligence against its falsity.

In as much as discourse carries with it a claim to having done such due diligence, the claim would be false. And if he knows he has not done due diligence, he is a liar, though the lie is about having performed due diligence, not about his knowing that the information is false.

Out-and-out lying travels with a vast entourage of shabby norms and shabby understandings of the duties of due diligence. Related here would be the large topics of denialism, self-deceit, self-delusion, and hypocrisy (for Adam Smith's treatment of self-deceit, see in Klein 2023, ch. 20). The terminus is cynicism, baseness, and miserableness.

The word *lying* is itself polysemous. Let's distinguish between stiff and loose. Stiff lying is speaking falsehoods that the speaker knows to be false. Loose lying are falsehoods that involve on the part of the speaker some kind of deception, but "deception" here is used loosely, so as to include self-deceit and self-delusion. I have called the "misinformation" stratagem a category error. Instead, we are tempted to call it a lie. That might work if we understand it as loose lying, not stiff lying. The category error involves taking stock in interpretations of the nature of knowledge, interpretations that are bad. It involves, at minimum, self-deceit and self-delusions—specifically, delusions that allow one to persist in committing the category error—and thus are instances of loose lying. Instead of calling the erring a sort of lying, we are tempted to use such words as *sham*, *travesty*, *quackery*, or *folly*, but those words connote an inconsequentialness; it is like calling Jacobinism, Bolshevism, Naziism, or Maoism a *sham*, *fraud*, *travesty*, *quackery*, or *folly*. Those terms do not seem to accommodate the heinousness of such movements.

In ordinary private-sector affairs, outside of politics and outside of heavily governmentalized affairs, shams and frauds usually do not persist. Lying at the level of information is naturally checked and counteracted. Again, "information" implies reference to working interpretations. Getting things right should not be difficult or tricky—issues there are all *within* the *working* interpretation. Sure, mistakes are made; but such mistakes are readily and easily corrected.

Liars who lie about information lose the trust of their voluntary associates, whether those voluntary associates are friends, customers, trading partners, or employees. If liars lie about simple features of their products or their services, they could be subject to law suits from their trading partners, to public criticism, and to rival exposé by competitors. In ordinary private-sector affairs, everyone has reputational incentives not to lie systematically about information. Again, the concept of information presupposes a basic working interpretation, akin to a grammar. The thing about grammar, and this is something that makes it different from aesthetics, is that feedback on one's grammar is only negative (beyond grammar school, anyway). That is, when you make grammatical mistakes, you get criticism, but when you get your grammar right, you do not get praise. Putting out false information, is similar. When crooked people falsify records or statistics, they might try to cover it up by making the primitives behind the records unavailable. We might call that misinformation, because we have norms that say that such primitives should be disclosed and honestly reported. So misinformation happens, sometimes by innocent mistake (the supermarket-aisle example) or by fraud. But when it is fraud, it risks very serious reputational and legal repercussions. It also risks jeopardizing functionality within one's relationship, within the organization, and within one's own habits of personal management. "You see, Pinocchio, a lie keeps growing and growing, until it's as plain as the nose on your face." Most of us have strong moral incentives within ourselves against lying, especially about cut-and-dried things. We dread the disapproval of "the man within the breast"—an expression Adam Smith used for the conscience.

So, you might ask: If private actors without government privileges and immunities scarcely spread false information dishonestly and programmatically, is disinformation really a thing? Before addressing that question directly, let's turn to the Godzilla of programmatic lying.

7.7 Propaganda: Government's Programmatic Lies

It is government, especially, that lies programmatically. The lying can be at the level of information, but it usually makes more sense to say that its lying is at the level of interpretation: The government promotes *interpretations*—for example, *The Covid virus came from nature*— interpretations that it, the government, itself does not particularly believe. It lies about the virus having come from nature, as it lies about many other big interpretations. It propagates big lies.

And it lies with confidence. Government is the only player in society that initiates coercion in an institutionalized way. Its coercion is overt. What's more, it does so on a colossal scale. That is the most essential feature of government. Every government is a Godzilla, and we must learn to live with our Godzilla and mitigate the destruction it wreaks.

The traditional term for government's programmatic lying is propaganda—a word that once did not necessarily imply falseness (instead signifying simply the propagation of ideas or the ideas so propagated, https://www.etymonline.com/search?q=propaganda), but is now generally used in that necessarily-pejorative sense, and that is how I use it here. The falsehoods of propaganda are typically stiff lies, in that the propagandizers usually do not particularly believe the claims they propagate, but sometimes they are only loose lies.

Government can lie programmatically because it does not depend on voluntary participation for its support. It subsists on coercion, including restrictions on competitors and opponents, and takings from taxpayers. Organizations in heavily governmentalized settings can also lie programmatically. Crony private organizations sustain large programmatic lying only when they enjoy privileges, immunities, and protections from the government.

7.8 "Misinformation" and "disinformation" as Censorious Stratagems

Gurri (2023) suggested that, so often, "disinformation" "means, 'Shut up, peasant.' It's a bullet aimed at killing the conversation." The term "disinformation" scarcely existed before 1980, as shown in Figure 7.1. The figure contains data through 2019, and it is likely that the recent surge has continued.

Gilbert Doctorow writes of "the introduction of the word 'disinformation' into common parlance." Doctorow writes:

> The word "disinformation" has a specific context in time and intent: it is used by the powers that be and by the mainstream media they control to denigrate, marginalize and suppress sources of military, political, economic and other information that might contradict the official government narrative and so dilute the control exercised by those in power over the general population.
>
> (Doctorow 2023)

Gurri and Doctorow are describing what is now the main way, or at least the most troubling and most terrible way, that "disinformation" is used. It must be noted, however, that the word has also been used simply as a synonym of propaganda—and thus something that governments, too, perpetrate. But, now, "misinformation" and "disinformation" are most conspicuously a propagandistic term—a loose lie, and, again, a category error—used in the manner described by Gurri and Doctorow. In that sense, "disinformation" is not a general synonym for propaganda, but is, rather, a word that propagandists use to smear and persecute miscreants.

In fighting against propaganda-plus-censorship, honest people, too, now resort to using "disinformation," as a synonym for propaganda, to fling that specific word back onto the propagandists. Doctorow exemplifies what I mean. He justly writes:

> In reality, it is these censorious states and the mass media that carry their messages with stenographic precision into print and electronic dissemination who are the ones that day after day feed *disinformation* to the public. It is cynically composed and consists of a toxic blend of 'spin,' by which is meant misleading interpretation of events, and outright lies.
>
> (Doctorow 2023)

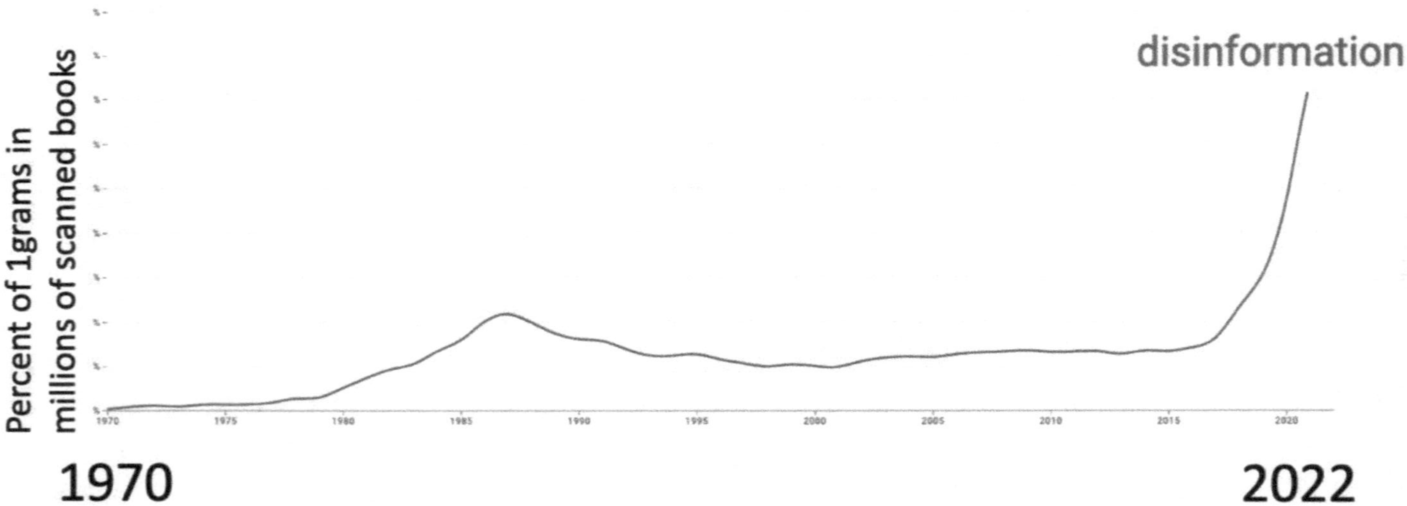

Figure 7.1 “disinformation” as percent of all 1 grams, 1970–2022.

Source: Google Books Ngram Viewer. http://books.google.com/ngrams (https://books.google.com/ngrams/graph?content=disinformation&year_start=1970&year_end=2022&corpus=en&smoothing=0&case_insensitive=false)

Time and again we find ourselves having to use the degraded verbalisms of the anti-liberals to address and combat their abuses. Sometimes it seems like our civilization revolves around trying to keep the anti-liberals from burning down the house.

7.9 Base Humans Tend to Weaponize Things

But aren't governments accountable to checks and balance, divisions of power, and the rule of law? Haven't we learned to tame Godzilla, to chain down Leviathan?

It is true that the government of a rule-of-law republic, checked by an honest media, might be quite limited in its programmatic lying and censorship. But that's not how it is today, where the legacy media is morally base in the extreme and dissent is being tarred as "mis-" and "disinformation." Today, regimes are increasingly despotic, and despotic regimes are much less checked and limited.

The rule of law means, first and foremost, the government even-handedly applying the rules posted on its own website. Governments today don't do that. Law is applied politically, that is, with extreme partiality, upon a double-standard. Laws are selectively enforced and punishments are selectively meted out. Moreover, rule-making around censorship grows vague and arbitrary—to the effect of, "Something is misinformation if we or our allies say it is." Anti-liberals avail themselves of show trials, kangaroo bodies, and galleries filled with stooges. The "anti-misinformation" agenda is misrule.

Despotism despoils checks and balances. Despotism centralizes power formerly divided. It destroys the independency and autonomy that, theoretically, branches and units, divided and balanced, had once enjoyed. Despotism usurps powers once distributed and balanced. Despotism is unbalanced power.

Under an anti-liberal regime, the coercive institutions unique to government become weaponized by the anti-liberals and their allies. They turn them against their opponents. But weaponization is itself always somewhat constrained by cultural norms. The existence of government implies the existence of a governed society, and the existence of society implies the existence of some basic norms, for example against theft, murder, and lying. David Hume famously pointed out that the governed always vastly outnumber the governors, and hence government depends on "opinion"—if only the opinion to acquiesce to those governors:

> Force is always on the side of the governed, the governors have nothing to support them but opinion. It is therefore, on opinion only that government is founded; and this maxim extends to the most despotic and most military governments, as well as to the most free and most popular.
>
> (Hume 1994, 32)

I wonder whether the shut-them-up projects of Naziism, Stalinism, and Maoism tarred their opponents with labels akin to "misinformation" and "disinformation." Even National Socialists and Communists gave some lip service to social norms, with their show trials and righteous objections to "the lying press" (*Lügenpresse*). But did their languages, at those times, have words that corresponded to the English words *information*, *interpretation*, and *judgment*, along the lines of the distinctions made here? Was their vocabulary for knowledge like that of English, and did they abuse the presuppositions involved in those distinctions the way that "anti-misinformation" projects do today?

7.10 The Contested Claims Go Far beyond Information

Disagreement usually arises over interpretations and judgments as to which interpretations to take stock in or believe. We make judgments, "good" and "bad," "wise" and "foolish," about interpretations, "true" and "false."

Again, "anti-misinformation" projects presuppose the information dimension where such a presupposition is inapt. When anti-liberals declare something to be "misinformation," the discourser—say, John Campbell, Peter McCullough, Robert Malone—unlike the clerk in the supermarket example—does *not* readily accept the supposed correction. That is proof that presuppositions of the information dimension do not apply. The matter is clearly beyond information.

The anti-liberals tend to invoke certain organizations as the definitive, authoritative sources of "information." They say, in effect: "The CDC, the WHO, the FDA says the mRNA injections are safe and effective, so anything that suggests otherwise is misinformation." The farce here is pretending that everyone's working interpretation consists of the dicta of some such particular organization. Never has an organization or agency had such a Mount-Olympus status for determining, throughout society, working interpretations of complex matters. And to suggest such a Mount-Olympus status for an organization with the foul characters and track-records of the CDC, WHO, FDA makes plain what is afoot. The similitude to the Soviet Union under Stalin is obvious.

To be worth a damn, estimations of wisdom and virtue must emerge from arrangements not heavily governmentalized, liberal arrangements, in society, in science, and in public discourse. We shall look not to Godzilla but to certain among the human beings who check Godzilla. A big part of the interpretation dimension is the estimation of the wisdom and virtue of those who contend for authority. Government is a Godzilla; it is not a validator of an organization's wisdom and virtue.

7.11 What the Sincere Human Looks Like

I wrote above of "quite decisive proof that presuppositions of the information dimension do not apply," in noting that Peter McCullough does not readily accept the supposed correction. But what if McCullough is a liar? Then it would be no surprise that he does not readily accept the purported correction. What, in other words, about the possibility of *dis*information? An insincere disinformationist would stand by his informational statements and persist in misinforming his listeners.

7.12 What Does Sincere Engagement Look Like?

Sincere engagement is sincere in the desire to become better aligned with the larger good, which would correspond to a universally benevolent beholder. The sincere human does not claim to be universally benevolent. He does not even claim to be more benevolent than the average person. But, compared to the average person, the sincere human scrupulously strives to align his conduct with universal benevolence.

The sincere human *wants* to be corrected. He *welcomes* correction. Sincerity is evident in the human's openness to engagement. The sincere human welcomes deep-dive conversation, debate, and challenge. He is eager to learn.

If the sincere human rejects a purported correction, he is eager to explain the interpretations and judgments that motivate his rejection of the purported correction. He explains why he rejects it. And he welcomes a response to his explanation. He is agreeable to continuing the engagement.

The sincere human wants to sit down, human-to-human, and hash things out. He wants to enter into the mind of his intellectual adversary and see why the adversary says what he says. The sincere human wants to hear about the adversary's portfolio of possible interpretations. The sincere human is eager to compare the adversary's portfolio to his own portfolio of interpretations.

In comparing the portfolios, the sincere human may see some interpretations that are not in his own portfolio and wish to consider those as candidates for incorporation into his own. The sincere human wants to probe their soundness, their worthiness. The sincere human may also see that the adversary's portfolio lacks certain interpretations that are in his own and will want to understand why those are lacking from the adversary's portfolio.

By hashing things out, the two prattlers should aim to get the contents of their respective portfolios onto the table, making a larger union of the contents of the two portfolios of possible interpretations. They can then explore together the reasons, or causes, for their difference in how they judge among the possible interpretations. They try to dwell in one another's mind, sympathetically, to get a feeling for the ways of the other's judgment. After doing so, each can then make a moment in the other's judgment into an object up for examination, an object for interpretation and estimation. "But why do you draw *that* conclusion?"

The sincere human is frank and open about the calls of his own judgment. He invites the other human to ask, "But why do you draw *that* conclusion?" Adam Smith ([1790], 337) wrote: "Frankness and openness conciliate confidence."

When two sincere humans disagree, it is as if they say to one another:

> We both purport to orient ourselves upward, toward alignment with the good of the whole. We both understand that our thinking must focus on the most important things in the issue at hand. We both look at the same world—our interpretations are, as it were, interpretations of the signals presented to us in the book of nature. And yet we draw different conclusions. Let us explore

> the sources of that difference, in the hope that as a result there will be an improvement, for the good of the whole, in the joint effect of (your revised outlook and my revised outlook), after your outlook and my outlook have been revised by virtue of our conversation.

That is what the sincere human looks like. He is open, frank, and eager to participate in conversation and debate with adversaries. He is eager to sit down and hash things out. He is eager to delve into the fine points, to nail down the details, to respond to challenges, to document the evidence, to continue the conversation. He relishes engagement as a sort of adventure of the mind. He takes joy in argumentation and scholarship, as actualization of the human potentiality for virtue—of serving a benevolent beholder, as it were.

The sincere human looks like—from what I can tell—Peter McCullough.

I single out Peter McCullough as exemplar simply to single out someone. All of those who are eager to engage adversaries illustrate the most salient feature of the sincere human, and the more that that eagerness fits the rest of my description above, the more sincere that human likely is.

The sincere human loves life, and hence loves the most rewarding, most sublime of life's experiences. For scholars, researchers, thinkers, and indeed for *Man Thinking* everywhere, as humans in continual discourse about our duties to the good and our dependence on interpreting the book of nature, one of the most rewarding, sublime experiences is the sort of civil engagement described above. The sincere human, then, holds the norms, practices, and institutions that foster and safeguard that sort of civil engagement to be sacred. The sincere human, therefore, is not only a liberal in the pre-political senses of the word, but also in the political sense christened "liberal" around the 1770s by Adam Smith and other Britons (Klein, forthcoming). That is the political outlook that best sacralizes the norms, practices, and institutions of sincere engagement.

7.13 What the Unsincere Human Looks Like

We now turn to characters opposite of the sincere human. One would be insincere, but I wonder whether another is the human without either sincerity or insincerity. I will use "unsincere."

The features of the unsincere human are generally the opposite of the just-described ways of the sincere human. The unsincere human is not open. He is averse to sitting and hashing out differences with adversaries. He may issue brief, peremptory messages. He avoids challenges. He ignores criticism. He does not explain. He refuses engagement.

The most vicious humans hate to see adversaries finding platforms and channels to challenge their projects; they work to shut them up. Other humans fall in with, or at least stays silent about, the assaults on liberal norms and institutions, such as "anti-misinformation" projects.

7.14 Freedom Beats Unfreedom

I have asserted that for matters of mere information, voluntary, private-sector affairs—without contaminants of governmentalization—have natural incentives to communicate information accurately and to correct mistakes in information. I have asserted that information tends to be autocorrecting under liberal arrangements.

But what about the higher (or deeper) realms of knowledge, of interpretation and judgment? Are they autocorrecting? Do liberal institutions—free speech, free markets, limited government—handle those nicely, as though the system were guided by an invisible hand?

The present paper is not about that. But, briefly, certainly one could make a strong case that, under liberal institutions and liberal attitudes, interpretation and judgment tend to be autocorrecting. Those arrangements allow people to criticize and challenge bad interpretations and bad judgments.

Big lies need to be torn to shreds, and a free marketplace of ideas allows people to do that. Freedom means that critics of big lies will be safe from being coerced by government for their speech acts. And the less that social affairs are governmentalized, the less weight will the government have to pressure its satellites to shut down speech it does not like.

The free marketplace of ideas is far from perfect. Indeed, Adam Smith suggested that few individuals ascend to higher wisdom and virtue. But the question is always: Compared to what? The more the marketplace of ideas is governmentalized, the more that certain interpretations and judgments will be privileged and protected—by largesse and favor, by prestige, and by coercion. Does government handle interpretation and judgment as though it were guided by the invisible hand of a universally benevolent conductor of the cosmos? What possible theory could maintain that such an invisible hand has the upper hand?

More important than imagining *the best* that a system might achieve is to ponder *the worst*. I think it is clear that heavy governmentalization can enforce outcomes far worse than anything we could have to fear from a free marketplace of ideas.

7.15 Fact

Earlier in this essay I theorized the three chief facets of knowledge (information, interpretation, and judgment). Now I add *fact* and offer a spiral diagram. I think that getting the understanding across can be useful to sincere efforts to advance the good. (At the end of this paper is an Appendix listing of a few philosophers whose thinking my thinking dovetails with.)

Consider the saying, *Facts are theory-laden*, a saying that got started in the 1960s. To relate that saying to my terminology, think of "theory" as *interpretation judged worthy or superior*. Theory, then, refers to the dimensions of interpretation and of judgment.

Facts are theory-laden is a useful saying, for it reminds us that what one person calls "fact" can be opened up to examination and challenge by another person—or even by the same person, a moment later, after having called it "fact." The simple truth is that we could, if we had cause to, dig interpretation and judgment out from underneath any of our facts.

Facts are theory-laden, but when "we" all embrace the laden theory, we call the statements fact. To call something fact is to declare that the laden theory is *not* the matter under discussion. Fact, then, is a facet of knowledge, but not a chief one. Fact designates statements that no one among "us" wishes at all to take issue with. Facts are noncontroversial, at least for the discussion within which they are treated as facts.

A diagram may be helpful.

Communication picks up midstream of human experience. We proceed upon working interpretations. "Information" is what we call the facts as seen within the working interpretation.

Figure 7.2 offers four phases (or facets) of knowledge, shown in each loop of the spiral. "Facts" reside in a more basic interpretive frame—more basic than what I have called "the working interpretation"—in which "factual" statements are presumed acceptable to all parties of the communication. When Jane and Amy "argue over the facts," they are, as it were, revisiting what is to be treated as factual.

The loops flow one into the next, through time, from outer loops to inner loops. We travel in the clockwise direction. The spiral image on your screen is two-dimensional, but imagine a third. We hope that the spiral winds upward in wisdom and virtue, such that the inner loops are higher than the outer loops.

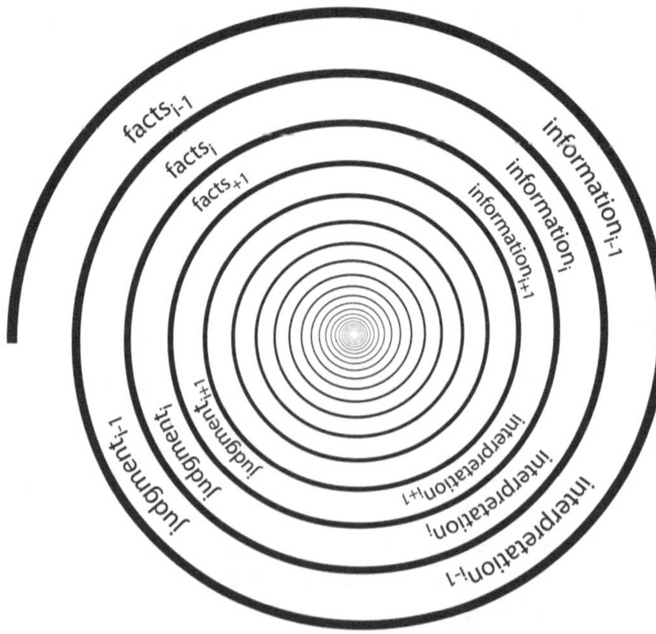

Figure 7.2 The spiral of knowledge, with four phases: fact, information, interpretation, and judgment.

Source: The author's creation

Suppose we sit down together with a telephone book. We call the ink markings "the facts." Neither of us thinks to dispute statements about the printed numbers on the pages. We then proceed to talk plainly of them as *phone numbers*. We often forget this working lens—interpreting the facts as phone numbers—because we see through it.

One of us, however, may propose another interpretation: Might the list of "phone numbers" contain secret knowledge encoded by spies?

Thus, we have multiple interpretations of the ink markings that some understand as "phone numbers." Those quotation marks signal: What the facts are called when they are seen through the working interpretation. But we may more directly speak of *multiple interpretations of the information*, as opposed to multiple interpretations of the facts. Thus, rather than interpretively pivoting off the "fact"-level interpretation—that the line reads 678-3554—let's pivot interpretively off of what I have called "the working interpretation"—that 678-3554 is a phone number—a level *up* from the factual, and there the pivot then turns to open up the interpretation dimension: "Maybe the phone number is a secret encoded message?" Again, universal acceptance among the "we" is built into "the facts": None of us disputes that the line says 678-3554. Wherever you want to accommodate interpretive pivoting, move "factual" to somewhere *down* from there.

Meanwhile, life rolls on, and we are called to act. The pitch races toward the plate. If the batter waits for a better interpretation, he may be called out on strikes. Again, the action facet of knowledge is judgment. As speaker, we judge of judgments—those of our interlocutors and of agents existing within the descriptions we give of things. We convey our judgments of their judgments using judgmental terms.

If, among our circle of "we," judgment is shared, then those judgments may now predicate a further conversation among us, and, thusly, those judgments present statements now *treated as fact*. Thus, we have completed the phases of the spiral and have moved from one loop to the next, where the sequence of phases may recur.

7.16 Anti-liberal Contempt for Our Circle of "We"

Again, what is labeled and attacked as "misinformation" or "disinformation" is not a matter of true or false information, but of true or false *knowledge*. Recognizing that knowledge, not merely information, is at issue is a matter of common decency.

The dignity of sincere discourse involves an openness, in principle a universal openness, to other human "we's" and their pursuits upward in wisdom and virtue. As we can see, the chief facets of knowledge—information, interpretation, and judgment—operate both behind and ahead of our current position in the spiral. Trying to shut us up is to show a despotic contempt for our way of weaving through the phases of knowledge. It is contemptuous toward the development of the *many loops* within which our sense-making has made a home and now operates.

By weighing interpretations and making judgments, we settle certain beliefs as fact, to predicate our further conversation. Those beliefs reflect a "we" with those beliefs. Meanwhile, in the wider world, different "we's" are forming and are addressing the public at large, representing different sets of belief, different ways of making sense of the world. We might call a "we" a distinct *sense-making community*.

The sincere human of any one of these communities is eager to learn from other communities. The sincere human has certain commitments which make it belong to the sense-making community it belongs to, but it is not wedded to that community. In fact, the entire population of that community—that is, the set of people who currently share that way of sense-making—may remake their community's way of sense-making. Those who learn from other communities may become leaders of intellectual change within their own community.

Sincere humans favor the freedom of speech and the norms of frank and open discourse *for all communities*. Besides favoring that freedom, they welcome engagement across communities, for all the reasons given earlier.

The "anti-misinformation" despots show contempt for communities at odds with their dicta and diktats. Not only are the members of the "anti-misinformation" community unwilling to engage in civil debate, but they promulgate "anti-misinformation" propaganda so as to intimidate their adversaries, to crush dissent.

I have explained that the "misinformation" characterization of the disagreement is false. The anti-liberals are presupposing that it is a matter within the information dimension of knowledge, when clearly the disagreement involves contentions in the interpretation and judgment dimensions. Under pretense of combatting misinformation, they are really just stomping on adversaries. It is akin to Naziism, Stalinism, and Maoism, regimes that likewise showed despotic contempt for sense-making communities at odds with their own. "Anti-misinformation" projects are a sham, just as "anti-racism" projects are a sham.

7.17 A Few Words about "Hate"

> We're a hate group … We hate.
> (Get Smart)

Just as "anti-misinformation" projects are anti-liberal, so too are "anti-hate-speech" projects (Holden 2023). The failure is again one of bad semantics and false presuppositions. "Anti-misinformation" despots tar their opponents with "misinformation," making an "information" category error based on a false presupposition. "Anti-hate speech" projects tar their opponents with "hate," again making a category error, for they treat hatred as necessarily hateful—that is, improper. Figure 7.3 shows the recent onset of "hate speech" and "hate crime."

But hatred is a necessary and organic part of any coherent system of morals. A coherent system of morals holds love and hate to be counterparts to one another. In a coherent system of morals, love is to be felt toward objects that are loveworthy, and hatred is to be felt toward objects that are hateworthy, although the bounds of

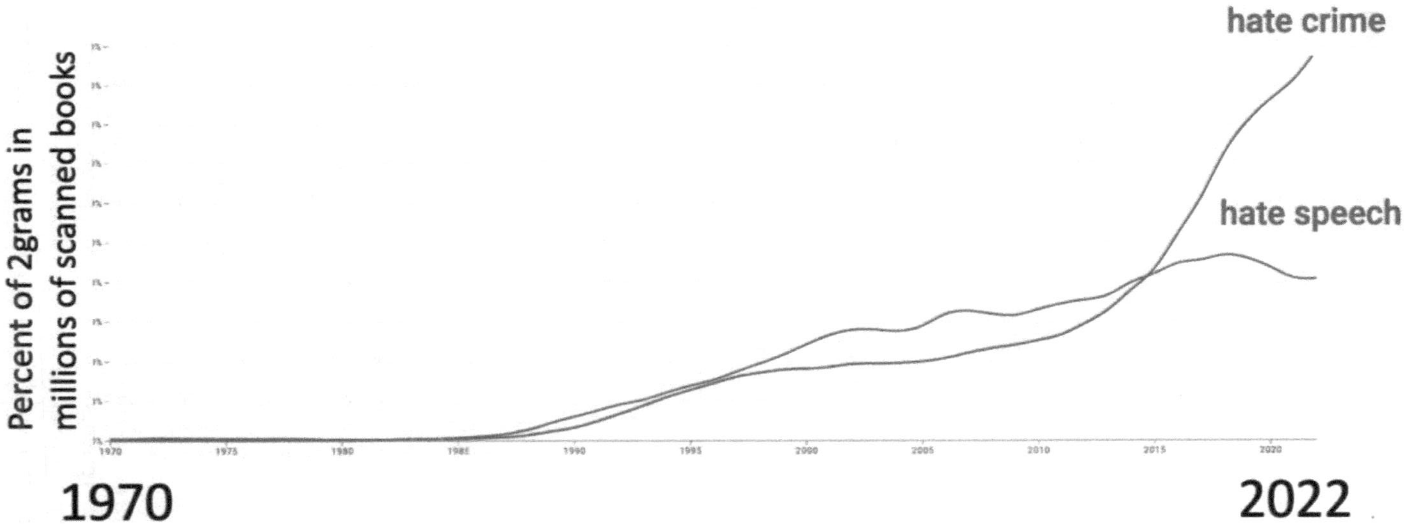

Figure 7.3 "hate speech" and "hate crime" are new.

Source: Google Books Ngram Viewer. http://books.google.com/ngrams (https://books.google.com/ngrams/graph?content=hate+crime%2Chate+speech&year_start=1970&year_end=2022&corpus=en&smoothing=3&case_insensitive=false)

propriety for the intensity and expression of the two respective feelings are importantly different, as Adam Smith explained (see esp. [1790] Part I, Sect. II, Chaps. 3 & 4 on the "unsocial" and "social" passions).

The two respective sets of objects bear a counterpart relation to one another, for that which works systematically against the loveworthy is hateworthy. As Edmund Burke (2022, 150) wrote: "They will never love where they ought to love, who do not hate where they ought to hate."

The implicit denial by anti-liberals that hatred is necessary and organic is parallel to their implicit denial, in treating interpretive matters as informational matters, that asymmetric interpretation is necessary and organic. Just as "mis-" and "dis-information" are words they use to shut you up, "hate speech," "hate group," and "hate crime" are words they use to shut you up, ratified by show trials and kangaroo bodies. A proper court of hate would presuppose a distinction between proper hate and improper hate, just hate and unjust hate. In a liberal civilization such "courts" are not governmental. Rather, they remain in the judgment and interpretation of the individual's own being. If hate is policed in the manner that outward action is policed by governments,

> we should feel all the furies of that passion against any person in whose breast we suspected or believed such designs or affections were harboured, though they had never broken out into any actions. Sentiments, thoughts, intentions, would become the objects of punishment; and if the indignation of mankind run as high against them as against actions; if the baseness of the thought which had given birth to no action, seemed in the eyes of the world as much to call aloud for vengeance as the baseness of the action, *every court of judicature would become a real inquisition.*
>
> (Smith [1790], 105 italics added)

7.18 Concluding Remarks

In 1787, James Madison wrote: "As long as the reason of man continues fallible, and he is at liberty to exercise it, different opinions will be formed." Differences in interpretation and judgment are what our civilization has striven to accommodate and keep peaceful. Censoring those differences is untrue to who we are as a civilization.

At the opening of this chapter, I quoted Hayek's *The Road to Serfdom*, in particular the chapter "The End of Truth." Hayek explained that propaganda relies on censorship, lest big lies be ripped to shreds. To get back to truth, polities must reverse course.

In this chapter I have argued that knowledge cannot be flattened down to information. In seeing that interpretation and judgment operate beyond information, that knowledge is richer than information, we see that counter-narrative claims attacked as "misinformation" are far beyond the information dimension. The attackers commit a category error. We expose their "anti-misinformation" projects for what they are, namely, censorship. And we expose the verbalisms "misinformation" and "disinformation" as a stratagem in service to that evil.

Seeing the richness of knowledge, we see that the "anti-misinformation" projects are miscarriages of civility, decency, and the rule of law. We must rediscover the norms of openness, tolerance, and free speech that dignify humankind. Science depends on confidence, and confidence depends on those liberal norms. Those norms are the parents of good science, healthy sense-making, and civil tranquility. There are two roads. The virtuous road is that of freedom, openness, confidence, truth-tracking, dignity. The vicious road is that of despotism, concealment, diffidence, bad science, serfdom, and servility. Let's get back to the right road.

Appendix: Philosophical affinities

FWIW: My take on knowledge has affinities to the philosophizing of David Hume, Adam Smith, Friedrich Hayek, Michael Polanyi, Thomas Kuhn, Iain McGilchrist, and many others. It also has affinities to the pragmatists William James and Richard Rorty, but I regard pragmatism—seeing one's belief as the product of one's choosing an idea among alternative ideas, and seeing the chosen idea's betterness (better, that is, compared to actual future-oriented alternative ideas, *not* to past days of innocence, which wisdom might have made unrecoverable) as necessarily the chief basis for what one shall count as true—as a phase situated on one side of a spiral, counterposed, on the other side of the spiral, by an phase that we may call Humean natural belief. Humean natural belief is belief that has emerged from depths beyond the loop in which we pass between the two phases; Humean natural belief is, within that loop, not to be treated in terms of choice; it is what we would call, as we dwell within that loop, brute reality. I think of Hume saying: I am not prepared to affirm that God exists, but I believe that backgammon with my friends exists and in a way that I could scarcely believe otherwise and, so, the belief is scarcely a product of past choice nor an object of future choice. To open such a part of reality up to the pragmatist phase—Does backgammon with my friends exist?—would mean acceding to another loop of the spiral. We have, then, within a loop two phases: (1) belief, and (2) pragmatist revisiting and possible revision of belief. Within a loop they bear a subscript corresponding to that loop. Now, it is important to understand that in the theory of knowledge offered here there is no first (or lower-most) loop and no final (or upper-most) loop. The spiral is indefinite. Hence, certain realities at some loop remain brutish, certain beliefs remain natural (in a sense of primitive), for any finite conversation. And, in this world, all conversations are finite, even when produced in a spirit of the eternal.

Note

1 This paper is a significantly revised and more academic version of the working paper "Misinformation Is a Word We Use to Shut You Up," posted at Brownstone Institute and Independent Institute.

References

Burke, Edmund. 2022. *Edmund Burke and the Perennial Battle, 1789–1797*. Edited by D.B. Klein and D. Pino. CL Press. https://clpress.net/books/edmund-burke-and-the-perennial-battle-1789-1797/.

Doctorow, Gilbert. 2023. *The Western Media Disinformation Campaign: Fall of Bakhmut, a Case in Point*. Gilbert Doctorow website. https://gilbertdoctorow.com/2023/05/21/the-western-media-disinformation-campaign-fall-of-bakhmut-a-case-in-point/.

Forbes. 2024. KBJ Creates 'Teens Jumping Out of Windows' Hypothetical to Address Limits of Government Censorship (video). YouTube, March 18. Link: https://www.youtube.com/watch?v=SvF-U0b5MBA

Glennon, Michael. 2024. Democratic Attorneys General Support Censorship. *Reason*. January 19. https://reason.com/2024/01/19/democratic-attorneys-general-support-censorship/.

Grotius, Hugo. 1853 [1625]. *Grotius on the Rights of War and Peace*. Abridged trans. W. Whewell. Cambridge: J.W. Parker.

Gurri, Martin. 2023. Disinformation Is the Word I Use When I Want You to Shut Up. *Discourse*, March 30. https://www.discoursemagazine.com/culture-and-society/2023/03/30/disinformation-is-the-word-i-use-when-i-want-you-to-shut-up/.

Gutentag, Alex. 2023a. US Military Contractors Used Counterterrorism Tactics against the American People, New Documents Show. *Public* (Substack), December 4. https://public.substack.com/p/us-military-contractors-used-counterterrorism.

Gutentag, Alex. 2023b. Pentagon Was Involved in Domestic Censorship Scheme, New CTIL Whistleblower Files Show. *Public* (Substack), December 7. https://public.substack.com/p/pentagon-was-involved-in-domestic.

Gutentag, Alex. 2023c. Censorship Industrial Complex Leaders Were Also Behind Trump-Russia Collusion Hoax. *Public* (Substack), December 15. https://public.substack.com/p/censorship-industrial-complex-leaders.

Hayek, Friedrich A. 1944. *The Road to Serfdom*. Chicago, IL: University of Chicago Press.

Holden, Paul. 2023. The 'UK Files': A History of the Center for Countering Digital Hate. Racket News, November 14. https://www.racket.news/p/the-uk-files-a-history-of-the-center.

Hume, David. 1994. *Essays, Moral, Political, and Literary*. Edited by Eugene F. Miller. Indianapolis: Liberty Fund.

Iannaccone, Laurence. 1992. Sacrifice and Stigma: Reducing Free-riding in Cults, Communes, and Other Collectives. *Journal of Political Economy* 100(2): 271–291.

Klein, Daniel B. Forthcoming. 'Liberal' as a Political Adjective (in English), 1769–1824. *Journal of Contextual Economics–Schmollars Jahrbuch*.

Klein, Daniel B. 2012. *Knowledge and Coordination: A Liberal Interpretation*. Oxford: Oxford University Press.

Klein, Daniel B. 2023. *Smithian Morals*. CL Press. https://clpress.net/site/assets/files/1091/smithian_morals_11.pdf.

Malone, Robert W. 2023. How a 'Cybersecurity' Agency Colluded with Big Tech and 'Disinformation' Partners to Censor Americans. *Robert Malone* (Substack), July 1. https://rwmalonemd.substack.com/p/how-a-cybersecurity-agency-colluded.

Select Subcommittee on the Weaponization of the Federal Government. 2023. The Weaponization of 'Disinformation' Pseudo-Experts and Bureaucrats: How the Federal Government Partnered with Universities to Censor Americans' Political Speech. U.S. House of Representatives, November 6. https://judiciary.house.gov/sites/evo-subsites/republicans-judiciary.house.gov/files/evo-media-document/EIP_Jira_Ticket_Staff_Report_11-6-23_Clean.pdf.

Shellenberger, Michael. 2023. The Censorship-Industrial Complex, Part 2. *Public* (Substack), November 30. https://public.substack.com/p/the-censorship-industrial-complex-c21.

Smith, Adam. 1982 [1790]. *The Theory of Moral Sentiments*. Edited by D.D. Raphael, A.L. Macfie. Oxford: Oxford University Press/Liberty Fund.

Taibbi, Matt. 2023. 'Anti-Disinformation' Is a Partisan Con. *Racket News*, November 29. https://www.racket.news/p/anti-disinformation-is-a-partisan.

Part III

Market Institutions and Economic Growth

8 Unfettered Money

Juan E. Castañeda

8.1 A Change in the Monetary Paradigm: A New 'monetary veil'

As Milton Friedman put it in 'The Counter-Revolution in Monetary Theory' in 1970, 'A counter-revolution, whether in politics or in science, never restores the initial situation. It always produces a situation that has some similarity to the initial one but is also strongly influenced by the intervening revolution'.

At the present time a new paradigm in monetary economics is needed, one that challenges New Keynesianism[1] (1990s–) as the foundation of monetary theory and policy. This chapter is not an attempt to do so, rather a more modest reflection on the principles of a monetary policy framework more compatible with a monetary stability and a stable economy in the long term. To this end, we will use the experience of the gold standard as a reference and a benchmark to propose a change in how monetary policies are conducted today. We will emphasise the differences between the framework and principles we are proposing with those of the current paradigm – the one that has been governing monetary policy since the effective adoption of the New Keynesian model three decades ago as the mainstream model, in both assessing the economy and making monetary policy decisions. Our alternative proposes that money is governed *as if* there were a separation between the real economy and money. This would mean a drastic change in the roles played by central banks (and by extension, governments) in market economies, as monetary policy would not be designed to affect the running of the economy along the business cycle.

8.1.1 The Gold Standard Principles as a Benchmark

Central banks and governments seem to have disregarded the foundations of a solid monetary system in recent decades. Money is managed by national central banks without reference to the effects of excessive money growth on the economy, which are more noticeable over the medium to the long term, both in the business cycle and in inflation. The reaction of policymakers to both the Global Financial Crisis (GFC) and the COVID-19 episode has resulted in greater monetary instability and large business cycle fluctuations: A period of monetary expansion during the three years before the outbreak of the GFC (2004–07) was followed by sharp monetary deceleration and monetary contraction in the aftermath of the crisis in 2009

DOI: 10.4324/9781003504412-12

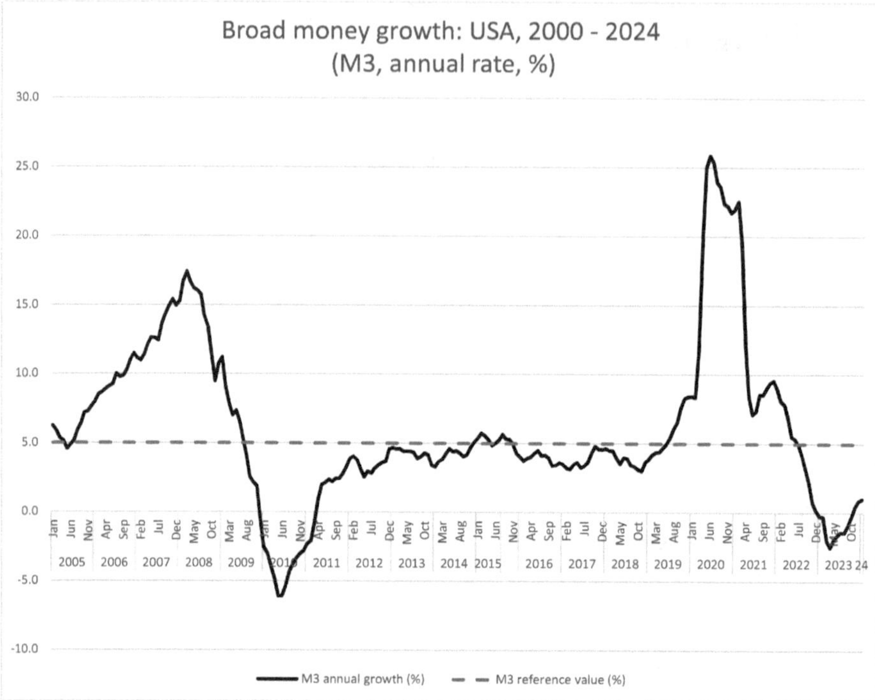

Figure 8.1 Monetary stability?

Source: M3 from the US Federal Reserve up to 2006; from 2006 on, from Shadow Government Statistics. A 5% reference value for M3 growth was calculated following the Quantity Equation, assuming a 2% inflation target, a trend rate of output growth of 2% and an annual decline in money velocity of –1%.

(see Figure 8.1), accompanied by deflation and recession, while a surge in the amount of money in 2020–21 led to an inflationary boom in 2022 followed once again by money deceleration and monetary contraction in 2023.

Quite often, the classical gold standard period (1870s–1913) is taken as the template of what it is considered to be 'sound money', a system that preserved monetary stability and the purchasing power of the currency over a long period of time. It was a system managed by the government through privately owned central banks with monopoly power to issue currency, but with effective restrictions ('rules' in the modern jargon, see Bordo and Kydland, 1995) that prevented the systematic mismanagement of the currency by the government or the central bank. Should we then aim at restoring the gold standard as it used to work before 1914? Leaving other complications aside, such as the relative scarcity of gold that would need to be reflected in the exchange rate between gold and the national currencies, the most important barrier to adopt it lies in a 'credibility problem'.

On the one hand, we are where we are now and we should not think – quite naively – that, should we so desire, we would be able to return simply to the paradigm of monetary and financial stability under the operation of the gold standard as it operated from the latter part of the 19th century until the outbreak of World War I in 1914. Expectations and credibility matter and since the abandonment of the gold standard in the inter-war period, central banks, along with their policies and the involvement of the government in the economy, have developed in a very different direction. The state – broadly defined – is now much more involved in the running of the economy. National central banks now belong to the treasury and have been given a remit to intervene more actively and more often in the economy, usually in order to achieve a specific macroeconomic target (which since the 1990s in most economies has been an inflation target[2]). The size of the government in the economy has tripled (from approximately 15% to 45% of the GDP) and so have the borrowing needs of the government.

On the other hand, there is the 'credibility problem' – namely, once the public knows that it is possible to abandon the commitment to the gold standard, they would anticipate that if it suited policymakers, they would have no hesitation in changing the parity rate or perhaps even quitting the gold standard altogether. As George Selgin put it a few years ago at the 'Think Conference' for the Institute of Economic Affairs in 2016 (see Selgin, 2018), now that the gold standard has been abandoned, any decision to adhere to a re-established gold standard would not now be perceived by the public as credible – as they know that abandoning the system is an option – and thus any commitment of the monetary authorities would not be as firm and lasting as it was assumed to be by all[3] at the time of the classical gold standard period.

During the classical gold standard period, in Britain along with other leading economies the central bank committed to the convertibility of the bank notes issued into gold on demand at the parity rate set at the time. This rarely changed and would only be altered in very extraordinary circumstances such as wartime. Convertibility imposed an effective restriction on the ability of the monopolist money issuer to over-expand, thus preserving the value of the currency in the long term. There was no need to pursue any other goal. Thus, the position of the central bank at that time was quite passive, absent a banking crisis or a liquidity panic. By 'passive' I mean that, compared to central banks nowadays the central bank did not, for example, seek to achieve a set price level or an inflation target. In those days, prices more transparently reflected changes in the economy; in particular, changes in productivity in what were much more open and free markets. These changes could be explained as follows: if the amount of money stays the same, should the production of goods and services increase in relatively open and competitive markets, then prices will tend to fall (as it did happen at the time, see evidence in Bordo et al., 2004), an outcome the central bank did not need to react to or offset with the creation of more money. There was no 'price stabilisation' or 'inflation stabilisation' policy by the central bank at the time, whose principal goal consisted of maintaining the convertibility of the notes issued in gold at the set parity. This contributed to an economy where the issuer of the currency did not intend to alter prices and the information they convey in a market economy – thus minimising distortions in the economy coming from changes in the supply of money.

In addition, during the second half of the 19th century, the Bank of England learned how to react to banking crises in order to maintain financial stability (see more details in Capie, 2020; Wood, 2000), thus becoming what we can consider as a 'modern central bank' – in other words, a central bank willing to act as the Lender of Last Resort in times of a banking crisis (see Anson et al., 2017; Capie, 2020). For example, the Bank of England responded actively to the 1866 banking crisis by lending promptly and against collateral at a high interest rate, effectively ensuring that the failure of Overend & Gurney that year did not result in any contagion which might affect other banks, thus avoiding the collapse of the payments system. The Bank had learned by then what we now call the 'Bagehot criteria' (Bagehot, 1873) to intervene in case of a banking crisis: (1) to be ready to lend promptly to banks in need of liquidity; (2) to lend against collateral; and (3) at a high interest rate. These were the principles that the Bank followed since then until the outbreak of the GFC, which resulted in a period of financial stability in Britain which lasted more than a century without any financial crisis as defined by A. Schwartz in 1986.[4]

In the case of Britain, the outcome of the working of the gold standard was a succession of episodes of mild deflation and mild inflation which, on average, led to true price stability. By 'true' price stability I mean that the price level back in the 1810s would be very similar to that in 1913 (see Figure 8.2), immediately before

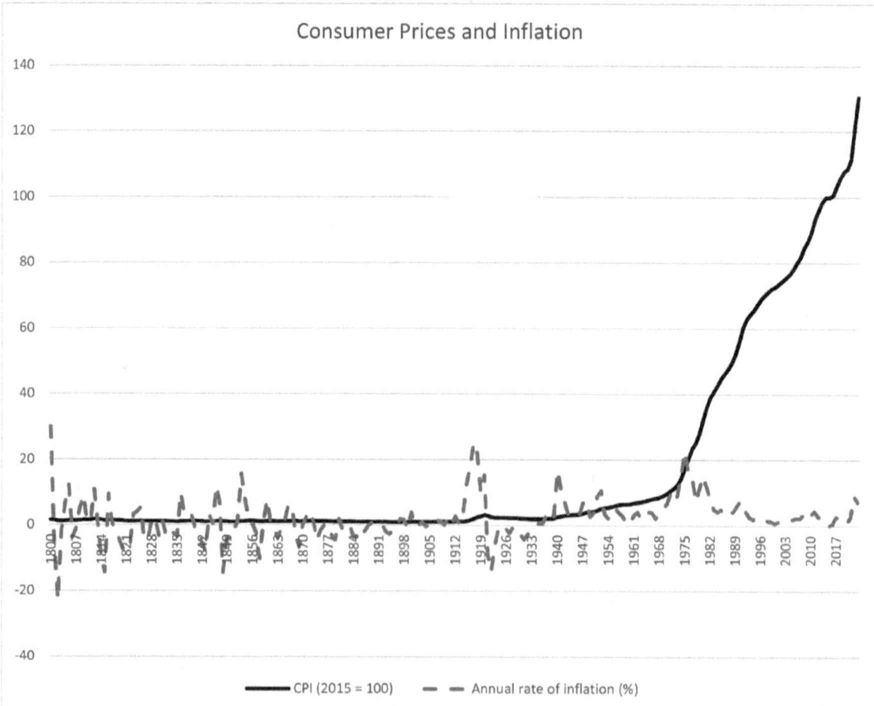

Figure 8.2 Inflation over two centuries (1800–2023).

Source: Data from the Bank of England and ONS.

the outbreak of the First World War. As Capie (2020) has pointed out, a simple observation of the graph below highlights how systematic inflation has very much been a 20th-century phenomenon.

8.2 Monetary Policies and the Debate on 'Money Neutrality'

Under the gold standard, the Bank of England was still a bank, mainly committed to maintaining the convertibility of its notes (a liability for the Bank), as well as being – at least by the end of the 19th century – increasingly conscious of its role in preserving the stability of the financial system. Under this system, the likelihood of monetary distortions that could potentially harm the real side of the economy was considerably reduced. I am not claiming that changes in the amount of money, even in a well-run gold standard system, were 'neutral', in the sense that they did not have any impact on the decisions made by individuals and companies as regards how much they wanted to consume, save or invest (see Hume, 1752[5]). It would be virtually impossible to foresee (or to anticipate correctly) the expected changes in the economy resulting from a change in the amount of money; the more so the more volatile and frequent changes in the monetary conditions are. The way money is introduced into the monetary market by central banks, through lending to commercial banks against collateral, results in changes in relative prices across different sectors in the economy, ultimately having an impact on who benefits most from the monetary expansion (this is explained by the operation of the so-called 'Cantillon Effect'[6]). A new monetary equilibrium will be met, as agents will try to get rid of the excess of cash in their portfolios by increasing their demand for alternative assets to money as well as their demand for goods and services, thus increasing asset prices and ultimately consumer prices. Overall, once the necessary adjustments in the market have been completed and a new monetary equilibrium has been reached, the result of a monetary expansion is ultimately an increase in the price level, provided that everything else stays the same (see Friedman, 1970).

However, the monetary expansion and the subsequent re-equilibrium mechanism briefly explained above would not be neutral. The structure of production and relative prices in several markets would inevitably have changed (see Hayek, 1931). But at least under the gold standard, monetary matters were not intentionally manipulated to alter the fluctuations and the outcomes of the economy in order to achieve a preferred inflation rate or to mitigate business cycle fluctuations connected with the potential of the economy, as it is the case nowadays. During that time, the institutions allowed for the running of the currency and the financial system *as if* there were a separation between the monetary and the real side of the economy, which is referred to as the 'classical dichotomy'. In such a world, money was meant to be a 'veil' because of its stability and predictability, so that market actors could see through the veil and focus on the real determinants of their decisions. A credible monetary anchor allowed for agents to rely on prices as a guide to make and plan their decisions, under the assumption that monetary decisions would not be made to change market prices deliberately.

The experience of abundant 'monetary mismanagement' by central banks across the world both in the years leading up to and during the last two crisis episodes (the GFC in 2007–09 and the COVID-19 episode in 2020–21) confirms that a profound deviation from the monetary standards and the principles compatible with monetary and financial stability discussed above had taken place. I am not going to suggest that we just return to the gold standard but that we use the principles in which that system was based on to achieve greater monetary and financial stability. Monetary policy in the last two decades has created greater monetary instability (see Figure 8.1) as well as turning national central banks into the biggest holders of their own government's debt, thus blurring the line between monetary and fiscal policies (Selgin, 2020). In the next two sections we will see why the decisions made in the last two crises have resulted in even more discretionary and unstable monetary policies.

8.3 Central Bank Models and Rationale (1990s–2024)

Leading central banks' models do not longer use money to make monetary policies. As the Chair of the US Federal Reserve declared in a testimony in the US Congress (February 2021): 'the growth of M2 … doesn't really have important implications for the economic outlook'. And a few months later (December 2021), in an US Senate hearing he added that the link between money and inflation 'ended about 40 years ago'. In the Eurozone, a new monetary strategy was announced by the European Central Bank in 2021 and the 'monetary pillar' that highlighted the relation between changes in broad money to inflation/deflation was effectively abandoned (see European Central Bank, 2021; Castañeda and Congdon, 2017). As the European Central Bank (2021) explained this decision (the emphasis is mine):

> The monetary analysis has shifted from its main role of detecting risks to price stability over medium to longer-term horizons towards a stronger emphasis on providing information for assessing monetary policy transmission. *This shift in focus reflects a weakening of the empirical link between monetary aggregates and inflation, ….*

In the UK, the Bank of England's quarterly Monetary Policy Report had not even mentioned money or referred to monetary analysis in decades, until the Autumn of 2023 when it once again started to discuss the rate of growth of money.

This disregard for monetary analysis reflects central bank preference for other models that explain inflation as a result of (1) changes in inflation expectations and (2) how close or far the economy is from its potential output (i.e. the size of the output gap). Following a New Keynesian model with expectations and price rigidity, changes in policy rates do enter directly into the Investment-Savings (IS) equation and affect the size of the output gap (y), which in turn will have an impact on inflation (p) through the Philips Curve (see equations 8.1–8.2).

$$\text{IS equation: } y = f\,[(-)\text{ policy rate; }(+)\text{ Expected } y] \qquad (8.1)$$

$$\text{Philips Curve: } p = f\,[(+)\,y; (+)\,\text{Expected } p] \qquad (8.2)$$

Therefore, with this model the central bank can control both prices and fluctuations of output during the cycle without any reference to how changes in the amount of money (or the demand for money) may affect spending and prices. Furthermore, in the New Keynesian model prices are 'sticky' in the short term and changes in interest rates will have an impact on spending in the direction intended by the policymaker – in other words, greater spending levels with lower policy rates and vice versa. It is a model that presumes that active monetary policies can achieve price stability (or rather, a steady rate of inflation) and at the same time, minimise deviations of production from potential. This is known as a 'flexible inflation targeting' strategy, one by which the central bank is committed to achieving a low rate of inflation in the 'medium term' (around two years), so that output fluctuations during the cycle are also minimised. Following equations 8.1 and 8.2, if inflation expectations are well anchored around the central bank's inflation target, this model provides the theoretical rationale for central banks to change policy rates as needed in order to produce 'optimal' policy decisions, that is, those compatible with inflation stability close to the central bank target and output gap stability along the cycle, in a nutshell, heaven on earth.

In the real world, these models require of a considerable amount of information to operate as intended. There are many uncertainties, in particular, the size of the output gap, which is by definition an indicator that must be estimated as it cannot be directly calculated.[7] As with many other models, the New Keynesian model works relatively well under stable conditions, but this was not the case during the GFC and its aftermath, or during the COVID-19 episode, when there were large fluctuations in the amount of money and great uncertainty in the economy.

The strategies developed by leading central banks in response to the last two crises have resulted in more discretionary (less rule-based) policies. The adoption of asset purchase programmes (so-called Quantitative Easing [QE]) back in 2008 was not undertaken to conform to any particular monetary growth measure, but rather in the determination to bring down short- and long-term bond rates (see Neely 2016 for a discussion on this question). In addition, QE has produced a notable expansion in central banks' balance sheets very much linked to the financial needs of their respective governments. National central banks have become major creditors of their governments which puts them in a difficult position when it comes to maintaining their credibility and their independence from the government. With the need to raise policy rates to rein in inflation in 2022–23 along with assets sales (so-called Quantitative Tightening), central banks are already running financial losses that would need to be covered by the government. This is all further blurring the separation between monetary and fiscal policy. True, following Capie and Wood (2013), when it really matters (i.e. in times of a severe crisis) central bank independence becomes ineffective, as the national central bank is inevitably constrained to provide financial support to the government. But the expansion of QE during the COVID-19 episode reveals a more permanent exposure of central banks to their governments which may undermine central bank credibility (see Ueda, 2023). As Friedman (1962) suggested, rather than central bank independence, the emphasis should be put on the adoption of a credible rule that binds the hands of the issuer of the currency, thus contributing to achieving monetary stability over the long term.

8.3.1 Central Bank Strategies

One way or another, leading central banks have been following an 'inflation targeting' strategy for over three decades, supported by the New Keynesian model to make policy decisions. When it was first adopted by the Reserve Bank of New Zealand back in 1989, this strategy was considered a welcome approach to policymaking, as it provided a more reliable and transparent framework for making decisions based on achieving a low rate of inflation, and would enable more regular communication with the market. However, the implementation of such a strategy in the last two crises has been based on models that do not incorporate important determinants of inflation in the medium and long term, such as the rate of change in the amount of money. This is reflected in the extraordinary deviation of inflation forecasts by central banks in 2020 and 2021 from the actual rate of inflation that ensued. Let us take the Bank of England's inflation forecasting record during the pandemic as a case-study. By the end of 2020 (see Figure 8.3a) the Bank of England expected inflation to rise moderately and stay within the 1–3% range from 2021 up to 2023. By November 2021, however (see Figure 8.3b), inflation was already above the 2% target. Even though the Bank of England revised its forecasts upwards, they did not remotely consider the likelihood of inflation above 8% in their official 'fan charts', and the Bank's central projection (see the darkest area in the figure) shows that inflation would peak at 4–5% in 2022, returning to the inflation target in 2023. As we know, Consumer Price Index (CPI) inflation actually reached a peak of 11.1% in October 2022 – more than twice higher than the Bank's central projection a year before – and it remained significantly above target during 2023. This means that the Bank of England's core inflation projections deviated from actual inflation by more than a 100% margin of error.

In addition, central banks have made other innovations and changes to their strategies which have not resulted in more credible policies. For example, the experiment of 'forward guidance' by the Bank of England or the Riksbank (among others) has not made central bank policies more predictable (see Andersson and Jonung, 2019). Worse still, in 2020 the US Federal Reserve changed its monetary strategy, adopting 'average inflation targeting' based around a 2% rate of inflation. However, the Fed has not disclosed the time period around which inflation will be

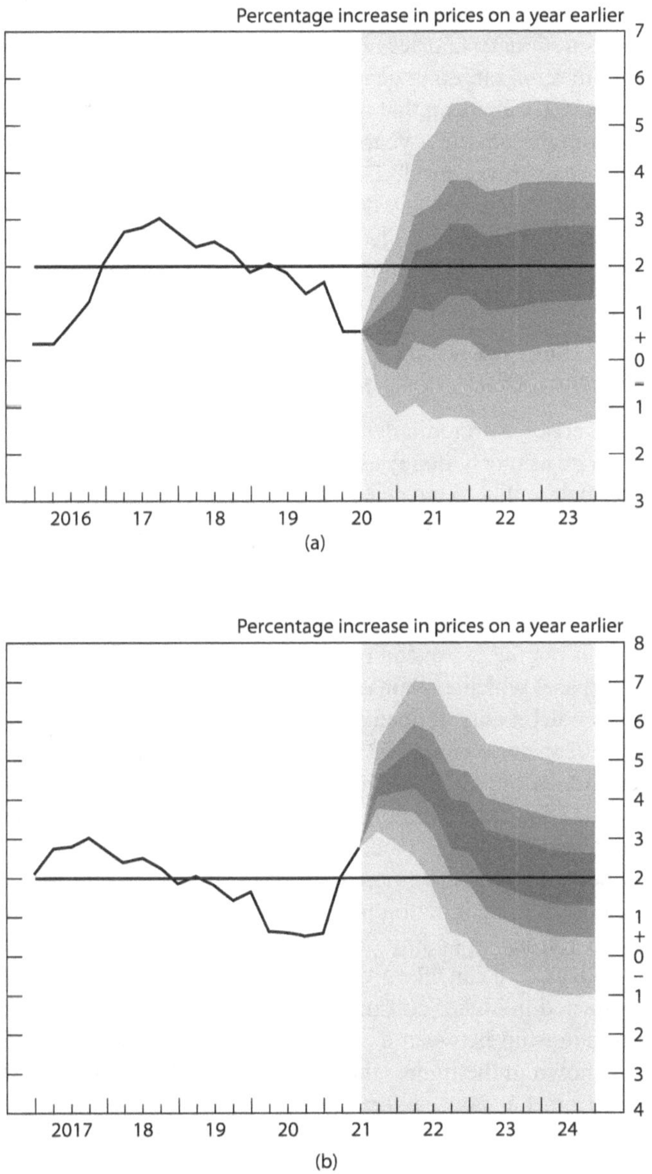

Figure 8.3 Bank of England's inflation forecasts. (a) Inflation forecast (November 2020). (b) Inflation forecast (November 2021).

Sources: (a) Bank of England's Monetary Policy Report (November 2020). This is Chart 1.5 (page 7) from the report available at https://www.bankofengland.co.uk/-/media/boe/files/monetary-policy-report/2020/november/monetary-policy-report-nov-2020.pdf. (b) Bank of England's Monetary Policy Report (November 2021). This is Chart 1.4 (page 6) from the report available at https://www.bankofengland.co.uk/-/media/boe/files/monetary-policy-report/2021/november/monetary-policy-report-november-2021.pdf.

averaged. Rather than enhancing transparency, the US Fed's monetary policy has become more discretionary and less credible (see Dorn, 2020). If the Fed is following average inflation targeting as a policy strategy, would the seriously above-target inflation in 2021–23 mean that monetary policy is going to target disinflation or even deflation in the next few years in order to ensure inflation averages out at 2% during some given time period? This is something we are yet to find out though the bias of central banks against any deflation makes it difficult to believe that they will abide by their own strategy. The lack of a realistic policy by the Fed could eventually impact its credibility and market inflation expectations.

8.4 Unfettered Money: Lessons from the Global Financial Crisis and the COVID-19 Episode

Both these recent crises are a reminder that, under a fully fiat monetary system, central banks can create as much money as they wish. In other words, there is no practical limitation to their ability to create money. However, this does not mean that their actions have no consequences. Blurred by the apparent lack of relation between the adoption of QE (i.e. expansion of central banks' balance sheets) and consumer inflation in the aftermath of the GFC, central banks did not only resume QE but augmented its volume in 2020–21, yet with the expectation that it would have no impact on inflation. However, it is not the expansion or contraction of central banks' balance sheets (or the monetary base) which explains spending patterns or inflation, but changes in the amount of money broadly defined (see Congdon, 2021; Greenwood and Hanke, 2022; Reynard, 2023; Borio et al., 2023; Castañeda and Cendejas, 2023.).

In the aftermath of the GFC, QE caused an increase mainly in bank reserves (see Congdon, 2017 for more details). However, in 2020–21 QE resulted in both an increase in bank reserves and in bank deposits (i.e. broad money). True, the relationship is neither automatic nor immediate. Typically, an excess in the amount of money results in asset price inflation in the very short term (1–3 months), followed by an increase in nominal spending (after 6–9 months more), and later on in consumer inflation. Overall, it can take around two years for an excess in the amount of money to be reflected in higher consumer inflation. Figure 8.4 shows this medium to long-term relationship between an excess in money growth and inflation. The five economies shown in the figure (the USA, the UK, Eurozone, Switzerland and Japan) suffered from the same external (exogeneous) shocks in 2020 and 2021, but did not expand the amount of money to the same extent (see Figure 8.4b). The annual rate of broad money growth was much higher at the peak of the pandemic in the USA (25%), the UK (15%) and the Eurozone (12%), than in Switzerland (less than 7%) and Japan (less than 6%). These differentials in money growth were not neutral. Once the economies started to return (gradually) to normality towards the second half of 2021, money velocity started to recover too,[8] which led to a strong increase in spending and later on in consumer prices, though at a different scale in different economies as Figure 8.4a shows. In particular, the countries with lower inflation were those which had registered lower rates of broad money growth 1–2 years earlier.

(a)

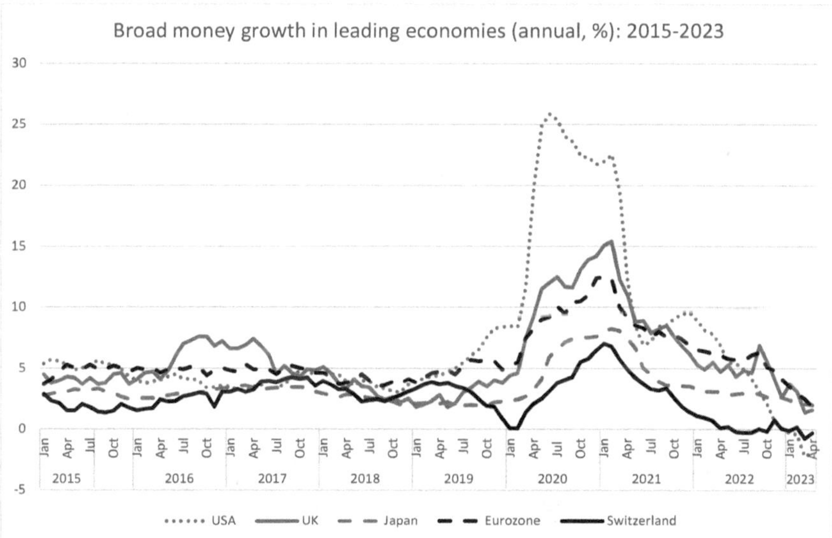

(b)

Figure 8.4 Inflation and monetary growth in leading economies (2015–2023). (a) CPI inflation. (b) Monetary growth.

Sources: (a) From Trading Economics (online), as collected from several national sources, including the US Bureau of Labor Statistics, the (UK) Office for National Statistics, Eurostat, the Japanese Ministry for Internal Affairs & Communications and the Swiss Federal Statistics Office. (b) Data collected from their respective national central banks.

There are two lessons to be learnt from the last two crises. First, the amount of broad money growth is critical in explaining spending and inflation patterns; and second, central banks have followed more discretionary policies that have lacked in a credible nominal anchor. A further important lesson is worth mentioning: an attempt to follow the New Keynesian model (see section above) and rely entirely on inflation expectations to drive monetary policy can be misleading and potentially result in destabilising policies. Inflation expectations are a reflection of central bank policy record in the past and its credibility, but not a good (early) indicator of future inflation. There is no question that a sound monetary policy builds up the central bank's 'credibility capital', thus contributing to aligning market expectations with the central bank's inflation target. This allows for a more effective monetary policy, which in turn gives central banks enough room of manoeuvre to respond to shocks in the short term with a certain degree of discretion.[9] However, this does not mean that market expectations drive inflation, nor that the central bank can expand the amount of money as it wishes provided that inflation expectations are 'anchored' (i.e. aligned with the inflation target). In 2020 – and even for several months in 2021 – leading central banks seemed to rely on the stability of market inflation expectations as if this would prevent inflation from rising in the future. This is what the former Governor of the Bank of England, Mervyn King (2022), called the 'King Canute theory of inflation', a view shared by a former member of the Monetary Policy Committee, Charles Goodhart (2021). Once early signs of increased spending and producer inflation became evident in the second half of 2021, inflation expectations did rise, but it was already too late to prevent consumer inflation from rising very fast in 2022 and 2023.

And lastly, those who claim that an expansionary monetary policy, defined as slashing policy rates interest rates to virtually zero, is an effective tool to foster spending and achieve economic growth in the long term will find it difficult to reconcile this position with the experience of the post-GFC years. Growth is explained over the long term by several factors but not by loose demand-side policies or 'easy money'. What monetary policy can do is to contribute to a stable economic framework for agents to plan their actions absent of monetary distortions.

8.5 An Attempt and a Proposal to Return to Monetary Stability

After decades of activist monetary policies, a different framework is needed to run monetary policies *as if* there were a veil between money and the real economy, one by which monetary policy focuses on maintaining the purchasing power of the currency over time. Within this framework, the demand for the currency would be enhanced over time and so will be the *seigniorage* gains of the central bank (i.e. the government).

8.5.1 Less Discretion, Greater Central Bank Accountability

In the aftermath of the GFC, John Taylor (2011) proposed a legislated monetary policy rule in the USA. He argued that the US Federal Reserve should report to Congress regularly, explaining what the rule consists of and, in case of deviations from the rule, to explain the reasons why it had happened, along with the policies needed to rectify the situation. This rule, whether decided by the Fed in the exercise of its operational independent or imposed by Congress, would limit the degree of discretion of the policymaker but as Taylor (2011) remarks, it would not eliminate it totally. It would also certainly enhance the accountability of the central bank. After the COVID-19 pandemic and the surge in money growth and ultimately, inflation, Tim Congdon (2023) has propounded some specific proposals aimed at making monetary policy less discretionary while enhancing central bank accountability. In the case of the Bank of England, he suggests that the Governor must report to Parliament when money growth exceeds certain upper and lower bounds and that the Governor and the Deputy Governor in charge of monetary policy must resign if inflation is significantly above or below the inflation target. This proposal preserves the independence of the central bank in making monetary policy decisions, while binding the hands of the central banks more firmly, with the need to report specific criteria on how monetary policy is conducted.

8.5.2 A More Neutral Monetary Policy

A policy rule should be designed to enhance the demand for the currency on a long-term basis. This should be the primary goal of the bank which issues the currency. If the operation of the rule is successful, the central bank would be expanding its seigniorage gains provided that the demand for the currency grows over the medium to the long term. In a fiat system, with no convertibility of bank notes into an asset (be it a precious metal or any other asset), the currency will be more accepted (and thus the demand for it will be greater) if it keeps its purchasing power over time. As White (1999) puts it, seigniorage gains can be explained as tax receipts; they can result from an expansion of the demand for the currency (i.e. the tax base) or the rate of inflation (i.e. the tax rate). This is a very effective way to understand what a successful monetary policy rule is, as we must not forget that a continuous increase in the rate of inflation can adversely affect the demand for the currency and thus reduce seigniorage over time. After all, ultimately, with any extremely inflationary policy there is no demand for the currency.

$$\text{Seignoriage} = \text{Demand for the currency} \times \text{Inflation rate} \tag{8.3}$$

In this framework, the central bank's primary concern should be fundamentally of a financial nature, namely how to increase the demand for its currency on a long-term basis. Maintaining monetary stability would be the key to this strategy. For this purpose, the rate of growth in the supply of money would be linked to a credible anchor; be it the trend rate of growth of real output under a 'monetarist rule' or the trend growth of nominal spending under a 'nominal income (rate) rule'. There are important differences between the two, but either of them would reduce the degree of activism in current monetary policymaking, thus resulting in a more *neutral*[10] monetary policy. With a monetarist rule (see Eq. 8.4), the central bank would set up a rate of growth of money compatible with price stability in the long term; money growth would then approximately match that of real output. With a nominal income rule (see

Eq. 8.5), the rate of growth of money would target the rate of growth of real output and prices (i.e. the rate of growth of nominal spending). As regards a demand-side shock, both rules would prescribe a similar policy reaction. However, in the event of a supply-side shock, the nominal income rule would recommend a more conservative policy, one that allows for prices to fall in case of a positive productivity shock and vice versa. Whichever of these two rules were to be adopted in the event of a banking crisis, the issuing bank would find it beneficial to intervene promptly and keep payment systems running following the 'Bagehot criteria',[11] thus preventing a collapse in the amount of money broadly defined.

$$m = p* + GDP_{real} - v \tag{8.4}$$

$$m = GDP \text{ nominal}* \tag{8.5}$$

(NB: p* and GDP nominal * are the inflation and nominal income growth targets, respectively)

In these more rule-based monetary strategies, unconventional monetary policies such as QE would only be undertaken within the rationale of the rule. For example, the amount of QE would be calibrated (and announced to the public) in order to achieve a set rate of growth of money compatible with either a monetarist or a nominal income rule. Following this rationale, unconventional monetary policies would be restricted by the operation of the chosen rule, thus avoiding the use of QE as a discretionary policy tool.

Not perfect, not Heaven on Earth, but an arrangement that will produce more stable money, a necessary condition to resume economic growth over the long term.

Notes

1 See, among others, the seminal works on the New Keynesian model by Clarida et al. (1999) and Woodford (2004).

2 The US Federal Reserve is an anomaly among leading economies, with the so-called 'plural mandate', which states that it must achieve price stability, maximum employment and stability in long-term interest rates (with no hierarchy among them).

3 After the suspension of the convertibility of the pound in 1931, a member of the previous government is reported as saying, 'Nobody told us we could do that'. The remark has been ascribed to various people, but never definitely. That shows how embedded in the system the institutions of the gold standard were at the time.

4 Anna Schwartz defines a financial crisis as '... fuelled by fears that means of payment will be unobtainable at any price and, in a fractional reserve banking system, leads to a scramble for high powered money .... In a futile attempt to restore reserves, the banks may call in loans, refuse to roll over existing loans, or resort to selling assets' (Schwartz, 1987).

5 When describing the effects of an increase in gold and silver on prices, D. Hume explains that 'tis only in this interval or intermediate fituation, betwixt the acquifition of money and rife of prices, that the encreafing quantity of gold and filver is favourable to industry' (Hume, 1752).

6 Those agents receiving the money first will benefit the most, as they can increase their spending at prices that have not yet reflected the increase in the amount of money.

7 The estimate of the output gap is controversial and subject to a significant margin of discrepancy and error. See Orphanides and Norden (2002) and Orphanides (2003) for the analysis of the output gap estimates in real time and the policy effects resulting from different estimates of the output gap.
8 Money velocity changes and tends to decline at –1 or –2% per year, but the series is mean reverting. This has very important policy implications: the exceptional increase in the amount of money in the USA in 2020 was accompanied by an equally extraordinary fall in money velocity (i.e. an exceptional increase in the demand for money), but this situation would not last forever. And it is precisely the return of money velocity towards its average, in combination with the previous expansion in the amount of money, what explains the significant increase in spending and in inflation from the second half of 2021 (more details in Castañeda and Congdon, 2020; Castañeda and Cendejas, 2023).
9 This is how Mervyn King referred to a successful policy rule – 'constrained discretion' (King, 2000).
10 By *neutral* we mean a monetary policy that does not add monetary disturbances to real ones (see Castañeda 2005 for details).
11 See Wood (2000) for details.

References

Andersson and Jonung, L. (2019): The Tyranny of the Tenths. The Rise and Gradual Fall of Forward Guidance in Sweden 2007–2018. Working paper 14. Economics dpt. Lund University.

Anson, M., Bholat, D., Kang, M. and Thomas, R. (2017): 'The Bank of England as lender of last resort: new historical evidence from daily transactional data'. Working Paper No. 691. Bank of England.

Bagehot, W. (1873): *Lombard Street: A description of the Money Market* (3rd edition). London: Henry S. King.

Borio, C., Hofmann, B. and Zakrajsek, E. (2023): 'Does money growth help explain the recent inflation surge?' BIS Bulletin, 67, January.

Bordo, M. and Kydland, F. (1995): 'The Gold Standard as a Rule. An Essay in Exploration'. In *Explorations in Monetary History*, 32, pp. 423–464.

Bordo, M., Lane, J. and Redish, A. (2004): Good versus bad deflation: Lessons from the gold standard era. NBER Working Paper Series 10329, February.

Capie, F. (2020): 'What should central banks do in a great financial crisis?' IIMR Conference Papers Series, November 2020.

Capie, F. and Wood, G. (2013): 'Central Bank Independence: A Victim of the Crisis?'. In *Economic Affairs*, 33 (3), pp. 379–385, October.

Castañeda, J. (2005): 'Towards a More Neutral Monetary Policy: Proposal of a Nominal Income Rule'. In *Economic Affairs*, 25 (4), pp. 61–67, December.

Castañeda, J. and Cendejas, J. L. (2023): 'Money Growth, Money Velocity and Inflation in the US, 1948–2021'. In *Open Economies Review*, November. https://doi.org/10.1007/s11079-023-09739-0

Castañeda, J. and Congdon, T. (2017): 'Have central banks forgotten about money?: The case of the European Central Bank, 1999 – 2014'. In Tim Congdon (ed.), *Money in the Great Recession. Did a Crash in Money Growth Cause the Global Slump?* Cheltenham, pp. 101–131. Edward Elgar.

Castañeda, J. and Congdon, T. (2020): 'Inflation: The next threat?'. Institute of Economic Affairs. COVID-19 Briefing 7, June.

Clarida, R., Gali, J. and Gertler, M. (1999): 'The Science of Monetary Policy: A New Keynesian Perspective'. In *Journal of Economic Literature*, 37(4), pp. 1661–1707, December.

Congdon, T. (2017): *Money in the Great Recession. Did a Crash in Money Growth Cause the Global Slump?* Cheltenham, Edward Elgar.

Congdon, T. (2021): 'Can Monetary Policy Run Out of Ammunition? The Role of the Money-Equities Interaction Channel in Monetary Policy'. In *Economic Affairs*, 41 (1), pp. 21–37, February.

Congdon, T. (2023): 'Inflation: Why Has it come back? And what can be done?' Politeia. https://www.politeia.co.uk/wp-content/uploads/2023/04/Congdon.pdf

Dorn, J. (2020): The Fed's Policy Drift. Alt-M blog, 30 September 2020. Cato. Available at: https://www.cato.org/blog/feds-policy-drift#:~:text=Average%20inflation%20targeting%20is%20the,an%20unfalsifiable%20%E2%80%9Cscientific%E2%80%9D%20claim.

European Central Bank (2021): 'An overview of the ECB's monetary policy strategy'. European Central Bank. Available online at https://www.ecb.europa.eu/home/search/review/html/ecb.strategyreview_monpol_strategy_overview.en.html

Friedman, M. (1962): "Should There Be an Independent Monetary Authority?" In L. B. Yeager (ed.), *Search of a Monetary Constitution*, pp. 219–43. Cambridge, Harvard University Press.

Friedman, M. (1970): The Counter-Revolution in Monetary Theory. IEA Occasional Paper, no. 33. London.

Goodhart, C. (2021): Remarks at the ECB Forum on Central Banking 2021. Part 4 – Panel 1: The future of inflation. Accessed on video online: https://youtu.be/w6KQi2tnmIM.

Greenwood, J. and Hanke, S. (2022): 'On Monetary Growth and Inflation in Leading Economies, 2021–22: Relative Prices and the Overall Price Level'. In *Economic Affairs*, 42 (2), pp. 288–306.

Hayek, F. (1931): Prices and Production. In the Collected Works of F. Hayek. Business Cycles. Part 1. March, 2017. Liberty Fund. Indiana.

Hume, D. (1752): *Essays. Moral, Political and Literary*. (2nd edition). *Discourse III. Of Money*. Google books.

King, M. (2000): Monetary Policy: Theory in Practice. Bank of England. Accessed online. https://www.bankofengland.co.uk/speech/2000/monetary-policy-theory-in-practice

King, M. (2022): 'Monetary Policy in a World of Radical Uncertainty'. In *Economic Affairs*, 42 (1), pp. 2–12, February.

Neely, C. (2016): 'A survey on the empirical literature on US unconventional monetary policy'. Presentation at the IIMR 2016 Conference (November). Available on YouTube.

Orphanides, A. (2003): *Historical Monetary Policy Analysis and the Taylor Rule*. Washington, DC, Federal Reserve Board.

Orphanides, A. and van Norden, S. (2002): ''The Unreliability of Output-Gap Estimates in Real Time'. In *The Review of Economics and Statistics*, 84 (4), pp. 569–583, November.

Reynard, S. (2023): 'Central Bank Balance Sheet, Money and Inflation'. In *Economic Letters* 224. March.

Selgin, G. (2018): *Financial Stability without Central Banks*. London, Institute of Economic Affairs.

Selgin, G. (2020): *The Menace of Fiscal QE*. Washington, DC, Cato Institute.

Schwartz, A. (1987): 'Real and Pseudo Financial Crisis'. In A. Schwartz (ed.), *Money in Historical Perspective*, pp. 271–288. Chicago and London University of Chicago Press.

Taylor, J. (2011): 'Legislating a Rule for Monetary Policy'. In *Cato Journal*, 31 (3), pp. 407–415.

Ueda, K. (2023): 'Central Bank Finances and Monetary Policy Conduct'. Speech at the 2023 Autumn Annual Meeting of the Japan Society of Monetary Economics. 30 September 2023. https://www.boj.or.jp/en/about/press/koen_2023/data/ko230930a.pdf

White, L. (1999): *The Theory of Monetary Institutions*. Oxford, Blackwell.

Wood, G. (2000): 'The Lender of Last Resort Reconsidered'. In *Journal of Financial Services Research*, 18 (2), pp. 203–227.

Woodford, M. (2004): *Interest and Prices: Foundations of a Theory of Monetary Policy*. Princeton, Princeton University Press.

9 Economic Growth and the Size of Government

Do the Drivers Differ in Democracies vs. Authoritarian States?

Christian Bjørnskov

9.1 Introduction

In the tradition of classical political economy, the scope of government intervention is limited and the optimal size of government is therefore small. However, whether government consumption, government-directed investment activity, and state ownership contribute positively or slow down economic growth has been hotly disputed since the 1930s. Immediately after World War II, both the pre-war intellectual climate as well as the experience of managing a war economy led many economists and politicians to expect that government could productively direct the economy. Similarly, in 2021 and 2022, something resembling the 'Spirit of 1945' arose as politicians claimed that the societal lockdowns proved that government could control the economy (yet, see Herby et al., 2023; Zinberg et al., 2023). The question if government intervention and at a broader level restrictions of citizens' economic freedom help or hinder growth is therefore back on the political agenda.

A long literature since Dawson (1998) has rather clearly documented the positive association between economic freedom and long-run economic growth. Subsequent studies have explored the causality of the association, whether it only arises under specific political conditions and which elements of economic freedom are responsible for the association (see, e.g., Heckelman and Stroup, 2000, 2005; Justesen, 2008; Bergh and Henrekson, 2011; Rode and Coll, 2012; Justesen and Kurrild-Klitgaard, 2013; Bergh and Bjørnskov, 2021). Most of the literature finds robust effects of two components of economic freedom – the size of government and the quality of the legal system – while a smaller subset also finds evidence of other influences.

While most studies find that the size of government – at least above some level surpassed by most developed countries decades ago – appears harmful to growth, it nevertheless remains open questions which elements of government size are particularly harmful to long-run growth and whether government spending and production are equally harmful depending on the state of democracy. While the overall effect is robustly negative, one could easily conceive of a situation in which an overall negative effect hides that some elements are beneficial to growth while others are destructive. Spending on the provision of basic public goods such as functioning legal institutions, basic education and necessary infrastructure would,

DOI: 10.4324/9781003504412-13

all other things being equal, contribute to growth, as Adam Smith emphasised. Similarly, funding such spending by a tax structure consistent with the Ramsey Rule would be minimally distortive, as would other spending also following such rule.[1] However, other elements of public spending may have particularly strong incentive effects, for example driving out entrepreneurship and reducing the labour supply of the most productive or innovative members of society (Bjørnskov and Foss, 2016; Mertens and Montiel-Olea, 2018).

In addition, Bergh (2020) provides another perspective on the discussion by introducing the concept of 'Hayekian welfare states'. His argument is that to minimise the adverse incentive effects of public spending and government intervention, one would ideally prioritise spending and activities that are minimally epistemologically demanding. This would preclude most government investment, practically all industrial policy, and most transfer and subsidy schemes that are either not simple or for which any side effects are known with considerable precision. Bergh's (2020) requirements for 'good' spending thus complement other aspects, but also raise the interesting question why politicians would restrict themselves to epistemologically modest interventions.

These considerations imply that not all government spending, investment, or taxation may be equally harmful for long-run growth, but also that it is a priori difficult to predict which types are more harmful, which types may be directly beneficial, and whether democracy is a moderating institution or the opposite. This chapter is therefore an exploration of the topic, distinguishing the available data on the size of government in two different ways: by exploring effects in different political regimes and exploring effects across five broad types. The findings from estimating the association between the size of government, as measured by the Economic Freedom of the World indices, and economic growth suggest that transfers and subsidies appear to be the most harmful types of spending. While the association between size of government and growth is uncertain in single-party autocracies, I find relatively little robust evidence that multi-party autocracies and democracies differ systematically.

The rest of the chapter is structured as follows. Section 9.2 describes the data and estimation strategy used in Section 9.3, which outlines the main results, results across types of interventions, and a set of robustness tests. Section 9.4 concludes with a discussion of the likely mechanisms behind the findings.

9.2 Data and Estimation Strategy

I derive data from a number of sources used in much of the literature to explore the association between the size of government and economic growth. First, I use real purchasing-power adjusted GDP per capita from the Penn World Tables, mark 10 (Feenstra et al., 2015). From the same source, I also calculate trade volumes as per cent of GDP and a relative investment price as the price level of capital divided by the price level of private consumption. In all specifications, the dependent variable is growth in real GDP per capita in consecutive five-years periods between 1975 and 2015, where I add the logarithm to initial GDP to capture convergence effects.

Second, I follow most of the vast literature on economic freedom by using the size of government index as well as the legal quality index (i.e. areas 1 and 2) from the annual Economic Freedom of the World report (Gwartney et al., 2022).[2] Both follow the logic of the index such that higher values mean more economic freedom; in all cases, the data are scaled between 0 and 10. Throughout this chapter, it must therefore be kept in mind that higher values on government size indicators imply smaller government consumption, lower tax rates, etc. I also decompose the size of government index into its five elements: government consumption as per cent of all consumption, transfers and subsidies as per cent of GDP, government enterprises and investment as per cent of GDP, the highest marginal tax rate, and state ownership of the economy (covering more than just enterprises).

In order to separate democracies from authoritarian states, I turn to the regime types and regime change dataset in Bjørnskov and Rode (2020), which categorises regimes in two different ways. I mainly use the categorisation into either single-party autocracies (including those without elections), multi-party autocracies in which regular elections are held but the incumbent government in practice cannot lose, and full electoral democracies. In an additional test, I use an alternative feature, which allows me to separate multi-party autocracies into military dictatorships and civilian autocracies. As further robustness tests, I use Henisz's (2000) Political Constraints III indicator, which measures the strength of political veto players on a scale from 0 to 1, the parliament fractionalisation index from the Database of Political Institutions (Scartascini et al., 2021), or Gründler and Krieger's (2021) continuous quality of democracy indicator, based on a machine-learning approach. I add these measures as alternatives to the three-category regime variable. These additional variables thus capture three aspects of how democracies may differ from other regime types and thus how the consequences of the size of government could theoretically differ (Table 9.1).

The estimation strategy is relatively simple and follows common practice in the literature on economic freedom (cf., Bergh and Bjørnskov, 2021). I include a full

Table 9.1 Descriptive statistics

Variable	*Mean*	*Standard deviation*	*Observations*
GDP growth rate, 5-yr	.087	.179	1343
Lagged log GDP per capita	8.932	1.249	1343
Trade volume	.501	.489	1502
Investment price	1.271	.662	1502
Single-party autocracy	.309	.462	1616
Multi-party autocracy	.243	.429	1616
Military dictatorship	.139	.346	1616
Civilian autocracy	.259	.438	1616
Democracy	.449	.498	1616
Size of government	6.039	1.621	1385
Legal quality	4.891	1.577	1572
Political Constraints III	.219	.220	1490
DPI fractionalisation index	.441	.311	1300
Gründler-Krieger index	.525	.399	1493

set of period and country fixed effects, which implies that all common international trends as well as all approximately time-invariant factors – geography, culture, climate, historical factors etc. – are fully accounted for. To test the main question of this chapter, i.e. whether growth effects of different aspects of the size of government differ between liberal democracies and authoritarian states, I add an interaction between the size of government indicator and the regime type indicator used in separate regressions. In all cases, I calculate conditional marginal estimates with proper conditional standard errors, using the Delta method (Brambor et al., 2006).

The strategy implies that I do not directly confront the potential causality problem endemic to studies of this particular question. The primary concern is that a spuriously negative association between government spending or government investment may exist for two reasons. First, if governments conduct countercyclical fiscal policy, it will bias short-run estimates as government reactions to economic downturns will be correlated with large spending, larger government investments, or tax cuts. Second, even if fiscal policy is neutral, an economic downturn may result in a negative correlation between GDP and spending because the nominator when measuring the size of government is usually GDP itself. However, in practical terms, there are good reasons to suspect that endogeneity or simultaneity bias is not a major empirical problem.

Recent research for example shows that fiscal policy is often pro-cyclical, not counter-cyclical (De Haan and Gootjes, 2023) and demonstrates that the broader effects of economic freedom can be identified by exploring major reform episodes (Grier and Grier, 2021). To the extent that pro-cyclicality is more common than counter-cyclicality, any endogeneity bias will operate in the opposite direction and therefore lead to conservative estimates in the following. Another reason is that Bergh and Henrekson (2011), in a clever addition to the literature, documented that their medium-run growth effects were similar for measures of government spending and government income, although any endogeneity bias would be negative for the former but positive for the latter measure. Finally, most such concerns wash out over an entire business cycle, which implies that longer-run estimates – as those in this chapter – are likely to be more precise reflections of actual causal effects. These considerations of course do not dispel the potential problem, but make it substantially less likely to be a major concern.

9.3 A First Look at the Data

Figure 9.1 provides a first look by plotting average growth rates for either single-party autocracies, multi-party autocracies, or democracies for observations in each of the four quartiles of the size of government. In other words, the columns show average growth rates for societies with the 25% largest government sectors (smallest index scores), the 25 next per cent, etc.

The figure first of all clearly illustrates that single-party autocracies are different. If anything, single-party regimes appear to grow slower with smaller government sectors, although the particular group of observations that combine single-party regime and small government tend to be countries going through civil wars or similar

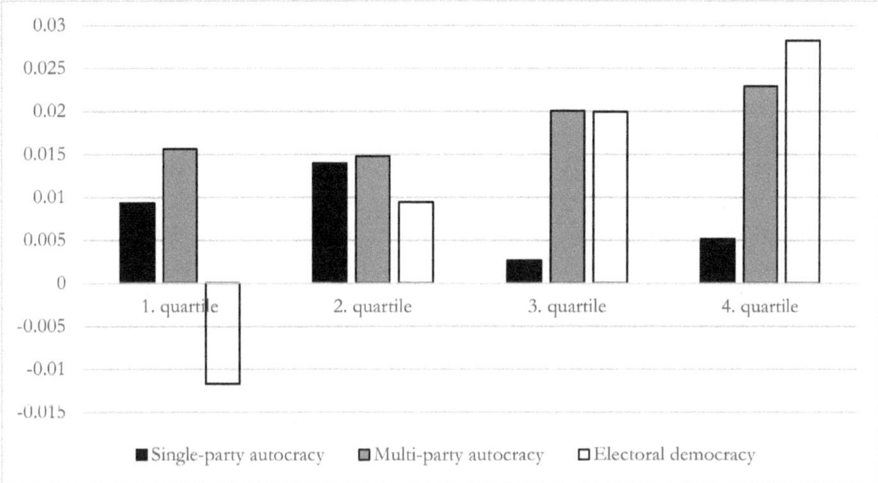

Figure 9.1 Growth in the four quartiles of the size of government.

events.[3] Conversely, one can see a clear progression among multi-party regimes as the size of government declines (the index increases). However, the figure also indicates that the size of government may be more consequential in democracies: the growth differences between the second, third, and fourth quartiles of size of government are all significant at $p < .01$ for democracies.

Figure 9.2 nevertheless raises the complication that the *structure* of government activities also differs across the three broad regime types. Overall, the government size index is much smaller in single-party autocracies (6.0) while

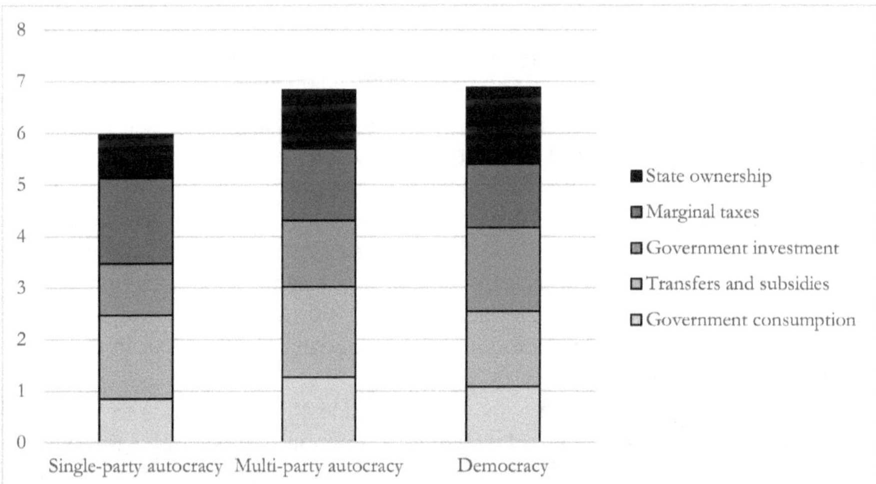

Figure 9.2 The structure of size of government, three regime types.

there is no systematic difference between multi-party autocracies and democracies (6.8 versus 6.9). However, the data reveal that the structure of the size of government varies systematically across regime types. On average, government consumption amounts to 27% of GDP in single-party autocracies, 19% in multi-party autocracies, and 22% in democracies. Conversely, the data show that there are usually substantially larger transfers and subsidies in democracies and substantially smaller government investments (21 versus 35 and 28%) and much less state ownership. Finally, democracies tax much more: the tax burden on average amounts to 18% of GDP in single-party states, 27% in multi-party autocracies, and 32% in democracies, although the difference between multi-party autocracies and democracies is substantially smaller (37 and 41%) when also adding payroll taxes. In other words, the most extensive government ownership and largest government investments are (not surprisingly) found in single-party regimes, while both components are smallest in democracies. Conversely, democracies tend to have much larger transfers and subsidies and higher tax rates than either type of autocracy. Whether these structural differences translate into different overall effects of the size of government is an open question, which I explore in the following section.

9.4 Empirical Estimates of Size of Government Effects

9.4.1 Main Results

Table 9.2 shows the main results, where columns 2–4 include interactions between the size of government and regime types; the conditional marginal effects are reported in the lower panel. Throughout the table, the control variables behave as expected: estimates of the initial GDP levels are significantly negative, indicating convergence, while trade volumes and the quality of the legal system are significantly positive. Conversely, investment levels are never significant. In column 1, where I do not interact regime types, the estimates are small and nowhere near significance.

Turning to the main variables, the estimate of the effects of the size of government in column 1, which can be interpreted as an average across regime types, is not only significant but of about the same size as in previous studies (cf., Bergh and Bjørnskov, 2021). However, when distinguishing between effects in single-party regimes, multi-party autocracies, and full electoral democracies in column 2, the estimates indicate that the average effect in column 1 is mainly driven by the latter group. The marginal effect in single-party regimes is tiny and far from significance, while the effect in multi-party autocracies is somewhat smaller than in democracies, but insignificant.

As the results in column 3 show, where I exclude all observations from single-party regimes, this difference is not driven by a potentially misleading comparison with the mostly socialist single-party regimes. Finally, column 4 further distinguishes between two types of multi-party autocracies: military dictatorships and civilian autocracies. Taking the additional institutional detail into account reveals

Table 9.2 Main results

	1	*2*	*3*	*4*
	All	*All*	*No single-party*	*No single-party*
Lagged log GDP per capita	–.261***	–.264***	–.313***	–.313***
	(.029)	(.028)	(.033)	(.033)
Trade volume	.082***	.073***	.08***	.079***
	(.027)	(.027)	(.027)	(.025)
Investment price	.007	.011	–.002	–.002
	(.012)	(.012)	(.015)	(.014)
Multi-party autocracy	–.011	–.104	–	
	(.021)	(.071)		
Civilian autocracy				–.183
				(.121)
Democracy	.012	–.185***	–.034	–.162
	(.023)	(.063)	(.078)	(.120)
Size of government	.013**	–.003	.018	.000
	(.006)	(.008)	(.011)	(.019)
Legal quality	.032***	.031***	.020*	.022**
	(.009)	(.009)	(.011)	(.011)
Size of government * multi-party autocracy		.018		
		(.011)		
Size of government * democracy		.033***	.007	
		(.010)	(.012)	
Size of government * civilian autocracy				.024
				(.019)
Size of government * democracy				.024
				(.019)
Country FE	Yes	Yes	Yes	Yes
Period FE	Yes	Yes	Yes	Yes
Observations	1252	1252	994	994
Countries	159	159	151	151
Within R squared	.279	.291	.314	.318
F statistic	17.76	18.30	15.99	14.50
Marginal effect of size of government at				
Multi-party autocracy		.015	.018	
		(.009)	(.011)	
Military dictatorship				.000
				(.019)
Civilian autocracy				.024**
				(.012)
Democracy		.029***	.025***	.025***
		(.007)	(.007)	(.007)

Note: Numbers in parentheses are standard errors clustered at the country level; ***, (**), and [*] denote significance at $p < .01$, ($p < .05$), and [$p < .10$], respectively.

that the insignificant estimate in multi-party autocracies in columns 2 and 3 is driven by an estimate, which is essentially zero in military dictatorships and of the exact same size in civilian autocracies as in democracies (although estimated with less precision).

9.4.2 Estimates of Single Components

As noted above, the structure of the size of government differs between regime types with substantially larger transfers and subsidies and higher taxes in democracies. If different elements of government activities and spending are either not substitutes or have similar economic consequences, the structural differences could potentially explain the different estimates in Table 9.2. In Table 9.3, I therefore re-estimate the specification from Table 9.2, column 4, but using each of the five sub-indicators of government.

Table 9.3 Results, subcomponents

	1	*2*	*3*	*4*	*5*
	No single-party	*No single-party*	*No single-party*	*No single-party*	*No single-party*
Full baseline specification included					
Civilian autocracy	–.033 (.095)	–.572** (.264)	–.023 (.049)	.013 (.068)	–.385*** (.123)
Democracy	–.033 (.098)	–.562*** (.118)	–.026 (.045)	.073 (.062)	–.358*** (.123)
Government consumption	.009 (.014)				
Transfers and subsidies		–.032** (.015)			
Government investment			–.001 (.006)		
Taxation				.023* (.012)	
State ownership					–.039** (.018)
EF variable * civilian	–.001 (.014)	.059** (.030)	.003 (.008)	–.008 (.013)	.056*** (.019)
EF variable * democracy	.003 (.014)	.060*** (.014)	.009 (.006)	–.015 (.012)	.057*** (.019)
Country FE	Yes	Yes	Yes	Yes	Yes
Period FE	Yes	Yes	Yes	Yes	Yes
Observations	924	848	903	813	1001
Countries	148	143	149	148	150
Within R squared	.323	.319	.309	.315	.319
F statistic	11.76	14.23	13.34	15.99	12.82
Marginal effect of size of government at military dictatorship					
Economic freedom variable	.009 (.014)	–.032** (.015)	–.001 (.006)	.023* (.012)	–.039** (.018)
Marginal effect of size of government at civilian autocracy					
Economic freedom variable	.009 (.006)	.028 (.028)	.002 (.006)	.015* (.008)	.017 (.012)
Marginal effect of size of government at democracy					
Economic freedom variable	.013** (.006)	.028*** (.006)	.008*** (.003)	.007** (.003)	.018** (.008)

Note: numbers in parentheses are standard errors clustered at the country level; ***, (**), and [*] denote significance at $p < .01$, ($p < .05$), and [$p < .10$], respectively.

Across the table, it is clear that although all estimates for democracies are significant, the smallest estimates are for tax burdens and the largest for transfers and subsidies. The large estimate for transfers and subsidies is identical for civilian autocracies, but insignificant as it is estimated with much less precision. Similarly, the estimates for government ownership are almost identical in democracies and civilian autocracies, but again much less precise in the latter regime type. Conversely, an interesting detail is that the estimated effect of taxation is larger in civilian autocracies than in democracies, and even larger still in military dictatorships. The results for military dictatorships and democracies nevertheless turn out to be driven by extreme growth periods, while that in civilian autocracies remains statistically significant with an estimate around .01. Hence, the only apparently counterintuitive result in Table 9.3, which holds up to simple robustness tests, is a significantly negative effect of the transfers and subsidies index in military dictatorships. This is contrasted by the largest positive effect across subcomponents in democracies.

A set of robustness tests reveal that some of these findings are unlikely to reflect either extreme events or other aspects of the size of government.[4] First, in order to avoid that one subcomponent reflects another I run a 'horserace' test between the five components, estimating two at a time. Although adding all five subcomponents to the same specification may create multicollinearity problems, doing so reveals that three subcomponents in democracies – government consumption, transfers and subsidies, and state ownership – and one in military dictatorships – the negative effect of the transfers and subsidies index – remain robust to adding another component. Second, I remove all extreme growth events (see in Appendix, Table A.2), defined as observations with the 5% largest and 5% smallest growth rates. This test again yields these four results robust while also indicating that the tax result for civilian autocracies may be considered robust, as the imprecision in estimates in Table 9.3 appears to be a reflection of episodes with very high growth rates.

9.4.3 What Is Special about Democracy?

Overall, with one exception, the robust and sizeable growth consequences of the size of government thus all seem to pertain to democracies alone. This begs the question: what is special about democracy that makes political decisions around government consumption, investment and transfers particularly consequential? In three figures, and the accompanying appendix tables (Tables A.1–A.3), I compare the estimates above with three alternative indicators of democracy or features associated with democracy: (1) Gründler and Krieger's (2021) continuous democracy indicator, which is based on a more maximalist conception of democracy; (2) Henisz's (2000) Political Constraints III index (PolCon III) of veto player strength, which captures the existence of effective checks and balances on political power; and (3) the quality of the legal system index from the Economic Freedom of the World dataset. In all cases, I interact these indicators with the overall size of government index.

The comparisons are relevant because each indicator both captures specific features of democracy, and because these differ across simple regime types. It therefore remains possible that the simple categorisation in three types may proxy for institutional differences across countries and that these differences – and not political differences – are responsible for different estimates across regimes. For example, in the present sample, Gründler and Krieger's democracy indicator averages .07 in single-party regimes, Henisz's PolCon III index of veto player strength is .03, and the legal quality index is 3.9. Conversely, democracy as captured by Gründler and Krieger averages .08, PolCon III .14 and legal quality 3.4 in military dictatorships, while the same averages are .12, .34 and 4.5, respectively, in civilian autocracies. Electoral democracies stand out by averaging .37 on the democracy indicator, .87 on PolCon III, and a legal quality rating of 5.9.

However, as is evident in Figures 9.3–9.5 (see Appendix), the confidence intervals of the estimates using the simple regime categorisation as interacting variable are visibly narrower than those of the three alternative indicators. Particularly when estimating effects interacted with the Gründler-Krieger measure of democracy, excluding single-party autocracies and thereby avoiding an arguably extreme comparison (illustrated by grey lines), the results exhibit no heterogeneity at all and a quite wide confidence interval. Conversely, adding an interaction between legal quality and size of government indicates that there may be relevant heterogeneity, although the confidence intervals here are also too wide to draw any significant conclusions. Although these comparisons do not reject any influence of veto player strength or institutional quality on the importance of government size, they serve to underline the robustness and precision of the overall estimates for democracies.

A final problem is endogeneity, which is not only an issue in much of the literature but also one that is extremely difficult to resolve (however, see Bergh and Henrekson, 2011; Grier and Grier, 2021). Two additional robustness tests can nonetheless provide a first impression of the severity of endogeneity bias: one in which I remove all extreme growth observations, defined as the 5% smallest and 5% largest growth rates in the sample; and another in which I remove the 25% observations with the lowest growth rates. The rationale for interpreting the findings as indicative of endogeneity bias in the overall results in Tables 9.2 and 9.3 is that if the size of government is either strongly countercyclical, as would be the case if governments followed Keynesian advice, pro-cyclical – which would be the case if governments induce political business cycle or otherwise spend in 'good times' – or if both patterns prevail, as suggested by Buchanan (1958), the estimates are likely to change when excluding particularly extreme or particularly poor growth observations. The second test is particularly strong if counter-cyclical fiscal policy creates positively signed endogeneity bias while the first is arguably more apt when the bias cannot be theoretically signed. While these tests arguably alleviate endogeneity bias, the latter test in particular is likely to yield very conservative estimates. If increasing government intervention causes large growth declines, this specific test will not capture such effects because the relevant observations are excluded. As such, one must consider the estimates in tests 2 and 3 as close to a lower bound of the 'real' causal effects.

The first test, reported in appendix Table A.2, renders the result pertaining to government investments in democracies insignificant. It also yields smaller estimates on government consumption and transfers and subsidies in democracies, although neither is significantly smaller than that obtained in the full sample. Somewhat interestingly, removing extreme observations yields much more precise estimates of the tax burden in civilian autocracies. The second and third tests (not shown), which are particularly demanding, yield generally smaller estimates. However, both only render one insignificant: that of government consumption in the second test and that of the tax burden in democracies in the third test. Keeping in mind that the size of government is already observed at the beginning of the period in the full estimates in Tables 9.2 and 9.3, these additional robustness results thus suggest that endogeneity bias may be present, but cannot account for the full estimates obtained in these tables.

Overall, exploring the effects of the size of government across regime types reveals that with one notable exception, all statistically significant effects are found only in electoral democracies. Why that is, and what it might tell us about how the size of government matters for growth, is the topic for the final discussion.

9.5 Discussion and Conclusions

The tradition of classical political economy since Adam Smith has held that substantial government intervention in society is likely to undermine future economic growth. Despite claims from Keynesians and several other strands in economics, empirical evidence in the last 25 years has found that larger government consumption and intervention is associated with lower growth rates. However, which elements of the size of government and whether the findings also apply in authoritarian countries have remained open questions.

The findings here indicate that the size of government is clearly associated with growth in democracies, while estimates tend to be insignificant in civilian autocracies – but of comparable size as in democracies – and either small or negative in military dictatorships. Disaggregating the Fraser Institute's overall index of government size in its five components – government consumption, transfers and subsidies, government investment, taxation, and state ownership – shows that only one component survives all robustness tests and simple causality tests: the transfers and subsidies component. Trying to get closer to an understanding of why effects are both larger and more precisely estimated in democracies, alternative interactions with the Political Constraints III index of veto player strength, Gründler and Krieger's continuous democracy indicator, and the Fraser Institute's assessment of the quality of the legal system revealed that none of the more exact indicators explain why effects mainly pertain to democracies.

What do these patterns tell us about the effects of government intervention in the form of consumption, investment, transfers and taxation? In particular, what do the regime differences tell us? The differences can have three types of sources: measurement problems, institutional details not captured by regime types, and differences in policy details.

A first issue is measurement problems, which may prevent precise estimates of institutional effects. These problems apply to both the measurement of the size of government, as emphasised by Cheang (2023) in the context of Hong Kong and Singapore's particular models of governance, and to national accounts in general (e.g., Magee and Doces, 2015; Martinez, 2022). Alvarez et al. (2024) for example show that these differences are not only more severe in non-democracies, but can also substantially bias the estimates of effects of institutions and economic freedom.[5]

The findings in this chapter cannot entirely dismiss the second problem, but do go some way in alleviating it. The most immediate institutional details suggested by previous research revolve around veto institutions and the overall quality of bureaucratic institutions. Additional estimates in an appendix fail to provide much evidence that the effects of government size are clearly mediated by veto institutions are some broader conception of democracy. This leaves the third complication as a relevant concern.

If the differences across regime types cannot be dismissed as measurement problems, the third option is that specific policy details tend to make transfers, subsidies and potentially also government investments more damaging to long-run growth in democracies. One way to understand these differences is to note that democratic policymaking is more subject to myopic concerns: democratic governments must gain the support of voters at regular intervals, and given that a new government may come to power in the next elections, special interests may lobby particularly hard for short-run measures. These factors may cause transfers and subsidies, and government investments, to be designed with myopic consequences in mind instead of avoiding long-run costs. In discussing what he calls 'Hayekian welfare states', Bergh (2020) asks a related question: do democracies choose epistemologically more challenging types of government consumption and interventions? The same problem of myopic policymaking could arguably cause democratic governments to not economise on the epistemological demands of policymaking and to choose policies with clear short-run intentions but unknown – and potentially unknowable – long-run effects.

However, how much owes to measurement errors and how much to epistemological concerns regarding policy design must remain questions for future research. Likewise, remaining questions include whether effects are homogenous across political ideology (cf., Aidt et al., 2018; Haini and Loon, 2021), if they are mostly due to labour supply or productivity effects (cf., Feldmann, 2007), and the degree to which reforms are likely.

The bottom line of this chapter is that the size of government and particularly larger transfers and subsidies hold back long-run growth in electoral democracies. Subsidising some voters and some interests therefore come with a price tag for all of society. This finding stands in stark contrast to claims made during and after the COVID-19 pandemic, which saw a historically large increase in government spending and intervention in most Western countries. Frank and Miller (2021), a health executive and a professor of health economics, for example claimed in an op-ed in *The Hill* that 'Government negotiation works — COVID vaccines are proof'. Many politicians across the world have made similar claims, and government spending in the United Kingdom in 2023 reached levels not seen since Clement Atlee's post-war government. The findings in this paper suggest that the newfound enthusiasm for big government could depress growth substantially.

Acknowledgements

I am grateful to Juan Castañeda, John Moynihan, Martin Rode, and participants of the 2023 Vinson Centre Classical Political Economy Conference (University of Buckingham) for help and comments on an earlier version. This publication was made possible through the support of Grant 62065 from the John Templeton Foundation. The opinions expressed in this publication are those of the author and do not necessarily reflect the views of the John Templeton Foundation. Additional financial support from Jan Wallanders och Tom Hedelius Stiftelse (grant P18-0162) is gratefully acknowledged.

Notes

1 The Ramsey Rule, named after the British mathematician and economist Frank Ramsey, states that an optimal tax system should be designed such that every good or activity experiences results in the same proportional reduction in compensated demand. In other words, a tax system that follows the Ramsey Rule will reduce economic activity but minimally given the revenue that the system is supposed to collect.
2 The literature on consequences of economic freedom is covered by Hall and Lawson (2014) and Lawson (2022) while that of its determinants is surveyed in Lawson et al. (2020). Berggren (2024) provides a set of chapters exploring aspects of economic freedom in more detail.
3 This group for example includes Guatemala, Burundi, and Chad in the early 1980s, Lebanon in the late 1980s when no elections were held, and Mali in several periods.
4 Most of these tests are not shown here to keep the chapter short. They are, however, all available upon request.
5 A specific set of estimates (not shown but available upon request) do not dismiss this problem. Excluding observations in which there are substantial differences between three GDP series in the Penn World Tables results in the removal of any odd negative estimates in military dictatorships but no other findings.

References

Aidt, Toke S., Vitor Castro and Rodrigo Martins. 2018. Shades of Red and Blue: Government Ideology and Sustainable Development. *Public Choice*, 175(3–4), 303–323.
Alvarez, Sean Patrick, Vincent Geloso and Mary Scheck. 2024. Revisiting the Relationship between Economic Freedom and Development to Account for Statistical Deception by Autocratic Regimes. *European Journal of Political Economy*, 85, 102577.
Berggren, Niclas (ed.). 2024. Handbook of Research on Economic Freedom. Cheltenham: Edward Elgar.
Bergh, Andreas. 2020. Hayekian Welfare States: Explaining the Coexistence of Economic Freedom and Big Government. *Journal of Institutional Economics*, 16(1), 1–12.
Bergh, Andreas and Christian Bjørnskov. 2021. Does Economic Freedom Boost Growth for Everyone? *Kyklos*, 74(2), 170–186.
Bergh, Andreas and Magnus Henrekson. 2011. Government Size and Growth: A Survey and Interpretation of the Evidence. *Journal of Economic Surveys*, 25(5), 872–897.
Bjørnskov, Christian and Nicolai J. Foss. 2016. Institutions, Entrepreneurship, and Economic Growth: What Do We Know? And What Do We Still Need to Know? *Academy of Management Perspectives*, 30, 292–315.
Bjørnskov, Christian and Martin Rode. 2020. Regime Types and Regime Change: A New Dataset on Democracy, Coups, and Political Institutions. *Review of International Organizations*, 15(2), 531–551.
Brambor, Thomas, William Roberts Clark and Matt Golder. 2006. Understanding Interaction Models: Improving Empirical Analyses. *Political Analysis*, 14(1), 63–82.
Buchanan, James M. 1958. Public Principles of Public Debt: A Defense and Restatement. Homewood, IL: Richard D. Irwin, Inc.

Cheang, Bryan. 2023. Economic Liberalism and the Developmental State: Hong Kong and Singapore's Post-war Development. London: Palgrave Macmillan.
Dawson, John W. 1998. Institutions, Investment, and Growth: New Cross-Country and Panel Evidence. *Economic Inquiry*, 36(4), 603–619.
De Haan, Jacob and Bram Gootjes. 2023. What Makes Discretionary Counter-Cyclical Fiscal Policy So Difficult? An Analysis of 32 OECD Countries. *CESifo Economic Studies*, 69(1), 1–20.
Feenstra, Robert C., Robert Inklaar and Marcel P. Timmer. 2015. The Next Generation of the Penn World Table. *American Economic Review*, 105(10), 3150–3182.
Feldmann, Horst. 2007. Economic Freedom and Unemployment around the World. *Southern Economic Journal*, 74(1), 158–176.
Frank, Richard and Mark Miller. 2021. Government Negotiation Works – COVID Vaccines Are Proof. *The Hill*, 22 May.
Grier, Kevin B. and Robin M. Grier. 2021. The Washington Consensus Works: Causal Effects of Reform, 1970–2015. *Journal of Comparative Economics*, 49(1), 59–72.
Gründler, Klaus and Tommy Krieger. 2021. Using Machine Learning for Measuring Democracy: A Practitioners Guide and a New Updated Dataset for 186 Countries from 1919 to 2019. *European Journal of Political Economy*, 70(Dec), 102047.
Gwartney, James D., Robert A. Lawson, Joshua C. Hall and Ryan Murphy. 2022. Economic Freedom of the World: 2022 Annual Report. Vancouver: The Fraser Institute.
Haini, Hazwin and Pang Wei Loon. 2021. Does Government Ideology Affect the Relationship between Government Spending and Economic Growth? *Economic Papers*, 40(3), 209–216.
Hall, Joshua C. and Robert A. Lawson. 2014. Economic Freedom of the World: An Accounting of the Literature. *Contemporary Economic Policy*, 32(1), 1–19.
Heckelman, Jac C. and Michael D. Stroup. 2000. Which Economic Freedoms Contribute to Growth? *Kyklos*, 53(4), 527–544.
Heckelman, Jac C. and Michael D. Stroup. 2005. A Comparison of Aggregation Methods for Measures of Economic Freedom. *European Journal of Political Economy*, 21(4), 953–966.
Henisz, Witold. 2000. The Institutional Environment for Economic Growth. *Economics and Politics*, 12(1), 1–31.
Herby, Jonas, Lars Jonung and Steve H. Hanke. 2023. Did Lockdowns Work? The Verdict on Covid Restrictions. London: Institute of Economic Affairs.
Justesen, Mogens Kamp. 2008. The Effect of Economic Freedom on Growth Revisited: New Evidence on Causality from a Panel of Countries 1970–1999. *European Journal of Political Economy*, 24(3), 642–660.
Justesen, Mogens Kamp and Peter Kurrild-Klitgaard. 2013. Institutional Interactions and Economic Growth: The Joint Effects of Property Rights, Veto Players and Democratic Capital. *Public Choice*, 157, 449–474.
Lawson, Robert A. 2022. Economic Freedom in the Literature: What Is It Good (Bad) For? Chapter 3 in Gwartney et al. (2022), 187–199.
Lawson, Robert A., Ryan Murphy and Benjamin Powell. 2020. The Determinants of Economic Freedom: A Survey. *Contemporary Economic Policy*, 38, 622–642.
Magee, Christopher S.P. and John A. Doces. 2015. Reconsidering Regime Type and Growth: Lies, Dictatorships, and Statistics. *International Studies Quarterly*, 59(2), 223–237.
Martinez, Luis R. 2022. How Much Should We Trust the Dictator's GDP Growth Estimates? *Journal of Political Economy*, 130(10), 2731–2769.
Mertens, Karel and Jose Montiel-Olea. 2018. Marginal Tax Rates and Income: New Time Series Evidence. *Quarterly Journal of Economics*, 133(4), 1803–1884.
Rode, Martin and Sebastian Coll. 2012. Economic Freedom and Growth. Which Policies Matter the Most? *Constitutional Political Economy*, 23, 95–133.

Scartascini, Carlos, Cesi Cruz and Philip Keefer. 2021. The Database of Political Institutions 2020 (DPI2020). Database and codebook, the Inter-American Development Bank, Washington, DC. Available at https://publications.iadb.org/en/database-political-institutions-2020-dpi2020 (accessed April 2023).
Zinberg, Joel M., Brian Blase, Eric Sun and Casey B. Mulligan. 2023. Freedom Wins: States with Less Restrictive COVID Policies Outperformed States with More Restrictive COVID Policies. Discussion paper, the Paragon Health Institute, Arlington VA.

Appendix

Table A.1 Using alternative indices

	1	*2*	*3*	*4*
	No single-party	*No single-party*	*No single-party*	*No single-party*
Full baseline specification included				
Civilian autocracy	–.183			
	(.121)			
Democracy	–.162			
	(.120)			
Political Constraints III		–.411*		
		(.242)		
Constraints = 0		–.164		
		(.104)		
Gründler-Krieger index			.026	
			(.111)	
Size of government	.000	.000	.022	.002
	(.019)	(.014)	(.014)	(.023)
Legal quality	.022**	.021*	.019*	–.005
	(.011)	(.011)	(.012)	(.028)
Size of government * civilian autocracy	.024			
	(.019)			
Size of government * democracy	.024			
	(.019)			
Size of government * constraints		.058*		
		(.035)		
Size of government * no constraints		.019		
		(.015)		
Size of government * democracy			–.001	
			(.017)	
Size of government * legal quality				.004
				(.004)
Country FE	Yes	Yes	Yes	Yes
Period FE	Yes	Yes	Yes	Yes
Observations	994	985	985	994
Countries	151	151	150	151
Within R squared	.318	.322	.311	.314
F statistic	14.50	14.35	15.61	17.19

(Continued)

Table A.1 (Continued)

	1	*2*	*3*	*4*
	No single-party	*No single-party*	*No single-party*	*No single-party*
Marginal effect of size of government at				
Military dictatorship	.000	.009	.022*	.017*
	(.019)	(.009)	(.012)	(.009)
Civilian autocracy	.024**	.012	.022**	.021***
	(.012)	(.008)	(.009)	(.007)
Democracy	.025***	.026***	.021***	.027***
	(.007)	(.008)	(.007)	(.008)

Note: Numbers in parentheses are standard errors clustered at the country level; ***, (**), and [*] denote significance at p < .01, (p < .05), and [p < .10], respectively.

Table A.2 Results, subcomponents without growth extremes

Variable	*Government consumption*	*Transfers and subsidies*	*Government investment*	*Taxation*	*State ownership*
	1	*2*	*3*	*4*	*5*
Marginal effect of size of government at					
Military dictatorship	–.002	.000	–.004	.007	.009
	(.007)	(.017)	(.004)	(.006)	(.010)
Civilian autocracy	.011**	.009	–.001	.012***	.021***
	(.005)	(.013)	(.003)	(.005)	(.006)
Democracy	.014***	.017***	.003	.006**	.014**
	(.004)	(.005)	(.003)	(.003)	(.006)
Observations	969	857	933	820	1065
Countries	151	146	151	149	153
Within R squared	.216	.219	.195	.257	.198
F statistic	16.00	14.79	12.09	20.70	16.90

Note: All estimates use the same specification as in Table 9.3 and exclude single party autocracies. The 5% observations with the smallest and 5% with the largest growth rates are excluded throughout. Numbers in parentheses are standard errors clustered at the country level; *** and (**) denote significance at p < .01, and (p < .05), respectively.

Table A.3 Results, subcomponents without growth declines

Variable	*Government consumption*	*Transfers and subsidies*	*Government investment*	*Taxation*	*State ownership*
	1	*2*	*3*	*4*	*5*
Marginal effect of size of government at					
Military dictatorship	–.003	.009	.001	.010	–.006
	(.009)	(.022)	(.005)	(.007)	(.012)
Civilian autocracy	–.003	.021	–.000	.015**	.010
	(.009)	(.027)	(.007)	(.006)	(.012)
Democracy	.004	.012*	.004	.008**	.023***
	(.005)	(.006)	(.003)	(.003)	(.009)
Observations	752	652	723	623	850
Countries	148	142	150	140	152
Within R squared	.231	.222	.278	.259	.268
F statistic	8.88	9.94	6.84	10.50	8.04

Note: All estimates use the same specification as in Table 9.3 and exclude single-party autocracies. The 5% observations with the smallest and 5% with the largest growth rates are excluded throughout. Numbers in parentheses are standard errors clustered at the country level; ***, (**), and [*] denote significance at p < .01, (p < .05), and [p < .10], respectively.

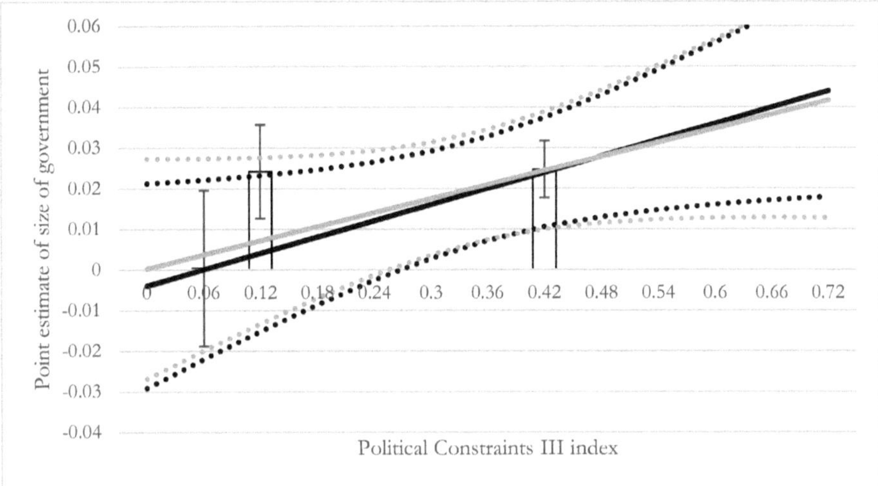

Figure 9.3 Marginal effects, interaction with Political Constraints III.

Note: Dotted lines indicate 95% confidence intervals

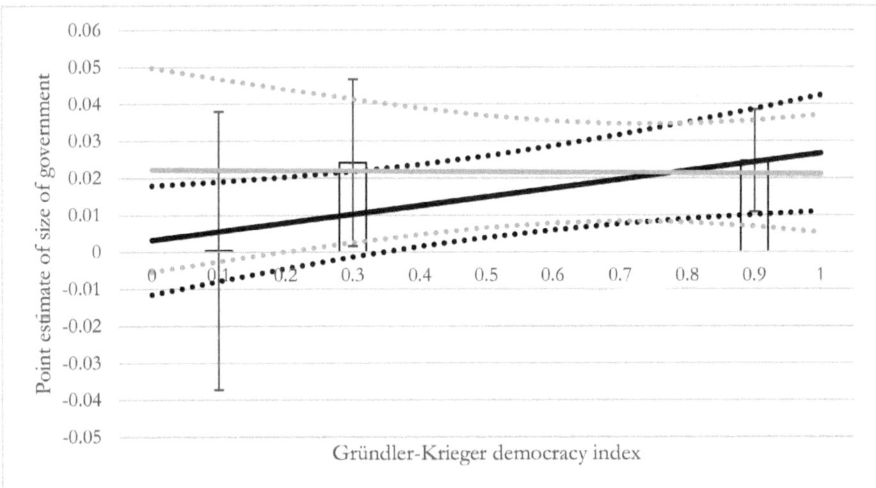

Figure 9.4 Marginal effects, interaction with Gründler-Krieger democracy index.

Note: Dotted lines indicate 95% confidence intervals

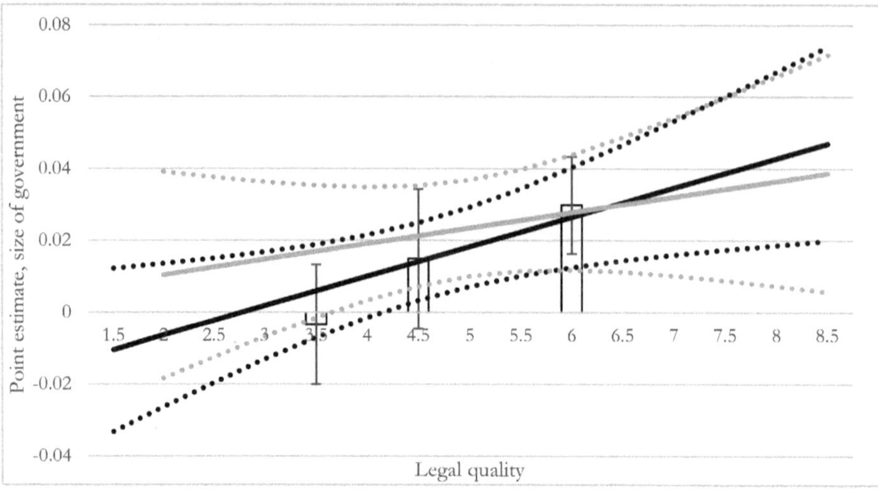

Figure 9.5 Marginal effects, interaction with legal quality.

Note: Dotted lines indicate 95% confidence intervals

10 Classical Liberal Solutions to the 'Productivity Puzzle'

Julian Jessop

10.1 Introduction*: What Is Productivity? And How Do We Measure It?*

Productivity "measures how efficiently production inputs, such as labour and capital, are being used in an economy to produce a given level of output. Productivity is a key source of economic growth and competitiveness" (OECD, 2024).

In more specific terms, productivity is the amount of goods and services produced by an economy, a business, or an individual, in a particular period of time, divided by the inputs required to produce those outputs.

The broadest measure of productivity is Total Factor Productivity (TFP), which takes account of all the inputs associated with production, including capital such as machinery, buildings and land, as well as labour. This can be hard to quantify. It is more common to focus on measures of labour productivity, notably 'output per hour worked'. This measure is generally preferable to 'output per worker', which can flatter economies where the average number of hours worked is higher.

'Output per head' of the population (or 'per capita') is occasionally used as a measure of productivity as well, but it has its flaws too. Variations in output per head can also simply reflect differences in the numbers of hours worked, rather than a genuine improvement in the efficiency of production.

In addition, differences in output per head between countries and over time could simply reflect differences in the proportion of the population that is (or could reasonably be expected to be) economically active. For example, a country with a relatively large proportion of children or elderly people in the total population might report a lower level of GDP per head, even though those who are in work could be relatively productive.

Nonetheless, output per head can still be a useful proxy for economy-wide productivity, especially over long historical periods when data on hours worked are not readily available. It can also be a better measure of average living standards for the population as a whole.

It is worth stressing that low productivity is rarely the fault of the individuals themselves. As the OECD explains further, "labour productivity only partially reflects the productivity of labour in terms of the personal capacities of workers or the intensity of their effort. The ratio between the output measure and the

DOI: 10.4324/9781003504412-14

labour input depends to a large degree on the presence and/or use of other inputs (e.g. capital, intermediate inputs, technical, organisational and efficiency change, economies of scale)" (OECD, 2024).

Other contributing factors to high or low productivity could include incentives and distortions created by the tax, benefit, and pension systems; the quality of healthcare and of physical infrastructure; the degree of international openness to trade and investment; and regulations covering everything from the terms of employment to the rules governing housebuilding and urban planning.

10.1.1 Why Does Productivity Matter?

The Nobel Prize-winning economist Paul Krugman once famously wrote that "productivity isn't everything, but in the long run it is almost everything ... a country's ability to improve its standard of living over time depends almost entirely on its ability to raise its output per worker" (Krugman, 1994).

This quotation is arguably the most over-used in the economic literature, but it is surely right. Gains in productivity allow 'intensive growth', which is when economies expand without using more resources. Indeed, the improvements in efficiency that drive productivity-led growth often allow firms and households to do 'more with less' (McAfee, 2019). This contrasts with 'extensive growth', which relies on an increase in the quantity of inputs and is the main target of the ire of those who advocate 'degrowth' (Susskind, 2024).

Gains in productivity are also a key driver of increases in real wages or, equivalently, a fall in the price of goods and services relative to the amount of work required to earn enough money to buy them. If workers are increasingly productive, they are worth more to their employer and so can command higher wages, work fewer hours for the same pay, or some combination of the two.

In contrast, low growth in productivity raises the risks of economic stagnation, making it harder to deal with social challenges including poverty reduction and climate change. It can also threaten debt sustainability and make it harder to raise the tax revenues that are needed to pay for public services.

The International Monetary Fund (IMF) has estimated that a widespread slowdown in TFP has accounted for more the half the decline in global economic growth since the early 2000s, with the rest mainly due to low private investment and adverse demographics (IMF, 2024a). In short, raising productivity is crucial to sustainable economic growth and improvements in living standards, without the social and environmental costs that might result from simply using more resources.

10.1.2 What Is the 'productivity puzzle'?

The British economist Michael Haynes has noted that "productivity is a puzzle because it is a problem to understand conceptually; it is a problem to measure; it is a problem to explain, and it is a problem to know how to improve it" (Haynes, 2020). These are all critical issues. However, the term 'productivity puzzle' is most often associated with the break in the long-term upward trend in productivity

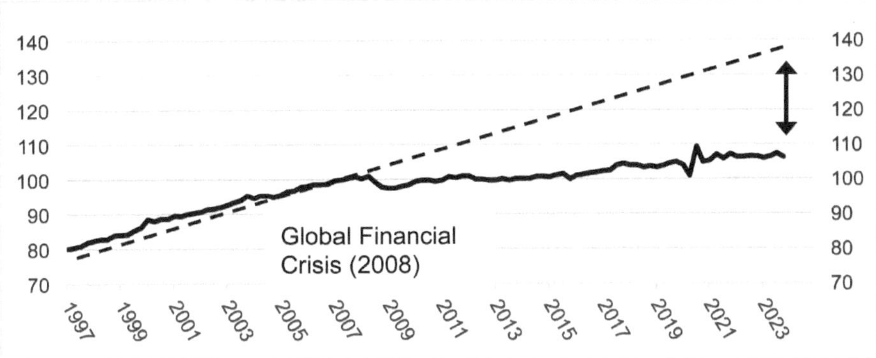

Figure 10.1 UK productivity (output per hour worked) (index where Q1 2008 = 100).
Data source: ONS

which occurred in most major economies in the wake of the Global Financial Crisis (GFC) of 2008–09. Growth had already begun to slow in the early 2000s, but the deceleration was particularly marked after the GFC.

For example, output per hour in the UK would now be more than a fifth higher if productivity had remained on its pre-GFC trend (see Figure 10.1).

Nonetheless, the UK is far from unique. As Figure 10.2 shows, productivity growth has slowed in other advanced economies too. Indeed, the UK performed relatively well in the period between 1990 and 2008, which makes the subsequent slowdown in UK productivity look worse than perhaps it is.

The US appears to have been least affected by the productivity slowdown, and the US has consistently topped the 'G7 league table' in terms of the *level* of productivity as well (as shown in Figure 10.3).

In short, we need to explain why productivity growth has slowed in all these major economies since 2008. There should also be lessons to the drawn from the

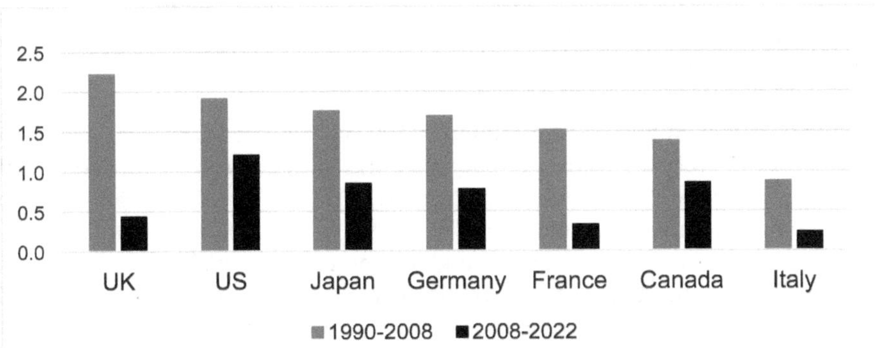

Figure 10.2 Average annual growth in output per hour worked (%).
Data source: OECD

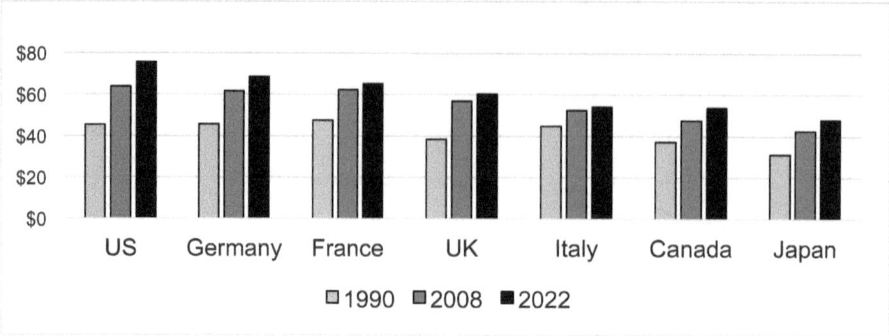

Figure 10.3 GDP per hour worked (US Dollars, PPP converted, constant 2015 prices).
Data source: OECD

relative resilience of productivity in the US and the sluggishness of productivity in the UK as well as other countries, notably Japan. The following sections will outline the most common explanations for the widespread slowdown in productivity, before presenting a Classical Liberal perspective and suggested policy options to address the 'productivity puzzle'.

10.2 'Secular stagnation'

Some economists think the productivity slowdown might be structural and potentially long-lasting. These explanations can be loosely linked to the heading of 'secular stagnation' (Backhouse and Boianovsky, 2016).

A number of different traditions point in the same direction here, including Karl Marx's ideas about the inherent tendencies of capitalism towards periodic crises as profits decline (Marx, 1867), the long-term 'super-cycles' suggested by the Russian economist Nikolai Kondratiev (Kondratieff and Stolper, 1935), Joseph Schumpeter's observation that technological advances tend to the cluster together in specific points in time (Schumpeter, 1934), and the theories of insufficient demand due to a surplus of private savings which were developed by John Maynard Keynes and Alvin Hansen (Keynes, 1936; Hansen, 1939).

One of the most pessimistic modern takes on 'secular stagnation' is found in the work of Robert J. Gordon, who has focused on the role of technological advances in driving productivity and growth. He attributed the more recent slowdown to "diminishing returns in the digital revolution that had its peak effect on business hardware, software, and best practices in the late 1990s but has resulted in little change in those methods over the past decade" (Gordon, 2015). Evidence for this included a decline in the dynamism of the economy, measured by the rate of new firm creation. In his best-known paper, Gordon noted that there was virtually no growth in output per head in the US or the UK before 1750, and thus there is no guarantee that growth will continue indefinitely

(Gordon, 2012). Instead, he linked periods of slow and rapid growth to the timing of the three industrial revolutions (IRs): IR#1 (steam, railroads) from 1750 to 1830; IR#2 (electricity, internal combustion engine, running water, indoor toilets, communications, entertainment, chemicals, petroleum) from 1870 to 1900; and IR#3 (computers, the web, mobile phones) from 1960 to the present day. His argument was that IR#3 had run its course. However, this amounts to a bet against human ingenuity. In fact, IR#3 appears to be gathering momentum again with the rapid development of Artificial Intelligence (AI) and its wider applications. This is potentially such a game-changer that it merits the label 'IR#4'.

For example, a study by economists at Goldman Sachs has suggested that AI could increase productivity growth in the US by as much as 1.5 percentage points annually over the next ten years, with similar effects in other major advanced economies (Goldman Sachs, 2023). Along the same lines, staff at the IMF have estimated that productivity gains from AI could range from 0.9 to 1.5% a year in the UK (Cazzaniga and others, 2024; IMF, 2024a).

Nonetheless, Gordon also identified no fewer than six other headwinds, namely "demography, education, inequality, globalization, energy [and the] environment, and the overhang of consumer and government debt" (Gordon, 2012). These often-overlapping points have all been developed in different ways by others, but three themes stand out.

The first is deficient demand due to rising inequality. This is particularly associated with the work of the French economist Thomas Piketty. In *Capital in the Twenty-First Century*, Piketty argued that higher returns to capital than those to labour would concentrate income and wealth among a small group of people with a lower propensity to spend (Piketty, 2014a, 2014b). Needless to say, this has been seized on by many to justify an increased focus on state intervention to redistribute income and wealth.

The second theme is that advanced economies are running up against natural limits, especially environmental and demographic constraints, which make expectations of continued growth both unrealistic and dangerous. These ideas are often associated with the 'green' economist Tim Jackson, who is one of many to argue that policy needs to refocus away from the narrow concept of GDP towards broader measures of 'wellbeing' (Jackson, 2021). The demographic headwinds have been particularly strong in Japan, but other countries, notably Germany, Italy, and the UK, are beginning to face the same problems of an ageing population.

The third theme is based around a more traditional economic point, namely that it may be impossible to lower interest rates sufficiently to boost demand when interest rates are already near their 'zero lower bound' (Krugman, 2013; Summers, 2015). The main policy prescription here is a more activist set of fiscal policies, notably increased public spending on investment. It is argued that as long as real interest rates remain low (specifically, lower than the real growth rate of the economy), higher borrowing need not push debt onto an unsustainable path.

10.3 Cyclical Factors

These 'structural' explanations cannot be entirely satisfactory, because it seems odd that they have all kicked in around the time of the GFC. Another (not necessarily mutually exclusive) set of explanations therefore focus on cyclical factors that might have depressed productivity in the wake of the recession after the financial crash.

One important insight here is that productivity usually falls during economic downturns, with the 'direction of causation' between productivity and economic growth therefore running in both directions: low economic growth can itself lead to weak productivity, as well as weak productivity being the driver of low growth.

For example, firms are typically less efficient at lower levels of output and capacity utilisation, because they do not benefit as much from factors such as economies of scale. Firms also tend to 'hoard labour' during economic downturns because firing and then rehiring workers can be expensive.

In addition, recessions cause a large amount of disruption and dislocation to the normal running of a business. Managers may have to spend a large amount of time, energy, and other resources simply finding new customers and suppliers to replace others that have gone bust, or new sources of finance. This is time that might otherwise have been devoted to making their businesses work better and improving productivity.

Finally, while there is a strong positive correlation between increases in capital investment and increases in productivity, it is also worth noting that investment itself is particularly cyclical.

All of these forces may have been especially powerful in the wake of the GFC. Nervous businesses were reluctant to invest in capital-intensive projects that might have raised productivity, especially when depressed wages meant that labour was relatively cheap anyway. At the same time, weakened banks (due in part to increased regulations) were reluctant to lend. The upshot is that the demand for and supply of finance for investment were both lower than they would otherwise have been.

Policy interventions also had a perverse effect. The normal operation of market forces should encourage resources to flow towards more productive uses, so that 'allocative efficiency' adds to the benefits of improvements in productivity within firms. But additional state subsidies and the long period of very low interest rates in the wake of the GFC made it easier for less productive businesses to stay afloat. This is the problem of 'zombie firms' which had already become a feature of Japan's first 'lost decade' in the 1990s (Caballero et al., 2008).

Moreover, the COVID-19 pandemic and then the global energy crisis were new shocks which have kept productivity down. Among other things, these new shocks were followed by sharp increases in government borrowing and debt, and by a further loosening of monetary policy, compounding the misallocation of capital.

An alternative (or complementary) diagnosis of the underlying problems is therefore that much of the productivity slowdown was a cyclical response to the GFC – albeit an unusually long one – as well as a permanent structural change.

What, then, can the Classical Liberal tradition add to this discussion?

10.4 The Classical Liberal View: The Importance of a Small State

The core tenet of Classical Liberalism is the priority given to individual freedom. This goes hand in hand with a small state, kept in bounds by clear rules. Applying this to the realm of economics, "prosperity comes through free individuals inventing, creating, saving, investing and, ultimately, exchanging goods and services voluntarily, for mutual gain – the spontaneous order of the free-market economy" (Butler, 2015).

These points about 'prosperity' also apply to *productivity*. Early Classical Liberal thinkers had a lot to say about 'productivity', even if they did not use that term.

For example, Adam Smith in the *Wealth of Nations* emphasised the benefits of specialisation and the division of labour as a means to increase the efficiency of production (Smith, 1776). The ability to specialise can make anyone more productive compared to the alternative of doing everything and providing for all their needs themselves.

David Ricardo took Smith's ideas further by showing that it is not even necessary for one country to have an absolute competitive edge in order for there to be gains from international trade. Instead, each party simply needs to focus on what they do best compared to the alternatives available to them. This is the concept of 'comparative advantage' (Ricardo, 1817).

John Stuart Mill developed the point that increased openness to trade boosts productivity, for example by allowing the import of better equipment, the sharing of knowledge, and additional competitive pressures on domestic producers (Mill, 1848).

More recently, Friedrich Hayek coined the term 'spontaneous order' to describe the emergence of complex social institutions – such as language or markets for goods and services – that are far more efficient than anything that central planning could come up with (Hayek, 1944, 1960).

The Classical Liberal approach to solving the 'productivity puzzle' would therefore focus on reversing trends which have undermined the efficient operation of free markets. One would be the increase in the tax burden, which discourages work and saving and diverts resources to priorities chosen by the state, thus reducing the dynamism of the economy. Moreover, public debt has still risen sharply, despite higher taxes, increasing the debt interest bill now and also adding to the burden on future generations.

Another new development would be the backlash against globalisation and the creep towards greater protectionism. This is a growing problem in the US, while the UK's departure from the European Union has initially increased frictions to trade.

The increasing emphasis on state intervention to redistribute of wealth and income is also problematic. This risks undermining the incentives for people to provide for themselves, including by work.

As Robert Lucas put it: "of the tendencies that are harmful to sound economics, the most seductive, and in my opinion the most poisonous, is to focus on questions of distribution [...] the potential for improving the lives of poor people by finding different ways of distributing current production is nothing compared to the apparently limitless potential of increasing production" (Lucas, 2004)

Or in more popular terms, politicians have become too concerned about the distribution of the cake, rather than creating the conditions that allow others to bake a bigger one.

Another headwind is the seemingly relentless increase in government regulation and state direction of the economy. A bigger state is sometimes defended in terms of the need to correct 'market failures'. These undoubtedly exist, such as 'externalities'[1] and the under-provision of 'public goods'[2] and as a consequence of the inevitable divergence from the ideal of 'perfect competition'. However, market-based solutions (such as 'Pigovian taxes' that correct for negative externalities) and measures to enhance competition between private companies are preferable to other forms of government intervention that amount to state planning.

In addition, the inevitable imperfections of an actual market economy are often compared unfavourably and unfairly to the idealised world of perfect government, or, equivalently, the reality of capitalism is compared to the ideal of socialism (Butler, 2018; Niemietz, 2019). In practice, there are government failures too. This is the focus of 'Public Choice Theory', where the 'public interest' is determined by a process which may simply favour the self-interest of a small number of participants (Buchanan and Tullock, 1962).

It is helpful here to contrast this with the more positive view of the role of the government which has been popularised by the Italian-born economist Mariana Mazzucato. She has argued that the state's influence in promoting innovation, investment, and hence productivity growth is underappreciated, citing the examples of the role of the US government in the development of internet and space exploration. In this perspective, the state is at least as effective at creating value as the private sector – and perhaps more so when a longer time horizon is needed (Mazzucato, 2013, 2018, 2021).

The state may indeed have some role to play in supporting the pure science that can lead to new inventions. But when it comes to innovation (creating commercial applications), or the diffusion of these innovations, there is overwhelming evidence that markets are more effective than any form of government planning (Ridley, 2010). For example, it was private companies that developed the full potential of the internet and mobile communications. And any innovations resulting from government investment in the US space programme need to be seen in the context of the vast amount of taxpayers' money spent on the project, which might have been better deployed elsewhere.

More generally, there is a growing body of evidence (summarised in Wennberg and Sandström, 2022) that 'mission-oriented' innovation policies rarely work in practice. Reasons include the self-interest of politicians and government agencies, inadequate information, rent seeking and regulatory capture, distortions to competition and incentives, and inadequate attention paid to opportunity costs.

10.5 Is the United Kingdom a Special Case?

We can illustrate many of these points by taking a closer look at the UK and by drawing out some contrasts with the US.

The 'productivity puzzle' has been a hot topic in the UK for many years – so much so that in 2019 the Royal Statistical Society (RSS) identified the average annual increase in UK productivity in the ten years since the financial crisis as the 'United Kingdom Statistic of the Decade'. This figure was just 0.3%, compared to the average of around 2% achieved between 1997 and 2007, and represented the worst decade since the early 1800s. The RSS noted too that "although productivity growth has also slowed in other advanced economies, the slowdown in the UK has been particularly marked" (Royal Statistical Society, 2019).

There are many possible explanations for the UK's apparently poor performance on productivity relative to other major economies since 2008. Starting with the raw data, the sharper deceleration in UK productivity since the GFC needs to be seen in the context of the relatively rapid growth in UK productivity between 1990 and 2008. If we take the entire period between 1990 and 2022, the growth in UK 'output per hour worked' was second only to the US among the G7 economies (OECD, 2024).

The difficulties of realising and measuring productivity gains in services may also have had a bigger impact on the data in the UK than in countries which are dominated by other sectors, notably manufacturing. Douglas McWilliams has coined the term 'flat white economy' to describe the growing importance of tech-led services in the UK (McWilliams, 2016). An independent review of UK statistics, led by Professor Sir Charles Bean, has suggested that if the digital economy were fully captured by official data, annual GDP growth could be between a third and two-thirds of percentage point higher (Bean, 2016).

10.5.1 Is There a 'finance curse'?

Others have suggested that the relative importance of financial services to the UK economy may have held back overall productivity. Output per hour worked has grown more slowly in manufacturing than in financial services and especially since 2008 (see Figure 10.4).

There are two opposing views here. For some this is not just a case of weak productivity growth in financial services dragging down the average. Instead, the sector itself is a blight on the economy. Some have even gone as far as describing many financial services activities as 'socially useless', and the apparent success of the City of London as a 'finance curse', leading to inflows of 'hot money', excessive financial speculation and short-termism, and an over-valued currency (for example, Shaxson, 2019).

In reality, the role of the City is much more benign. The UK has a 'comparative advantage' in financial services and is simply playing to its strengths. A strong

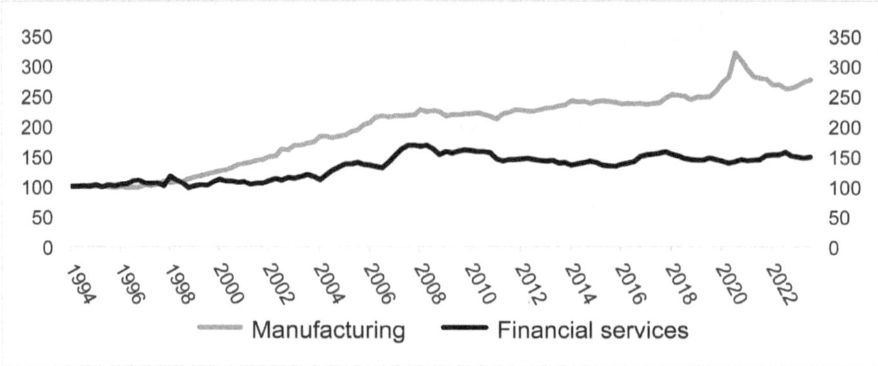

Figure 10.4 UK output per hour worked (Q1 1994 = 100).

Data source: ONS

financial sector also plays a crucial role in reducing transaction costs throughout the economy (Booth and Zuluaga, 2018). If the financial sector has become a problem for productivity, this largely reflects an increase in state intervention and regulation, and an over-reliance on bank finance over other more flexible forms of funding. The contrast here between the UK and the US is relatively nuanced. Both have large, globally important financial sectors, so that cannot explain the differences in economy-wide productivity. The UK also continues to score highly in surveys of financial sector competitiveness and investment attractiveness.[3] However, the UK has become more dependent on bank finance than equity finance. History has shown that the emergence of joint-stock companies has played a key role in the ability to translate new ideas into rapid economic growth. Indeed, this goes a long way towards explaining the relatively rapid development of the economies of Western Europe from the 17th century onwards, which the economic historian Robert Allen has described as the 'Great Divergence' (Allen, 2011).

Bank lending may be appropriate for established companies but less suitable for new and riskier firms that typically drive innovation and growth (especially in new areas such as AI). Unfortunately, there is a significant gap in the availability of risk capital between Europe and the US (Lagarde, 2024). The UK still outperforms the EU in this regard, but the US is the world leader.

The UK market is also hampered relative to the US by restrictions on listing rules, such as the prohibition on dual share classes (preferential voting rights are especially important to protect the interests of founders of start-ups) and by the UK government's 0.5% stamp duty on share transactions.

10.5.2 What Is the Role of 'austerity'?

Another often-mentioned factor is the tightening in fiscal policy from 2010 onwards in the wake of the GFC, commonly known as 'austerity'. The Conservative-Liberal Democrat coalition government which took power in the UK in 2010

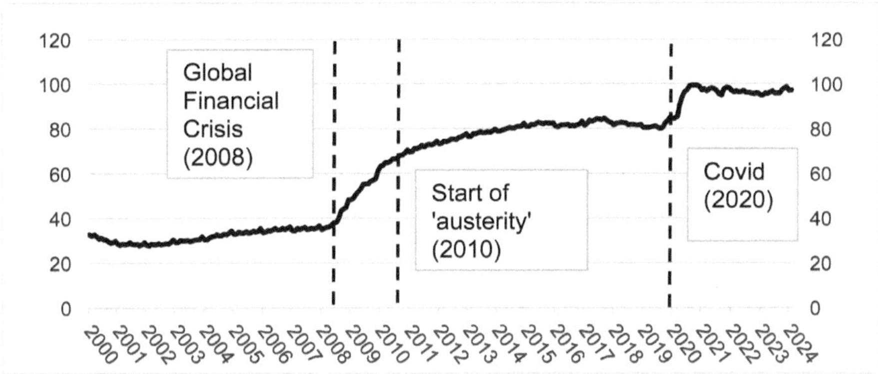

Figure 10.5 UK public sector net debt (% GDP).

Data source: ONS

enacted policies that aimed to reduce government borrowing through a combination of spending cuts and tax increases.

The official view at the time (supported by the IMF, among others) was that it was necessary to tighten fiscal policy, even at the cost of a weaker economic recovery, in order to prevent an even worse outcome. UK politicians and officials were particularly worried by the financial crisis then beginning to engulf Greece.[4] It was also believed that the economic drag from lower public spending would be at least partly offset by an increase in private spending, as the former helped to keep interest rates low. Supporters of 'austerity' also point to the apparent success of the policy in stabilising the ratio of debt to national income at around 80% by the second half of the 2010s, before another step increase in the wake of the COVID-19 pandemic (as shown in Figure 10.5).

In contrast, some economists believe that 'austerity' was a major policy mistake which contributed to the persistent weakness in productivity growth, via both the demand and supply sides of the economy.

In this view, the drag on spending and on both consumer and business confidence resulted in a slower economic recovery and hence compounded the cyclical weakness of productivity. Moreover, the restraint in public spending fell particularly hard on capital budgets, delaying what may have been much-needed investment in infrastructure and public services and reducing the resilience of the UK economy to subsequent shocks (notably COVID-19). According to this view, 'austerity' was precisely the wrong approach. Instead, the government should have taken advantage of low interest rates to increase spending, both to provide an immediate boost to demand and to increase investment for the longer term.

Critics of 'austerity' have also noted that the international creditworthiness of the UK was never seriously in doubt. In part this is because, unlike Greece, the UK was not member of the euro and therefore retained its independence on monetary policy, which helped the government to finance and service its debts.

Looking back, it is impossible to be sure which view is more accurate. This mainly reflects the difficulty of knowing the 'counterfactual' or what would have happened if fiscal policy had not been tightened. For example, opponents of austerity might argue that a more expansionary policy could have boosted growth and therefore lowered the debt/GDP ratio more quickly. Supporters of austerity might counter that interest rates would not have remained so low if fiscal policy had been loosened instead.

On this debate, we make three general observations. First, the degree of 'austerity' in the UK is often overstated – especially as compared to other countries. In our analysis we will use the change in the 'structural budget balance', which is an estimate of government borrowing adjusted for the stage of the economic cycle. An increase in the structural deficit implies that the government has chosen to loosen fiscal policy, while a reduction implies a discretionary fiscal tightening.

Figure 10.6 shows the data on structural budget balances for the UK, alongside Germany and the US (a negative number indicates a deficit). The UK government did tighten fiscal policy from 2010 onwards, reflected in a narrowing of the structural deficit, but so did governments in other advanced economies. German fiscal policy remained relatively conservative throughout this period (reflecting a relatively restrictive set of national fiscal rules).

More strikingly, the path of the structural budget balance was similar in the UK and the US until 2017, when the Trump administration began a major fiscal stimulus. This helps to explain the stronger performance of the US economy over the last few years. However, this may simply be storing up problems for the future – the debt dynamics of the US are relatively poor[5] – and other countries without the advantage of issuing in the world's dominant reserve currency might not be able to replicate this approach anyway. In other words, the US has larger 'fiscal capacity' than other economies because of the special status of the US dollar. But complacency on this point creates more risks both in the US and elsewhere through interest rate spillovers (IMF, 2024b).

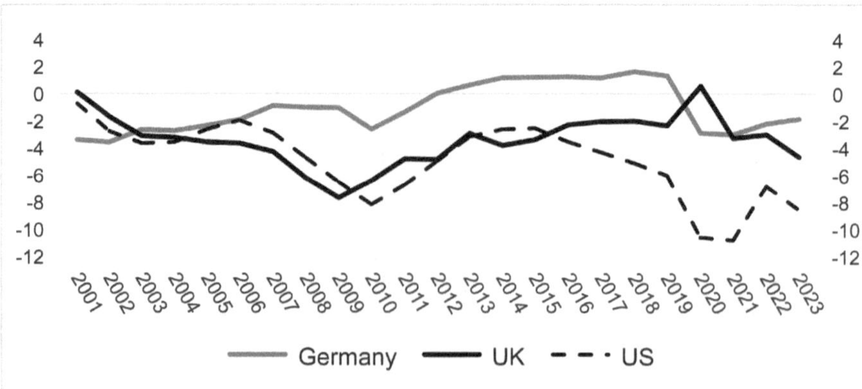

Figure 10.6 Government structural balance (% potential GDP).

Data source: IMF WEO Database April 2024

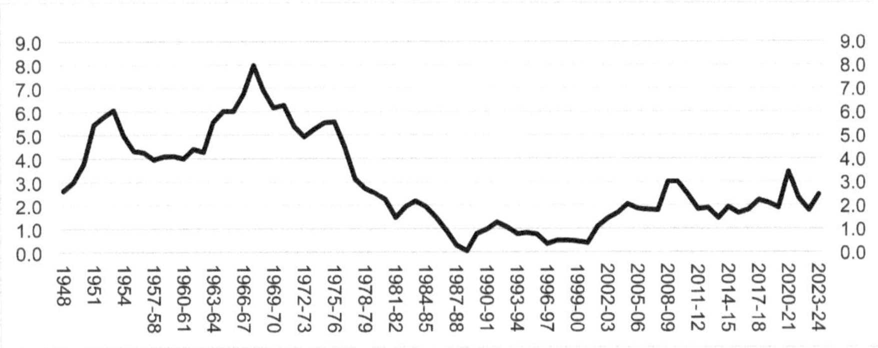

Figure 10.7 UK public sector net investment (% of GDP).

Data source: OBR

This fiscal expansion in the US and in other countries, including the UK, has also been facilitated by the widespread adoption of 'quantitative easing' (the purchase of government bonds by central banks using newly created money), which has blurred the lines between fiscal and monetary policy as well as saddled taxpayers with a growing bill as this policy is unwound.

The second observation about 'austerity' is that its impact partly depends on where the burden falls, including the balance between taxation and spending, and the distribution of spending restraint between different government programmes. One common argument is that the axe fell particularly hard on capital budgets. This claim is also somewhat overdone: public sector net investment averaged just under 2% of GDP in the 2010s (albeit flattered a little by the inclusion of student loans; see Figure 10.7 above).

However, the state probably did under-invest during this period in 'public goods' such as flood defences or the criminal justice system, and in other critical infrastructure projects such as nuclear power.

10.5.3 The Crisis in Public Services

Critics of 'austerity' also often focus on spending on public services, notably the National Health Service (NHS). In fact, government spending on healthcare continued to grow in real terms between 2010 and 2019, albeit at a slower pace than under the previous Labour government, before spiking during the COVID-19 pandemic. The upshot is that government (and total) healthcare spending was stable as a share of national income through the 2010s (see Figure 10.8).

It might still be reasonable to argue that health spending failed to keep up with the additional demand pressures from an ageing population. In contrast to the flat figure in the UK, the ratio of government healthcare spending to GDP rose by about half a percentage point in the 2010s in Germany and in France, and by nearly two percentage points in Japan.

However, it would be wrong just to focus on the amount of money spent on healthcare, or other public services, rather than the outcomes achieved, especially

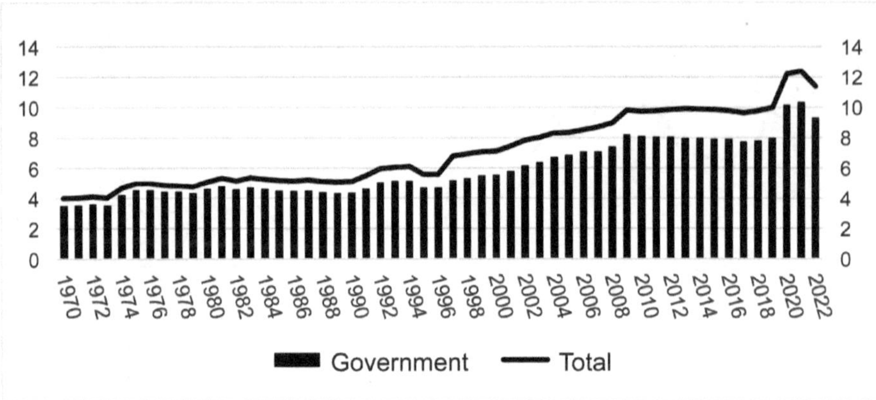

Figure 10.8 UK spending on healthcare (% of GDP).

Data source: OECD

in the context of a discussion about productivity. Indeed, the UK's productivity crisis appears to be most acute in the public sector. Productivity has at least continued to increase in the economy as a whole since the GFC, albeit at a slower rate. In contrast, output per hour worked in public services has been drifting down since the early 2000s and is now about 10% lower than it was in 1997 (as shown in Figure 10.9).

There are some important caveats. It is relatively hard to quantify the output of public services and to adjust for improvements (or deteriorations) in quality, compared to manufacturing. In particular, the biggest drags seem to be in health and education, which can partly be explained by the nature of these activities. They are inherently labour intensive and require lots of personal contact. For example,

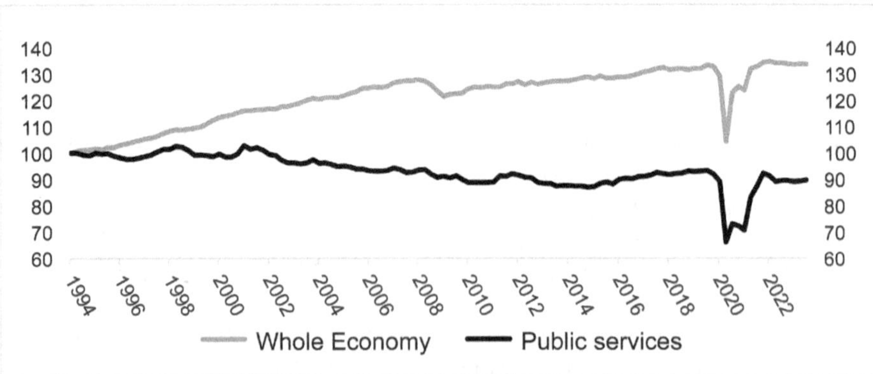

Figure 10.9 Output per hour worked (Q1 1994 = 100).

Data source: ONS

it is more difficult to raise the productivity of an individual teacher, given the constraints on class size, or for a surgeon to perform many more operations at the same time. Indeed, economies which are dominated by service can be expected to report slower rates of productivity growth. This is not necessarily a fundamental failing: William Baumol illustrated this point with the impossibility of improving the value of an orchestra by reducing the number of musicians (Baumol, 2012).

Above all, low productivity is rarely the fault of public sector workers themselves. That was certainly the case during the pandemic, when lockdowns and infection precautions made it more challenging for teachers and medical professionals to do their jobs as normal.

Nonetheless, productivity has improved in many areas where services are mainly delivered by the private sector. For example, output per hour worked has increased since the 1990s by more than 10% (and sometimes by much more) in retail, distribution, professional services, and office support. The reasons for the shortfalls in the public sector are not entirely clear.

We may want to consider four factors:

- First, the lack of competition in the large parts of the public sector. It is no coincidence that sectors where market pressures are strongest also tend to be those where productivity gains are greater.
- Second, the reliance on the UK Treasury for much needed capital spending. The appropriate amount of public investment in new hospitals or school buildings is debatable, but any business model that depends on political choices will always be vulnerable to under-funding (or wasteful spending).
- Third, the public services generally have higher rates of trade union membership and, in some cases, more militant unions. This is reflected in the increased number of strikes in the public sector and greater resistance to change.
- Fourth, and probably related to all the above, the public sector has been slower to adopt new technology. The scope for AI to transform the provision of public services is surely huge.

10.5.4 Is 'Brexit' to Blame?

Another possible explanation for the UK's sluggish productivity growth is the decision in 2016 to leave the European Union, known as 'Brexit'. This could have undermined productivity in three main ways, but the available evidence so far is weak.

First, the increased uncertainty and higher costs of capital could mean that business investment has been weaker than it would otherwise have been. Business investment did stall in around 2016 after the vote to leave the EU, though it now seems to be back on its long-term trend (see Figure 10.10). In the meantime, the UK has retained its high position in surveys of investment attractiveness, and for 'greenfield' investment, suggesting investment will continue to recover as uncertainty eases.

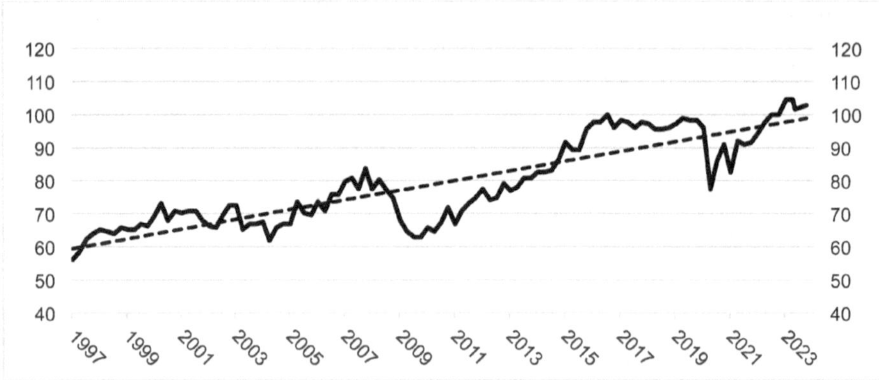

Figure 10.10 UK business investment (Q2 2016 = 100).

Data source: ONS

Second, the increased frictions to the UK's trade with the European Union have reduced the amount of trade being done. After the 2016 vote the Office for Budget Responsibility assumed that the volume of UK imports and exports will both be 15% lower than if the UK had remained in the EU and that the resulting reduction in the trade intensity of GDP will eventually lead to a 4% reduction in the potential productivity of the UK economy (OBR, 2024).

However, the jury is still out here too. UK trade in goods has grown relatively slowly since the vote to leave the EU, but trade in services has performed relatively well. This continues a longer-term trend: UK goods exports have grown by just 7% in real terms since 2010, compared with services exports growing by 63% over the same period (ONS, 2024).

Third, the end of 'free movement' of labour to and (especially) from the EU could have introduced new frictions into labour markets that have held back productivity. However, the post-Brexit migration regime is arguably a success story. The UK is now less dependent on low-cost labour from the EU, but overall levels of migration remain high (due in part to a very liberal approach to migration from Ukraine and Hong Kong).

In the longer run, there are some ways in which Brexit could boost productivity. It is fair to say that Classical Liberal economists are still split here. Some view the EU positively. Examples here include how the EU has curtailed intervention by national governments in regional trade, in the movement of capital, and in the flow of people, and how the creation of the euro has prevented countries that have adopted it from engaging in competitive devaluations. In principle at least, membership of the EU therefore involves states mutually restricting their powers – for mutual benefit.

There is clearly something in this. Many libertarians would have a favourable view of key aspects of how the EU works, including the free movement of goods and people within the bloc, the restrictions on state aid, and interventions to limit anti-competitive practices by multinational firms.

Other advantages of this 'pooling' of sovereignty might include the efficiency gains from coordinating rules and regulations, and an increase in bargaining power when negotiating free trade deals with the rest of the world.

But an alternative view is that the EU behaves like an 'overreaching superstate' in some areas and would like to be one in many others (including foreign and defence policy). Examples include an excessively cautious approach to regulation, notably in biosciences and AI, the follies of the Common Agricultural Policy, and the bias towards tax harmonisation. In short, EU membership adds yet another layer of government, with a unitary approach to both tax and regulation hampering constructive competition between nations.

Looking ahead, the crucial question is whether the UK will take advantage of its new freedoms to move in a more liberal direction. The UK government may have moved slowly but the direction of travel is clearly a more liberal one (at least in areas where policy was previously determined by the EU). Examples include the new system of agricultural subsidies (still too statist, but better than before) and the improvements to the regulation of the financial sector (including the so-called 'Edinburgh reforms'[6]).

The UK has also begun to sign new trade deals with third countries and to lower trade barriers unilaterally, for example by abolishing import tariffs on many products that the UK does not produce itself.

10.5.5 The UK Exposure to COVID-19 and the Energy Crisis

Finally, it is possible that the UK's economic growth and productivity were both hit relatively hard by the COVID-19 pandemic in 2020 and by the energy crisis that followed Russia's full-scale invasion of Ukraine in 2022. Two points in particular stand out in a comparison with the US.

First, the UK (like many other Western European economies) responded to the shock of the pandemic by protecting employment through a generous system of subsidies to keep people in their current jobs. (In the UK this was known as the 'Coronavirus Job Retention Scheme'.) This was at least a reasonable way to prevent the costs involved with businesses shutting down and then having to restart again (if they had not gone bust in the meantime). However, the US took an alternative approach, which was to subsidise household incomes rather than specific jobs. This led to a bigger spike in unemployment, but also resulted in a more efficient allocation of labour and capital to the most productive uses at the time and as the economy recovered from COVID-19.

The global energy crisis also had a more severe impact on the UK than the US, both because the US produces more of its own energy and because the UK has put more emphasis on promoting a 'net zero' agenda by setting high prices to encourage investment in renewables. This has added to the costs for households and businesses and discouraged investment.

The high fiscal costs of COVID-19 lockdowns and support with energy bills have also meant that the UK has seen the largest increase in the tax burden of any major economy (with the exception of Spain) between 2019 and 2024. This has been compounded by uncertainty about future tax policy, including changes of direction on both corporation tax and national insurance contributions, and frequent extensions to what was supposed to be a one-off 'windfall tax' on the profits of energy producers.

10.5.6 The US versus the UK

Summing up, there are a number of reasons why the US might have outperformed the UK (and other European countries) on both productivity and growth since the GFC, including a larger and more flexible financial sector; the adoption of policies during COVID-19 that encouraged the efficient reallocation of labour and capital; lower energy costs; and the earlier adoption of AI. But the recent outperformance of the US economy has also been flattered by the additional fiscal stimulus that is unlikely to be sustainable (or at least could not be replicated in other economies). It is also threatened by a lurch towards protectionism which could reduce productivity and raise inflation. From the UK perspective, the negative impact of both 'austerity' and 'Brexit' is generally exaggerated and dominated in any case by the impact of COVID-19, but it is important to acknowledge some ways in which they may have held back productivity too.

10.6 Conclusions: Market-Led Solutions to the Productivity Puzzle

A bigger state has actually contributed to the productivity slowdown, especially in the UK, rather than a further expansion of the state being an essential part of the solution. Indeed, the responses to the COVID-19 pandemic and then the energy global crisis have moved policymaking further away from the Classical Liberal ideal. The belief that the government will always 'have your back' runs directly counter to many key principles of Classical Liberalism. Joseph Schumpeter, who popularised the idea of 'creative disruption', wrote that "capitalism is by nature a form or method of economic change and not only never is, but need can be stationary" (Schumpeter, 1976), In contrast, the modern state seems determined to protect incumbents, with more regulation, more subsidies, and more planning.

What our analysis suggests is to revert to these basic principles, including: lower and simpler taxation, especially of investment; reforms of the tax and benefit system to make work and entrepreneurship pay; deregulation, such as liberalising planning rules and making it easier for private pensions to be invested in infrastructure; reducing barriers to international trade and cross-border investment; maintaining flexible policies on migration; market-based reforms of public services (notably the NHS in the UK); and the return of 'sound money', with central banks re-focused on monetary stability.

Above all, the Classical Liberal solution to the productivity puzzle would emphasise the role of free markets in encouraging innovation and the more efficient allocation of resources, including labour as well as capital.

Notes

1 'Externalities' are side-effects of an activity that are not directly reflected in the cost of that activity, such as the pollution that might result from driving a car.
2 'Public goods' are goods or services that are both *non-excludable* (people cannot be excluded from the benefits) and *non-rivalrous* (a benefit to one person does not reduce the benefit to others), such as national defence or flood protection.
3 Examples include the Global Financial Centres Index, available at https://www.longfinance.net/programmes/financial-centre-futures/global-financial-centres-index/, and the EY survey https://www.ey.com/en_uk/news/2023/06/uk-remains-europes-most-attractive-destination-for-financial-services-investment.
4 Indeed, the Greek economy was still 23% smaller at the end of 2023 than it was at the beginning of 2008 (Hellenic Statistical Authority, 2024).
5 The IMF expects the US government to continuing running large budget deficits for the foreseeable future, with the annual deficit still 6% of GDP in 2029. Gross government debt is then predicted to rise to 139% of GDP, compared to the global average of less than 100% (IMF, 2024b).
6 https://www.gov.uk/government/collections/financial-services-the-edinburgh-reforms.

References

Allen, R.C. (2011). *The Great Divergence*. Oxford: Oxford University Press.

Backhouse, R.E. and Boianovsky, M. (2016). 'Secular Stagnation: The History of a Macroeconomic Heresy'. *The European Journal of the History of Economic Thought*, 23(6), 946–970.

Baumol, W. (2012). *The Cost Disease; Why Computers Get Cheaper, and Healthcare Doesn't*. New Haven: Yale University Press.

Bean, C. (2016) "Independent review of UK economic statistics: final report". Available at https://assets.publishing.service.gov.uk/media/5a7f603440f0b62305b86c45/2904936_Bean_Review_Web_Accessible.pdf

Booth, P. and Zuluaga, D. (2018). *Socially Useless? The Crucial Contribution of Finance to Economic Life*. London: Institute of Economic Affairs.

Buchanan, J.M. and Tullock, G. (1962). 'The Calculus of Consent: Logical Foundations of Constitutional Democracy'. Available at https://oll.libertyfund.org/titles/buchanan-the-calculus-of-consent-logical-foundations-of-constitutional-democracy

Butler, E. (2015). *Classical Liberalism – A Primer*. London: Institute of Economic Affairs.

Butler, E. (2018). *An Introduction to Capitalism*. London: Institute of Economic Affairs.

Caballero, R.J., Hoshi, T. and Kashyap, A.K. (2008) '*Zombie Lending and Depressed Restructuring in Japan*'. *The American Economic Review*, Vol. 98, No. 5, pp. 1943–77.

Cazzaniga and others (2024). *Gen-AI: Artificial Intelligence and the Future of Work*. IMF Staff Discussion Note SDN2024/001, Washington, DC: International Monetary Fund.

Goldman Sachs (2023). 'AI may start to boost US GDP in 2027'. Available at https://www.goldmansachs.com/insights/articles/ai-may-start-to-boost-us-gdp-in-2027.

Gordon, R.J. (2012). 'Is U.S. Economic Growth Over? Faltering Innovation Confronts the Six Headwinds'. NBER Working Paper No. 18315.

Gordon, R.J. (2015). '*Secular Stagnation: A Supply-Side View*'. *American Economic Review*, 105(5), 54–59.

Hansen, A. (1939). "*Economic Progress and Declining Population Growth*'. *American Economic Review*, 29(1), 1–15.

Hayek, F.A. (1944). *The Road to Serfdom*. London: Routledge.

Hayek, F.A. (1960). *The Constitution of Liberty*. London: Routledge.

Haynes, M. (2020). *Productivity*. Newcastle, UK: Agenda Publishing.

Hellenic Statistical Authority (2024). 'Gross domestic product/4th Quarter 2023'. Available at https://www.statistics.gr/en/statistics/-/publication/SEL84/-
IMF (2024a). *World Economic Outlook – April 2024*. Chapter 3. International Monetary Fund, Washington, DC. Available at https://www.imf.org/en/Publications/WEO/Issues/2024/04/16/world-economic-outlook-april-2024
IMF (2024b). *Fiscal Monitor – Fiscal Policy in the Great Election Year*. International Monetary Fund, Washington, DC. Available at https://www.imf.org/en/Publications/FM/Issues/2024/04/17/fiscal-monitor-april-2024
Jackson, T. (2021). *Post Growth – Life after Capitalism*. Cambridge: Polity Press.
Keynes, J.M. (1936). *The General Theory of Employment, Interest and Money*. London: Palgrave Macmillan.
Kondratieff, N.D. and Stolper, W.F. (1935). '*The Long Waves in Economic Life*'. *The Review of Economics and Statistics*, 17(6), 105–115.
Krugman, P. (1994). *The Age of Diminished Expectations*. Cambridge: MIT Press.
Krugman, P. (2013). 'Bubbles, regulation, and secular stagnation'. The New York Times blog, 25 September 2013. Available at https://archive.nytimes.com/krugman.blogs.nytimes.com/2013/09/25/bubbles-regulation-and-secular-stagnation/#more-35680
Lagarde, C. (2024). 'Unlocking the power of ideas'. Speech by Christine Lagarde, President of the ECB, at Yale University (22 April 2024). Available at https://www.ecb.europa.eu/press/key/date/2024/html/ecb.sp240422~0f3299e7bb.en.html
Lucas, R. (2004). 'The industrial revolution: Past and future'. In 2003 Annual Report of the Federal Reserve Bank of Minneapolis (pp. 5–20).
Marx, K. (1867). 'Das Kapital'. Available at https://www.marxists.org/archive/marx/works/1867-c1/
Mazzucato, M. (2013). *The Entrepreneurial State*. London: Anthem Press.
Mazzucato, M. (2018). *The Value of Everything: Making and Taking in the Global Economy*. London: Penguin Books.
Mazzucato, M. (2021). *Mission Economy: A Moonshot Guide to Changing Capitalism*. New York: Harper Collins.
McAfee, A. (2019). *More from Less: The Surprising Story of How We Learned to Prosper Using Fewer Resources – And What Happens Next*. New York: Scribner.
McWilliams, D. (2016). *The Flat White Economy: How the Digital Economy Is Transforming London and Other Cities of the Future*. New York: Gerald Duckworth & Co Ltd.
Mill, J.S. (1848). 'Principles of Political Economy'. Available at https://oll.libertyfund.org/titles/mill-principles-of-political-economy-ashley-ed
Niemietz, K. (2019). *Socialism: The Failed Idea That Never Dies*. London: Institute of Economic Affairs.
OBR (2024). 'Economic and fiscal outlook – March 2024'. Pages 38–41. Available at https://obr.uk/efo/economic-and-fiscal-outlook-march-2024/
OECD (2024). *OECD Compendium of Productivity Indicators 2024*. Paris: OECD Publishing.
ONS (2024). 'Recent trends in UK trade volumes and balances: 2010 to 2023'. Available at https://www.ons.gov.uk/businessindustryandtrade/internationaltrade/articles/recenttrendsinuktradevolumesandbalances/2010to2024
Piketty, T. (2014a). *Capital in the Twenty-First Century*. Cambridge: Harvard University Press.
Piketty, T. (2014b). '*About Capital in the 21st Century*'. *American Economic Review*, 105(5), 48–53.
Ricardo, D. (1817). 'On the Principles of Political Economy and Taxation'. Available at https://www.econlib.org/library/Ricardo/ricP.html
Ridley, M. (2010). *The Rational Optimist – How Prosperity Evolves*. New York: Harper.
Royal Statistical Society (2019). 'The Royal Statistical Society announces its Statistics of the Decade'. Available at https://rss.org.uk/news-publication/news-publications/2019/general-news-(1)/rss-announces-statistics-of-the-decade/

Schumpeter, J.A. (1934). 'The Theory of Economic Development: An Inquiry into Profits, Capital, Credit, Interest, and the Business Cycle'. University of Illinois at Urbana-Champaign's Academy for Entrepreneurial Leadership Historical Research Reference in Entrepreneurship. Available at https://ssrn.com/abstract=1496199

Schumpeter, J.A. (1976). *Capitalism, Socialism and Democracy*, 3rd edition, London: George Allen and Unwin.

Shaxson, N. (2019). *The Finance Curse: How Global Finance Is Making Us All Poorer*. New York: Grove Press.

Smith, A. (1776) 'An Inquiry into the Nature and Causes of the Wealth of Nations'. Available at https://www.econlib.org/library/Smith/smWN.html

Summers, L. H. (2015). '*Have We Entered an Age of Secular Stagnation?*' IMF Fourteenth Annual Research Conference in Honor of Stanley Fischer, Washington, DC. *IMF Economic Review*, 63(1), 277–280.

Susskind, D. (2024). *Growth: A Reckoning*. London: Allen Lane.

Wennberg, K. and Sandström, C. (eds) (2022). *Questioning the Entrepreneurial State: Status-Quo, Pitfalls, and the Need for Credible Innovation Policy*. Berlin: Springer.

11 Liberalism and the Regulatory State

Cento Veljanovski

In this short chapter, I set out a classical liberal view of the role of the state and regulation. I use the term liberal in the English classical liberal sense rather than the corrupted progressive and libertarian senses as understood in the USA. Secondly, liberalism is a family of approaches which have evolved and differ (Fawcett 2014, Freeden 2015, Kahan 2023). Here I focus on what I term the "competitive liberalism" of Friedrich A. Hayek (1899–1992), a leading exponent of the Austrian School of economics.

I will show that while Hayek set out a coherent case for the superiority of the free market, his theory of state intervention and regulation is detached from his liberal theory and places insufficient constraints on the state's coercive powers. Nonetheless, important general principles can be extracted from Hayek's political theory to develop a Hayekian approach to regulation.

11.1 Background – The Rise of the Regulatory State

By the end of the First World War, *laissez-faire* liberalism no longer commanded wide political and intellectual support. In the ensuing collapse of the Weimar Republic, the 1929 Stock Market Crash, the Great Depression, the rise of National Socialism, of Bolshevism and WWII the world looked very grim. During the 1930s and 1940s some economic liberals such as Hayek replaced *laissez-faire* with competition as the basis of a liberal society.[1] However, the role they gave to the state and regulation differed considerably. John Maynard Keynes and William Beveridge, both liberals and contemporaries of Hayek, developed policies – Keynesianism and the welfare state respectively – which were greeted with horror by fellow liberals. Hayek, while often portrayed as a free market fundamentalist, most recently by Joseph Stiglitz (2024), assigned the state an active and "considerable" role. Others such as fellow Austrian School economists retained the *laissez-faire* view giving the state little more than a "night watchman" role.[2]

Hayek offered a distinctive approach to determining the boundary between the market and the state. He recognised that an appropriate legal framework was fundamental to the proper working of the free market and that the state could legitimately tax its citizens to finance a range of collective services and regulate to control externalities. Having accepted the case for "considerable" government

DOI: 10.4324/9781003504412-15

involvement Hayek sought to set out "the limits that a free society must place upon the coercive powers of government."

This task is just as urgent today. We are experiencing a cycle in which the demand and supply of regulation is growing rapidly. The rise of populism, nationalism, protectionism, industrial policies, identity politics, net zero, and related movements have spawned government policies which in large measure reflect a disdain for, and increasingly a rejection of, liberal values.[3] Whatever the purpose of regulation much impairs economic growth and individual liberties and is often "designed" to achieve laudable objectives with a disregard for their costs and effectiveness.[4] This is concerning since many economies are experiencing low economic growth and productivity which impinge on the ability to sustain regulatory burdens and social programmes.

11.2 Hayek's Competitive Order

Hayek's liberalism is based on economic precepts within an interdisciplinary analysis combining economics, law, history, cybernetics, cognitive science, and evolutionary theory. It is a grand theory filled with big ideas in the European tradition, mixing abstract normative and positive propositions about liberty, markets, laws, and politics.

Hayek's liberalism rests on several enduring insights, namely the "knowledge problem," competition as a "discovery procedure," the evolution of "spontaneous orders," and the rule of law.

11.2.1 Competition as a Discovery Procedure

Hayek's (1979: 68) fundamental insight is that competition is "a process in which people acquire and communicate knowledge." Markets, government, and the legal system all must deal with the "knowledge problem," and the way they deal with it determines their comparative efficiency and attractiveness (Hayek 1945a).[5]

The knowledge problem is much more than the usual claim that individuals are not perfectly informed or the existence of large asymmetric information costs or scientific knowledge. In a Hayekian world knowledge is the localised understanding of what Hayek (1948: 80) called "the particular circumstances of time and place" only known to each individual and dispersed among individuals. Such knowledge cannot be captured by statistical aggregates or "data."[6]

For Hayek (1967:88) "human intelligence is quite insufficient to comprehend the details of the complex human society, and it is the inadequacy of our reason to arrange in detail which forces us to be content with abstract rules." Knowledge emerges and is endogenously created by the market process and is often inarticulate and tacit. Indeed Hayek (1952) made original and early contributions to the theory of the mind (cognitive science) which underpins his political theory.

Unlike neoclassical economics which assumes that everyone knows everything (perfect information), individuals and firms in the market are ignorant of the circumstances surrounding the supply and demand of the goods and services they buy and sell, and the forces responsible for changing prices. Prices are informationally efficient in the comparative sense as the best available means for economising on and disseminating the dispersed knowledge and information on local conditions known only to each individual in the market. Individuals can then freely pursue their interests given the information conveyed by prices and the knowledge they possess and have acquired. As Hayek (1980 [1948]: 86) said: "[T]he most significant fact about this [market] system is the economy of knowledge with which it operates, or how little individual participants need to know in order to take the right action" Hayek likened it to a "system of telecommunications."

The radical nature of Hayek's view of competition has not been fully understood. Hayek turned the concept of competition on its head – a competitive market is a social organisation that efficiently deals with "irremediable ignorance." This is the opposite of the standard economics proposition which holds that consumer and producer ignorance causes market failure. For Hayek, the efficiency of markets does not rely on the assumption of perfect knowledge and economic rationality; it is free competition that creates the conditions for effective competition. Hayek deftly reversed causality in the way markets work, turning standard neoclassical assumptions of economic theory into outcomes of the competitive process. Hayek (1979: 75) rejected the assumption of individual rationality but not market rationality: "competition will make it necessary for people to act rationality to maintain themselves,"[7] and firms may not set out to maximise profits but only those that maximise profits survive under competition. It is competition that generates information and knowledge, creates a way of thinking among individuals, and leads to market rationality. Hayek's different approach may seem superficial since the conclusions are the same as neoclassical economic theory – competitive markets are efficient.

Free competition gives rise to a "spontaneous order" which coordinates buyers' and sellers' actions to produce an efficient outcome over time. By "order" Hayek meant "system" rather than some stable state of affairs, what today would be called an "ecosystem." Instead of decentralised decisions causing chaos, free competition generates a "spontaneous order" in which the expectations of buyers and sellers are rendered mutually compatible, and which adapts quickly to the continuous changes in circumstances and new information and allows for experimentation and entrepreneurship. "In the manner of Adam Smith's 'invisible hand': The whole acts as one market," says Hayek (1945a: 526), "not because any of its members survey the whole field, but because their limited individual fields of vision sufficiently overlap so that through many intermediaries the relevant information is communicated to all." While Adam Smith's invisible hand was guided by producers satisfying consumers' wants, Hayek's (1945a: 521) spontaneous order arises from markets making the "fuller use...of the existing knowledge" than any other system (Samuelson 1983).

Hayek (1945b: 45/6) tied liberty and the legal system to the knowledge problem. Liberty – defined as the absence of coercion or so-called "negative liberty" – in Hayek's schema is the ability to use one's knowledge and information for one's purpose. Free competition maximises the prospects of liberty.[8]

Many will be surprised to learn that Hayek's (2014: 386) intellectual case for the market, liberalism and economic freedom is not based on ideology or "ethical presuppositions" but ignorance:

> … the awareness of our irremediable ignorance of most of what is known to somebody is the chief basis of the argument for liberty. This is especially true in the economic field. If it appears that the market mechanism leads to the effective utilization of more knowledge than any directing agency can possess, this is the chief foundation of the case for economic freedom.

11.2.2 Appropriate Legal Framework

Hayek (1944: 39–40) stressed that the efficiency of free competition "depends above all on the existence of an appropriate legal system" which must be "intelligently designed and continuously adjusted." This "appropriate legal system" has several key features.

Hayek rejected the dichotomy between "law" and "market." Markets cannot function in the absence of private property and freedom of contract guaranteed by the state. Second the origins and nature of the legal framework matter. Hayek emphasised that laws are not exclusively handed down by the legislature. He distinguished between "grown" and "made" laws, i.e. those that evolved and those imposed by Parliament as regulation, respectively. Third, Hayek revitalised the rule of law as a limitation on the coercive powers of the state and as a method of distinguishing liberal from illiberal laws.

The proper functioning of a competitive market requires private property and freedom of contract. These should conform to David Hume's "three fundamental laws of nature, *that of stability of possession, of its transference by consent*, and *of the performance of promises*" (Hayek 1979: 40). However, private property – which Hayek confusingly calls "several property" – and freedom to contract cannot be absolute and unconstrained. Hayek recognised that private property is everywhere a bundle of rights, which depends on the state providing security for those rights and curtailing the exercise of private property where there are conflicting uses. As Hayek (1980 [1948] 113) put it: "We need only turn to the problems which arise in connection with land, particularly with regard to land in modern large towns, in order to realize that a conception of property which is based on the assumption that the use of a particular item of property affects only the interest of its owner breaks down."

Freedom of contract must also be constrained as "[N]o modern state has tried to enforce all contracts, nor is it desirable that it should. Contracts for criminal or immoral purposes, gambling contracts, contracts in restraint of trade, contracts permanently binding the services of a person or even some contracts for specific performances are not enforced" Hayek (1960: 230).

Hayek distinguished "law" from "legislation," calling them "grown" and "made" laws, respectively. Much legal theory treats the legislature as sovereign and as the sole authority for law. Hayek rejected this. Law can and does exist independently of the state. It can and does evolve from customary practices and experience enforced by judges. It is not planned or designed by humans "but the results of a process of evolution and selection, the distilled essence of experience of which ourselves have no knowledge."

Hayek regarded the English common law – which strictly means the law common to all subjects – as the embodiment of grown law.[9] Hayek (1979: 95) went as far as to describe the judge as "an institution of a spontaneous order" who decides cases based on "whether the conduct under dispute conformed to recognized rules." Irrespective of this caricature the judiciary is accepted, an independent judiciary is seen as an important bulwark against the encroachment of the state at least in common law countries and reinforces freedom in the market.

Hayek made both a normative claim and a positive factual claim about grown law. Normatively Hayek (1973: 94) treated judge-made law as "the law of liberty" and "just law." To this, he added the empirical claim that: "the ideal of individual liberty seems to have flourished chiefly among people where, at least for long periods, judge-made law predominated." Hayek believed, perhaps too optimistically and not without contradicting himself later, that the laws and institutions that survive are those that are the most "useful": "(N)o institution will continue to survive unless it performs some useful function" so that "the ineffective will be discarded and the effective retained." Hayek came very close to treating the survival of these laws and institutions as evidence of their moral superiority.[10]

Made law by which Hayek meant legislation, government regulation and code-based civil legal systems of the rest of Europe are designed by humans, and based on authority, coercion, purpose, and prescription. Hayek took a public choice position regarding the development of made law seeing it as inherently discriminatory and influenced by sectional interests or the majority democratic processes. He accepted and perhaps even foreshadowed the public choice view of regulation as largely driven by producer and sectional interests rather than the public interest (Stigler 1988). On the other hand, Hayek set out a normative public interest theory of regulation to define the role of the state in a free society.

11.2.3 The Rule of Law

To control the coercive powers of that state Hayek drew on the rule of law.[11] To Hayek (1960: 206) the rule of law was a "meta-legal doctrine or a political ideal" to protect individuals from the discriminatory and arbitrary coercive powers of the state. In an early analysis Hayek (1944: 54) defined the rule of law thus:

> Stripped of all the technicalities this means that government in all its actions is bound by rules fixed and announced beforehand – rules which make it possible to foresee with fair certainly how the authority will use its coercive powers in given circumstances, and to plan one's individual affairs on the basis of this knowledge.

The rule of law has three core attributes: "generality, equality, and certainty" (Hayek 1960 [2011]: 315/17) expressed through "general abstract rules" universally applied so that individuals can predict whether and how the law affects them. As Hayek (1960, 153) put it:

> The conception of freedom under the law … rests on the contention that when we obey laws, in the sense of general abstract rules laid down irrespective of their application to us, we are not subject to another man's will and are therefore free. It is because the lawgiver does not know the particular cases to which his rules apply, and it is because the judge who applies them has no choice in drawing the conclusions that follow from the existing body of rules and the particular facts of the case, that it can be said that laws and not men rule.

Hayek (1967: 80) tied the necessity of general abstract rules under the rule of law to the knowledge problem:

> It is, in other words, our restricted horizon of knowledge of the concrete facts which makes it necessary to coordinate our actions by submitting to abstract rules rather than to attempt to decide each particular case solely in view of the limited set of relevant particular facts which we happen to know.

The rule of law also entails the separation of powers; an independent judiciary, full judicial review of administrative and executive discretion where it affects individual liberty, and full compensation where individual rights are expropriated to ensure that the public benefits exceed private losses.

11.3 Hayek's Framework Applied to Regulation

Hayek claimed that the rule of law "provides the criterion which enables us to distinguish between those measures which are and those which are not compatible with a free system". It does not exclude all "general regulations of economic activity," but only those that involve arbitrary discrimination. While some state interventions can be justified on grounds of "economic expediency" (see below), others presumptively "run counter to the very principle on which a free system rests and which must therefore all together be excluded if such a system is to work" (Hayek 1960: 331). Specifically measures that "involve arbitrary discrimination between persons" including "decisions as to who is to be allowed to provide different services or commodities, at what prices or in what quantities – in other words, measures designed to control the access to different trades and occupations, the terms of sale, and the amounts to be produced or sold." "All forms of licenses, permits, allocations and price fixing would be impossible since all these methods imply that the government has to decide who gets what." The same for quotas, subsidies, and tariffs. As Hayek (2022 [1950]: 122) put it "direct controls which necessarily involve discrimination between persons, should be ruled out of court once and for all." Government cannot direct the means of production towards particular ends only "the conditions under which the available resources may be used". That is interferences with the price system are presumptively incompatible with the rule of law and hence illiberal.

Hayek (1947) recognised "that, in order to make efficient use of the means at its disposal, the government must exercise a great deal of discretion." To control this discretion Hayek (1960: 221) proposed that government actions "must be examined in each instance from the viewpoint of expediency." Expediency "is a test of whether discretionary actions are efficient in reaching their objectives; and economic analysis, especially the weighing of costs and benefits, is crucial in making such judgements" Hayek (1960: 213). As Hayek (1960: 222) states, where "the government merely undertakes to supply services which otherwise would not be supplied at all … the only question which arises is whether the benefits outweigh the costs." Hayek (1944: 80) saw the state as a "piece of utilitarian machinery."

More controversially Hayek (1960: 231/2) considered social justice and wealth (re)distribution as inherently discriminatory and incompatible with the rule of law: "Distributive justice requires an allocation of all resources by a central authority; it requires that people be told what to do and what ends to serve."

11.4 Competition Policy and Antitrust

The first duty of Government was deregulatory – to ensure that the government was not responsible for the creation and preservation of monopolies either directly or through laws that gave monopolists privileged positions. Hayek (1944: 203) believed that "[P]rivate monopoly is scarcely ever complete and even more rarely of long duration or able to disregard potential competition." He (Hayek 1978 [1973]: 145) supported "particular rules which favour the preservation of competition and restrain, so far as possible, the development of monopolistic positions." He opposed tariffs, subsidies, and intellectual property rights (patents, copyrights, and trademarks), which he saw as monopoly rights, and regarded company law as artificially extending firm size (see Veljanovski 2021, 2023). Where the Government produced goods and services "it must make the services available to all and not forcibly monopolise their provision or enjoy any special advantage in offering them." To Hayek (1960: 224) "what is objectionable … is not state enterprise as such but state monopoly." Further "any special advantages, including subsidies, which government gives to its own enterprises in any field, should also be made available to competing private agencies."

Hayek proposed a limited antitrust law which would make agreements in restraint of trade unenforceable and prohibit "bad" price discrimination, i.e. discrimination designed to exclude potential competitors. These laws would be enforced by the "potential competitors" harmed by these prohibited actions incentivised by the award of multiple damages and contingency fees paid to their lawyers (Veljanovski 2023, 2024).

11.5 The Positive Functions of the State

Hayek (1948:22) proposed that: "The state … ought to be only a small part of the much richer organism which we call society … the former ought to provide merely a framework within which free (and therefore not 'consciously directed') collaboration of men has the maximum scope." Hayek expressed this proposition many times, but his political theory of the state envisaged a much wider role.[12] Hayek (1960: 231) claimed that "the range and variety of government action that is, at least in principle, reconcilable with a free system is … considerable."[13] This includes the supply of collective goods and extensive intervention in the provision of education, health and safety regulation, social security measures, and so on.

Like most liberals, Hayek adopted Adam Smith's three legitimate functions for government – defence, the administration of justice, and the provision of public goods. These interventions were to be "determined chiefly by considerations of efficiency and expediency rather than justice" and satisfy at least three principles (Hayek 1973: 14):

> I am the last person to deny that increased wealth and the increased density of population have enlarged the number of collective needs which government can and should satisfy. Such government services are entirely compatible with liberal principles so long as,
>
> *firstly,* government does not claim a monopoly and new methods of rendering services through the market (e.g., in some now covered by social insurance) are not prevented.
>
> *secondly,* the means are raised by taxation on uniform principles and taxation is not used as an instrument for the redistribution of income; and,
>
> *thirdly*, the wants satisfied are collective wants of the community as a whole and not merely collective wants of particular groups.

Note that here Hayek is recognising that there is a legitimate dynamic to the growth of regulation.

Hayek (1944: 87) set out the main justification for his approach to regulation which as would be expected was tied to the failure of the price system to take proper account of social costs:

> There are, finally, undoubted fields where no legal arrangements can create the main condition on which the usefulness of the system of competition and private property depends: namely, that the owner benefits from all the useful services rendered by his property and suffers for all the damages caused to others by its use. Where, for example, it is impracticable to make the enjoyment of certain services dependent on the payment of a price, competition will not produce the services; and the price system becomes similarly ineffective when the damage caused to others by certain uses of property cannot be effectively charged to the owner of that property. In all these instances there is a divergence between the items which enter into private calculation and those which

> affect social welfare; and, whenever this divergence becomes important, some method other than competition must have to be found to supply the services in question. Thus neither the provision of signposts on the road nor, in most circumstances, those of the roads themselves can be paid for by each individual user. Nor can certain harmful effects of deforestation, of some methods of farming, or of the smoke and noise of factories, be confined to the owner of the property in question or to those who are willing to submit to the damage for an agreed compensation. In such instances we must find some substitute for the regulation by the price mechanism. But the fact that we have to resort to the substitution of direct regulation by authority where the conditions for the proper working of competition cannot be created, does not prove that we should suppress competition where it can be made to function.

Hayek (1979: 41) accepted that the state could legitimately exercise its coercive powers to raise "funds by taxation to provide services which for various reasons cannot be provided, or cannot be provided adequately, by the market." The resulting taxes must be uniform and not used to redistribute wealth. They should fund the provision of collective goods such as sanitary and health services, road construction and maintenance (except long-distance toll roads), urban amenities, and public works leaving their production and provision to private competitive entities where possible. The justification for government provision is that because collective goods once produced are available to all at zero marginal costs, it is either impossible or prohibitively costly to exclude non-payers.

To align the demand for and supply of collective goods Hayek (1979: 45/6) proposed that their provision should be delegated to local agencies "as the best way of ensuring that the burdens of and benefits from government action will be approximately proportional." Where possible the services should be provided by "competitive enterprises," not monopolised or otherwise interfere with the spontaneous market order. Hayek also briefly discussed what he called the "independent" sector principally local charitable or private institutions that provide collective goods either free or which can be priced such as hospitals, libraries, theatres, museums, and parks.

Hayek (1960: 341) recognised the need to deal with externalities and "neighbourhood effects" where "the costs involved in large numbers living in great density are not only high but to a large extent …do not fall … on those that cause them. The latter called for intervention "capable of better managing these "neighbourhood effects." Hayek (1960: 375) supported the expropriation of property at fair market value to provide such amenities as parks and recreation "so long as the community approves this in full awareness of the costs and alternatives."[14]

To Hayek (1944: 87) "an extensive system of social service" is compatible with a free market "so long as the organization of these services is not designed in such way as to make competition ineffective over wide fields." These included means-tested guaranteed minimum income and "[C]ompulsory insurance to provide for the extreme needs of old age, unemployment, sickness, etc., irrespective of whether the individuals could and ought to have made provision themselves" (Hayek 1960: 427). His support for these was not based on a concern for the disadvantaged but to relieve the public from the burden of dealing with the uninsured and to protect the competitive order from any hostility from those less well off.

Hayek (1960: 377) supported compulsory education to a minimum standard because, aside from its contribution to democratic governance, "all of us will be exposed to less risks and will receive more benefits from our fellows if they share with us certain basic knowledge and beliefs." He endorsed Milton Friedman's (1955) vouchers scheme.

Hayek (1960: 224/5, 1979: Ch 14) saw considerable regulation as compatible with a free society. These included regulation of the production and sale of phosphorus matches, building regulations, pure food standards, the certification of the professions, restrictions on the sale of certain arms, explosives, poisons and drugs, and "regulations for the processes of production and the provision of such public institutions as theatres, sports grounds, etc.," the "setting of standards of weights and measures; information gathered from surveying, land registration, statistics, etc." The "appropriateness of such measures must be judged by comparing the overall costs with the gain" and be subject to judicial review.

Hayek believed the state should have "far-reaching discretionary powers" and be exempt from the rule of law to deal with national security, internal insurrection, and natural disasters such as storms, floods, earthquakes, epidemics, avalanches, the spread of contagious disease, and fire. More controversially he supported compulsory universal military conscription because it was non-discriminatory and hence did not violate the rule of law.

11.6 Hayek's Constraint Will Not Control the Regulatory State

It will come as no surprise that Hayek's ambitious attempt to set out a comprehensive political economy of liberalism would have gaps and inconsistencies. It evolved over many decades against the background of a radically changing world, and it often lacks detail being at a general abstract level. Nonetheless, Hayek's approach to the positive role of Government and regulation was very different from his theory of markets – it is ad hoc and utilitarian – and his claim that the rule of law and cost-benefit analysis (CBA) would act as effective checks on the growth of regulation is overly optimistic.

First, Hayek's normative theory of regulation endorses the market failure framework (Bator 1958). Yet the market failure approach has routinely been used to justify wide-ranging technocratic interventions many of which he would consider illiberal (Spulber 2002). As Milton Friedman (1976) observed the public goods concept "can be used to justify a completely unlimited extension of government." The same can be said of externalities as pointed out by Ronald Coase (1960). Notwithstanding Hayek proposed a comparative institutions approach (Demsetz 1969) that took into account regulatory failure and costs which even today economists fail to do.

Yet Hayek never bothered to set out the details and practicalities of his numerous regulatory proposals. Indeed, it would be fair to say that many were no more than plausible responses to ill-defined market failures. For example, he advocated town planning to deal with "neighbourhood effects" without recognising that in practice planning laws restrict housing construction and interfere with the pricing system thereby creating shortages of housing and rented accommodation. His support for Government crisis management while plausible looks dubious following the COVID-19 pandemic lockdowns and responses. He supported universal military conscription because it was non-discriminatory and therefore consistent with the rule of law, whereas most liberals would advocate a voluntary army as more liberal and efficient.

But of more significance, Hayek did not address how the state is to overcome the knowledge problem that lies at the heart of his liberalism. Enumerating the areas for legitimate regulation does not provide practical guidance on the appropriate type and volume of regulation and collective goods. Hayek's powerful criticism that planners cannot obtain the knowledge necessary to simulate market outcomes applies equally to regulations designed to plug the gaps in the market economy. Bureaucrats and regulators do not have the knowledge,[15] do not have appropriate incentives to collect and faithfully analyse the necessary knowledge and information, and the regulatory process lacks an effective corrective, endogenous, and adaptive "discovery procedure" that would lead to liberal or efficient regulation.

Hayek's proposed "test of expediency" fails to address the problem. CBA is a "planning" technique not a solution to the knowledge problem nor an effective means of controlling bureaucratic discretion. It requires bureaucrats to collect and analyse information on costs, benefits, impacts and the secondary, often offsetting, effects. This knowledge is not available or known to politicians and bureaucrats. But more critically it is distorted and corrupted by partisan politics and bureaucratic processes to rationalise politically favoured policies. The public discretion that Hayek believed CBA would control will in practice subvert a CBA into a box-ticking exercise to justify favoured policies.

These are more than academic criticisms. CBA as a regulatory "tool" has been around since the 1980s when the Reagan Administration used it to freeze the growth of regulation (Baldwin and Veljanovski 1984) and has grown in popularity ever since.[16] It is a feature of the UK and EU regulatory systems, yet every detailed assessment of these regulatory impact assessments shows that not only do they fail to lead to better regulation but do not take proper account of the cost of regulation (e.g. Clougherty and Colville 2024).

Hayek's other claim that the rule of law places an effective constraint on the growth of (bad) regulation and the coercive powers of Government can be doubted. There is no doubt that the rule of law is essential for a liberal society and that it prevents discriminatory laws including those which interfere with the pricing system. Compared to a society where it does not exist it massively increases liberty and restricts the coercive powers of government. But in liberal democratic countries, it has not led to better regulation nor prevented illiberal interventions such as rent and price controls, tariffs and direct interference with the operation of the market. And indeed, by invoking the test of expediency Hayek accepted that the rule of law and evolutionary process were inadequate to support a free society. This is even before considering whether proposed regulations were designed to favour producer and sectional interests.

11.7 Return to the Common Law?

Following the UK's exit from the European Union, there was an attempt to distinguish future UK regulation from that of the European Community. *The Taskforce on Innovation, Growth and Regulatory Reform* (TIGRR Report) published in May 2021 proposed a "common law approach" to regulation. This has a Hayekian ring to it as consistent with his spontaneous order theory of liberalism and so warrants brief comment.

Recall that Hayek claimed that the common law evolved to maximise economic growth and liberty. There is evidence from the extensive empirical research on legal origins to support this claim (La Porta et al. 2008). But the common law at its apogee in England in the 1890s reflected *laissez-faire* liberalism which Hayek disparaged. What is Hayekian about the common law is that historically the common law judges were at the forefront of curtailing the coercive and monopolistic activities of the state. However, in the process, they gave Parliament absolute sovereignty over the growth of regulation.

The attempt to draw a stark contrast between the common and statutory laws is exaggerated. The common law – the term meaning no more than the law common to all in England – is as much a product of the state as it is of judges' decisions and legal precedent. Government regulation has existed as long as civil society and well before the common law. But more particularly the English common law is a product of the "State" (i.e. Monarchs starting with King Henry II) which integrated the different legal systems of England and brought the courts under state control during the Middle Ages. Hayek appreciated that the common law was not perfect nor efficient and would require legislative correction. This is because it could be slow to adapt to changing circumstances and/or become distorted by sectional and class interests including the prejudices of judges (Hayek 1973: 88). Hayek, like Adam Smith, did not regard the legislative correction of the common law by rules applied equally to all as government interference. This is not to detract from its attractive features of privatised enforcement, fact-based decision-making, and open-ended general principles that are often more attuned to economic reality than statutory law.

The evolutionary nature of the common law is however somewhat illusory. Hayek confused the English common law with customary law that developed in Anglo-Saxon times. The two are very different, and there is no presumption in the common law that custom is efficient. But of more significance, there is no "discovery procedure" governing the development of the common law similar to that of the market. In particular, there is no competitive supply of laws as the common law courts are monopoly state institutions which were "nationalised" by the King and Parliament centuries ago (Veljanovski 2008).

The TIGRR Report proposed to replace what it described as the EU legal "straitjacket" of prescriptive and restrictive codified law with a "modern, agile and effective approach to regulation," guided by the principle of proportionality not the EU "precautionary principle,"[17] and a "[R]eliance on case law … to regain the benefits of precedent-based, incremental regulation making." This proposed "new" approach was rich in adjectives – "simple," "agile," "proportionate," "adaptable," "forward looking," "outcome-focussed," "collaborative," "experimental," and "responsive" regulation – but low on its understanding of the common law.

The TIGGR Report's vision of post-Brexit has little to do with the common law (nor was it ever adopted). It claimed that the "common law approach allows more forward-looking, judgement-based regulation without needing … complex and exhaustive rules for every situation set out in advance." The common law is not forward looking; its backward looking resolving disputes about conflicts and breaches of the law that have already occurred. And while it is judgment-based (without an "e") and does not set out exhaustive and prescriptive regulation it is certainly not agile. But critically the proposed common law approach would proceed without a missing essential element. The then Conservative government regarded the judiciary as meddlesome activists usurping the will of Parliament by which it meant the executive. The TIGRR Report wanted regulation based on "case law and precedent" but without interference by the courts and judges. It is proposed to give the regulators and bureaucrats (the executive) vast discretion to invent and apply the law with no protections for individuals and firms, no appeal process, and no immediate constraints on the regulators' discretion. The control was to come from a parliamentary committee, in a committee system already weakened by the then Government, leaving the executive answerable only to itself.

11.8 Concluding Remarks: An Effective Set of Constraints on an Ever-Growing Regulatory State?

Hayek's central tenet is to "make(s) as much use as possible of the spontaneous forces of society, and resort as little as possible to coercion." These spontaneous forces are to operate within the "rules of the game" set by grown law augmented where necessary by regulation and taxation to fund a range of collective goods. Regulation should not impair the competitive process and should not interfere with the market process by directly controlling prices (such as rent and price controls) or directing resources or any protective measures such as tariffs, subsidies, and industrial policies, erecting barriers to potential competitors or confer government privileges. Any legal privileges given to trade unions or associations that enable anti-competitive behaviour should be removed. Where regulation is warranted, it should be in the form of abstract general rule applied equally to all and subject to the test of expediency to ensure that the benefits exceed the costs and to control the discretion of public officials.

Yet the technocratic constraints that Hayek proposed to control and guide the regulatory process – equality before the law and CBA – are manipulable and do not deal with the knowledge problem central to Hayek's liberalism. That is why Hayek (1973: 93) ultimately appealed to "community opinion": "[I]n a free society in which power rest on opinion, this ultimate power will be the power which deters nothing directly yet controls all positive power by tolerating only certain kinds of exercise of that power." This "opinion" is seen to come from society's "common cultural" view of what is right and wrong. These cultural values are however not external to the evolutionary process, but part of it.

The appeal to cultural values reveals an unresolved tension in Hayek's political economy of a just society. Hayek did not believe that liberalism was a natural philosophy or ideology; the way the free markets generated massive benefits was not understood, and their very success bred disdain for competition and pressures for more regulation. The implication is that for liberalism to survive and influence public policy politicians and the public must hold liberal views. If they do not and do not understand the nature of the competitive order, then technocratic attempts to control the growth of regulation will fail.

Hayekian liberals, and liberals generally, face a paradox – liberalism's success threatens the "extended order" and brings into place pressures for greater state intervention and policies that undermine market forces. Hayek's answer is not to wait for the spontaneous order to reject erroneous beliefs but for an intellectual elite who understands his political economy to engage in a constant "battle of ideas" to explain why the market is the best guarantee of freedom. But perhaps the better explanation is that societies swing between liberalism and socialism broadly defined in reaction to the prevailing inefficiencies or inequalities that each brings about. In this regard, one can have sympathy with Acemoglu and Robinson's (2019) thesis that liberty needs a strong state and a strong market as it operates in a "narrow corridor" between state despotism and *laissez-faire* capitalism. Hayek, I believe would agree.

Notes

1 Hayek's liberalism is in the tradition of Bernard Mandeville (1714) and Adam Smith (1776) and joined by liberal economists such as Henry Simons (1934), Lionel Robbins (1937), Walter Lippmann (1937), Karl Polyani (1944) and the early views of Milton Friedman (1951). Friedman (1962) and the Chicago School later became sceptical about the role and effects of government moving to a more libertarian position (see Jones 2012).

2 The Austrian School of Economics was founded by Karl Menger and Ludwig von Mises (1949). Hayek broke from his fellow Austrian economists who retained their *laissez-faire* position (e.g. Rothbard 1970).

3 Funke, Schularick, and Trebesch (2023) estimate that populist rule lowered per capita GDP by 10 per cent compared to non-populist rule.

4 Crain and Crain (2023) estimate that the costs of compliance with US Federal Government regulation run at around 12% of US GDP. Coffey, McLaughlin, and Peretto (2020) using data for 22 US industries over 35 years (1977–2012) estimated that regulatory restrictions had dampened GDP growth by around 0.8% since 1980 and absent these restrictions the economy would have been 25 per cent larger in 2012. Also, Broughel and Hahn (2022).

5 The New Institutional Economics kick started by Oliver Williamson's (1985) builds on the insights of Hayek (1945a), Simon (1982) and Coase (1960).

6 The approach differs from Stigler's (1961) information economics which adopts a rational marginal analysis to search and information gathering.

7 See Becker (1962) for an explanation of how individual irrational behaviour can lead to market rationality, and Alchian (1950) on firm survivorship under conditions of uncertainty.

8 See Hayek (1966, 1978 [1973]) for his views on liberalism.

9 Hayek was influenced by Bruno Leoni (1961).
10 Hayek (1960: 36): "[A]ll that we know is that the ultimate decision about what is good or bad will be made not by individual human wisdom but by the decline of the groups that have adhered to the 'wrong' beliefs."
11 The legal philosopher Joseph Raz (2012) states that "F.A. Hayek has provided one of the clearest and most powerful formulations of the rule of law."
12 Hayek (1973: 33): "Liberalism … restricts deliberate control of the overall order of society to the enforcement of such general rules as are necessary for the formation of a spontaneous order, the details of which we cannot foresee."
13 Hayek (1960: 220): "[F]reedom of economic activity had meant freedom under the law, not the absence of all government action."
14 On the exploitation of natural resources Hayek's (1960: 321) claims without explanation that: "[I]t cannot be denied that there are some facts concerning probable developments which the government is more likely to know than most of the individual owners of natural resources."
15 Hayek (1979: 85) rejected the public enforcement of antitrust laws on these grounds: "[T]he knowledge required … in order to prosecute successfully is not the kind of knowledge that any authority is likely to possess."
16 Governments across the world have tried to control the growth of regulation by requiring CBAs and similar techniques. See for example the European Commission (2017) 's *Better Regulation Guidelines* (SWD 2017, 250 final) and the better regulation toolbox available at https://ec.europa.eu/info/files/betterregulation-toolbox.
17 Ironically the TIGRR Report proposes that the EU "precautionary principle" be replaced with the "proportionality principle." However, both these are EU principles imported into UK law. The proportionality principle is a key feature of EU law (Article 5 TFEU), and a key aspect of the UK judicial review of Executive actions.

References

Acemoglu, Daron and James A. Robinson. (2019) *The Narrow Corridor: States, Societies, and the Fate of Liberty*. London: Penguin.

Alchian, Armen A. (1950) Uncertainty, Evolution and Economic Theory. *Journal of Political Economy* 58(3): 211–221.

Baldwin, Robert and Cento Veljanovski. (1984) Regulation by Cost-Benefit Analysis. *Public Administration* 62: 51–69.

Bator, Francis M. (1958) The Anatomy of Market Failure. *Quarterly Journal of Economics* 72(3): 351–379.

Becker, Gary. (1962) Irrational Behavior and Economic Theory. *Journal of Political Economy* 70(1): 1–13.

Broughel, James and Robert W. Hahn. (2022) The Impact of Economic Regulation on Growth: Survey and Synthesis. *Regulation & Governance* 16(1): 448–469.

Clougherty, Tom and Robert Colville. (2024) *The Future of Regulation*. London: Centre of Policy Studies.

Coase, Ronald H. (1960) The Problem of Social Costs. *Journal of Law & Economics* 3: 1–55.

Coffey, Bentley, Patrick A. McLaughlin and Pietro Peretto. (2020) The Cumulative Cost of Regulations. *Review of Economic Dynamics* 38: 1–21.

Crain, Nicole V. and W. Mark Crain. (2023) The Cost of Federal Regulation to the U.S. Economy, Manufacturing and Small Business, A Study Conducted for the National Association of Manufacturers. https://nam.org/wp-content/uploads/2023/11/NAM-3731-Crains-Study-R3-V2-FIN.pdf

Demsetz, Harold. (1969) Information and Efficiency: Another Viewpoint. *The Journal of Law & Economics* 12(1): 1–22.

European Commission (2017) *Better Regulation Guidelines* (SWD 2017, 250 final), Brussels: European Commission.
Fawcett, Edmund. (2014) *Liberalism – The Life of an Idea*. Princeton: Princeton University Press.
Freeden, Michael. (2015) *Liberalism – A Very Short Introduction*. Oxford: Oxford University Press.
Friedman, Milton. (1951) Neo-Liberalism and Its Prospects. *Farmand*, 17 February: 89–93.
Friedman, Milton. (1955) The Role of Government in Education. In Robert Solo ed. *Economics and the Public Interest*. New Brunswick: Rutgers University Press.
Friedman, Milton. (1962) *Capitalism and Freedom*. Chicago: University Chicago Press.
Friedman, Milton. (1976) Adam Smith's Relevance for 1976. Selected Papers No. 50 Graduate School of Business, The University of Chicago. https://www.chicagobooth.edu/~/media/9535E51706DF4136AB8ED7B59A873A57.PDF
Funke, Manuel, Moritz Schularick and Christoph Trebesch. (2023) Populist Leaders and the Economy. *American Economic Review* 113(12): 3249–3288.
Hayek, Friedrich A. (1944) *Road to Serfdom*. London: George Routledge & Sons.
Hayek, Friedrich A. (1945a) The Use of Knowledge in Society. *American Economic Review* 35(4): 519–30.
Hayek, Friedrich A. (2010) [1945b] The Road to Serfdom. *Readers Digest*. April. Reprinted London: Institute of Economic Affairs.
Hayek, Friedrich A. (1948) [1947] "Free" Enterprise and Competitive Order. In F.A. Hayek ed. *Individualism and Economic Order*. Chicago: University of Chicago Press.
Hayek, Friedrich A. (1948) The Meaning of Competition. In F.A. Hayek ed. *Individualism and Economic Order*. Chicago: University of Chicago.
Hayek, Friedrich A. (2022) [1950] The Meaning of Government Interference. In Paul Lewis ed. *The Collected Works of F.A. Hayek Volume 18 – Essays on Liberalism and the Economy*. London: Routledge.
Hayek, Friedrich A. (1952) *The Sensory Order – An Inquiry into the Foundations of Theoretical Psychology*. Chicago: University of Chicago Press.
Hayek, Friedrich A. (1960) *The Constitution of Liberty*. London: Routledge & Kegan Paul.
Hayek, Fredrich A. (1966) The Principles of a Liberal Social Order. *Il Politico* 31(4): 601–618.
Hayek, Fredrich A. (1967) Rules, Perception and Intelligibility. In F.A. Hayek ed. *Studies in Philosophy, Politics and Economics*. London: Routledge & Kegan Paul.
Hayek, Friedrich A. (1973) *Law, Legislation and Liberty: A New Statement of the Liberal Principles of Justice and Political Economy – Rules and Order* Vol. 1. London: Routledge & Kegan Paul.
Hayek, Friedrich A. (1978) [1973] Liberalism. In F.A. Hayek ed. *New Studies in Philosophy Politics, Economics, and the History of Ideas*. London: Routledge Kegan Paul.
Hayek, Friedrich A. (1979) *Law, Legislation and Liberty: A New Statement of the Liberal Principles of Justice and Political Economy – The Political Order of a Free People* Vol. 3. London: Routledge & Kegan Paul.
Hayek, Friedrich A. (2014) *The Market and Other Orders*. In Bruce Caldwell ed. *The Collected Works of F.A. Hayek*. Vol 15. London: Routledge.
Jones, Daniel S. (2012) *Masters of the Universe – Hayek, Friedman, and the Birth of Neoliberal Politics*. Princeton: Princeton University Press.
Kahan, Alan S. (2023) *Freedom from Fear*. Princeton: Princeton University Press.
La Porta, Rafael, Florencio Lopez-de-Silanes and Andrei Shleifer. (2008) The Economic Consequences of Legal Origins. *Journal of Economic Literature* 46(2): 285–332.
Leoni, Bruno. (1961) *Freedom and the Law*. Princeton: D. Van Nostrand Co.
Lippmann, Walter. (1937) *An Inquiry into the Principles of the Good Society*. Boston: Little Brown.
Mandeville, Bernard. (1714) *The Fable of the Bees: Or Private Vices Public Benefits*. Oxford: The Clarendon Press.

Mises, Ludwig von. (1949) *Human Action: A Treatise on Economics*. New Haven: Yale University Press.
Polyani, Karl. (1944) *The Great Transformation – The Political and Economic Origins of Our Time*. Boston: Beacon Press.
Raz, Joseph. (2012) *The Authority of Law: Essays on Law and Morality*. Oxford: Oxford University Press.
Robbins, Lionel. (1937) *Economic Planning and International Order*. London: Macmillan.
Rothbard, Murray. (1970) *Power and Market: Government and the Economy*. Menlo Park: Institute of Humane Studies.
Samuelson, Paul A. (1983) My Life Philosophy. *American Economist* 27: 5–12.
Simon, Herbert. (1982) *Models of Bounded Rationality* Cambridge. MIT Press.
Simons, Henry. (1934) *A Positive Program for Laissez Faire: Some Proposals for a Liberal Economic Policy*. Chicago: University of Chicago Press.
Smith, Adam. (1776) *An Inquiry into the Nature and Causes of the Wealth of Nations*. London: Strahan & Cadell.
Spulber, Daniel F. (2002) *Famous Fables of Economics – Myths of Market Failure*. Oxford: Basil Blackwell.
Stigler, George. (1961) The Economics of Information. *Journal of Political Economy* 69: 213–225.
Stigler, George J. (1988) *Chicago Studies in Political Economy*. Chicago: Chicago University Press.
Stiglitz, Joseph E. (2024) *The Road To Freedom*. London: Allen Lane.
Veljanovski, Cento. (2008) The Common Law and Wealth. In Stephen F. Copp ed. *The Legal Foundations of Free Markets*. London: Institute of Economic Affairs.
Veljanovski, Cento. (2021) Hayek on Competition and Antitrust in a Digital Age. In Victoria V. Hewson ed. *The Meaning of Competition in a Digital Age*. London: Institute of Economic Affairs.
Veljanovski, Cento. (2023) *Hayek on Competition – A Liberal Antitrust for a Digital Age?* The new Hobart Papers No. 1. London: Institute of Economic Affairs.
Veljanovski, Cento. (2024) Hayekian Competition Policy – A Historical Perspective. Paper delivered to The Royal Economic Society 2024 Annual Conference, Belfast. https://papers.ssrn.com/sol3/papers.cfm?abstract_id=4773219
Williamson, Oliver E. (1985) *The Economic Institutions of Capitalism*. New York: The Free Press.

12 Minerva in the Low Countries

Order and Prosperity in a Free Society

Forrest Capie and Geoffrey Wood

12.1 Introduction: Financial Development and Economic Growth

In the Musee de l'Hospice in Lille in northern France, there is a small painting. It is an oil on wood, painted in 1607 in Amsterdam. In English its title is "Minerva restraining the Government". An English translation of the text interpreting the picture is as follows:

> Minerva, although a warrior, symbolises wisdom, military strategy, arts and crafts. Seated, she is restraining a draped young woman wearing a tiara, the symbol of the Government. This allegory invites us to be wise and reasonable and avoid any precipitous action.

This paper is in effect a development, a more lengthy exposition, of the allegory. We consider how best a government can be constrained to allow freedom for individuals, while having the minimal, rarely changed and only after deliberation and avoidance of "precipitous action" set of laws needed for an efficiently functioning society.

That statement itself requires development. The freedom we have in mind is the freedom for individuals to do as they wish subject not to harming others, and with the objective of promoting economic growth over the long term, as such growth expands the range of choice in which individuals can do as they wish subject to not harming others.

Since we are concerned with encouraging economic growth, we focus first on how firms should be constrained in what they do and how they do it. We therefore contrast governance and regulation in that context. Then we turn to the role of law.

Our argument applies across the social, political, and economic spectrum. But within the economic sphere we argue it has particular importance in finance.

The study of the relationship between finance and economic development goes back a long way, certainly to the nineteenth century. But it has re-emerged in more recent times. In a summarising statement Ross Levine wrote, "Although conclusions must be stated hesitantly and with ample qualifications, the preponderance of theoretical reasoning and empirical evidence suggests a positive, first order relationship between financial development and economic growth. … There is even evidence that the level of financial development is a good predictor of future rates of economic growth" (JEL, 1997 pp. 688,9) This has been widely endorsed by

DOI: 10.4324/9781003504412-16

both economists and economic historians in the last decade or so (see, for example, Rousseau, 2003)

The case for England (/UK) does, at least at first glance, also look compelling. The industrial revolution is commonly written of as beginning in the eighteenth century, with recent work dating it from the 1740s or earlier. The origins were essentially a mid-eighteenth century phenomenon. It is equally well established that there was in England a financial revolution that preceded the industrial one. It was at the end of the seventeenth century, stretching from 1690 to 1720. A long list of innovations and changes can be given, from the establishment of the Bank of England in 1694 and the prospering of commercial fractional reserve banking, following its beginnings in the 1670s, through the reform of the coinage in 1696, and the establishment of credible government debt. There was also the appearance of a recognisable stock market in the 1690s. There was thus clearly a financial revolution ahead of the industrial revolution, and on the surface there would seem to be a good case for saying that British experience fitted the general story that is increasingly being told of financial development preceding growth in the real economy. The story is reinforced by the experience of the nineteenth century.

Research has also been showing that the rate of growth of the real economy in the eighteenth century was in fact quite low. It was sustained growth, but for the 50 years or so after 1740 it was probably no more than 1 per cent per annum (Crafts and Harley, 1992). So if there was little to get excited about on the growth front it should not be surprising that financial intermediation was less exciting than some have suggested. But the story still holds. The real spurt in the growth of the economy (something closer to 3 per cent per annum) comes closer to the middle decades of the nineteenth century. This spurt in growth was preceded by the de-regulation of banking and the important rise in financial intermediation.

Something that needs to be borne in mind here is that there were considerable constraints on finance in the mercantilist age that prevailed before the 1800s. There were usury laws. No joint stock banking was allowed.[1] Banks were restricted to being partnerships of no more than six partners. And so on. And that brings us to a key point. There may well be financial development but if regulation hampers activity less can be achieved. Our focus here is therefore on the realms of finance and on regulation and the need for it to be limited and never-endingly revised to ensure it is suitable for changing conditions, but at the same time not allowed to be cumulating unnecessarily.

State regulation, of course, should not be confused with self-regulation. The best substitute for regulation is a concern with reputation. Something that developed early in British financial institutions was a rigorous system of internal checking and inspection. This was motivated by a desire both to have, and to present, a well-run and reliable institution that would attract new custom and re-assure existing customers. It is the antithesis of *state regulation* where compliance with the rule-book takes over. The customer is not in the picture. The seller looks only to the regulator. Self-regulation is designed with the customer in mind.

A good reason for pursuing freedom in the economy is that free exchange, free speech, and so on promote ideas which in turn lead to innovation, a prime source of growth. However in finance, because of the burden of regulation that began to build in the second half of the twentieth century, innovation had more to do with finding ways to circumvent regulations. It may have helped to pave the way to greater output but it was not the purest form of innovation. There may be a sophisticated financial system but if resources are diverted to compliance with regulation or finding ways of defeating regulation, then output is distorted and damaged.

12.2 How Governments Control

There are two ways for governments to get firms to do what government thinks is in the public interest. One is telling them what to do. This can mean prescribing the outcome, prescribing the process, or even both together. These are forms of regulation. The other is explicitly to recognise that organisations are run by people, not by automata waiting passively to be told what to do. That recognition would suggest that rather than simply issuing instructions one should organise incentive structures such that these rational individuals, out of their own self-interest, do what the government wishes. The latter course can best be described as governance.

What, in more detail, do the terms "regulation" and "governance" mean? A clear definition of regulation was provided in 1975 by that most eminent of scholars of it (Stigler, 1975). Regulation, he wrote, is "… the exercise of coercive government power". It is, in other words, telling people what to do and punishing them in some way if they do not perform as instructed.

But there are is a problem with this definition. It is too wide. It seems to imply that any legal rule is regulation, so that a libertarian who wants state enforcement of contracts would be said to be in favour of regulation. But it does help capture a difference: regulation tells people what to do, while governance involves setting up structures, inside or outside organisations, so as to make it desirable for the organisations *in the best service of their own interests* to do what is thought also to be in the general interest. They may be told how to organise, but after that they are left to themselves; state-imposed governance can be thought of as a particular type of regulation, one which focusses on structures rather than on either processes or outcomes.[2]

Examples of regulation and of governance are helpful at this point. The setting of speed limits on roads, enforced by supervision and punished by one of a range of penalties, is an example of regulation. The repeal of the Bubble Act in 1825 is example, from English financial history, of governance – it *allowed a framework* the better to facilitate large-scale investment in risky projects and thus to facilitate a faster stage of industrialisation, but did not prescribe how that freedom should be used.

Three contemporary examples by use of which regulation and governance can be contrasted are as follows: the regulation of capital ratios for banks under the Basle accord, the regulation of investment trusts and the regulation of accounting standards. These are taken in turn.

12.2.1 Capital Ratios

Banks are frequently contrasted with other types of firms because of the interdependence between them. But there is interdependence between most types of firms. Should Marks and Spencer (a hypothetical example) be taken over, there can be little doubt that its relationships with its suppliers would be changed. Or suppose Marks and Spencer were to fail, to close down (presumably in an orderly manner). That would affect its suppliers – adversely and its competitors favourably.

It is there that the crucial difference between banks and other types of firms emerges. When a bank fails (again still using the term loosely), there is an immediate *and adverse* effect on its competitors. Certainly if the bank is large, there is some turmoil in financial markets. Second, to the extent that other banks had contracts with the failed bank, these contracts are at the least frozen. And third, confidence in banks generally is weakened, and this loss of confidence can lead to a "flight to quality" which in the last resort can become a flight to liquidity requiring central bank assistance.[3]

In summary, the interdependence between banks is different in kind from that between other types of firms. That of itself does not justify interest in them by government. But what *does* seem to justify that interest is the combination of that interdependence with the important role of banks in the economy. They transmit monetary policy (they are certainly one of the channels) and they transmit funds from lenders to borrowers.

This has led, surprisingly recently in the case of some countries, to governments (or central banks) imposing regulations on how much capital banks should hold. These regulations were initially devised by the Basel Committee of Central Banks and Supervisors. The first set of these regulations was known as Basel I and the second as Basel II.

The difference between Basel II and its predecessor, Basel I, was that in Basel II required capital ratios were related to risk in a much more complicated way. Thus, the more risky a bank's portfolio (of assets) the higher is the capital required. This seems eminently sensible. It is what prudent banks would do without prompting. But supporting Basel II because it produced what prudent banks would choose to do involves a dangerous misconception.

The fundamental point is that banks hold capital to use: they run it down as a result of negative shocks and build it up as a result of positive ones. In contrast, regulatory capital sets a floor below which capital is not allowed to fall. *Regulatory capital is not for using.*

Does this mean that banks should be left to choose their own capital?

They certainly were in the past; and some systems, notably the UK, proved robust.[4] Now, this is important. It is undoubtedly correct that regulators are concerned primarily about the above-discussed "external effects" of bank failures, while banks are concerned to survive to earn future profits. But despite this apparent difference of interest (note that it is difference, not conflict: both regulators and banks want banks to survive) in the past banks took heed of *both* issues. One can infer this from actions banks took to monitor other banks and to protect themselves from failures by others. See for example clearing houses, the famous Suffolk Banking System in the USA, and the note return arrangements in Scotland under free banking (see, for example, Rockoff (1991) and White (1984)). Why can we not rely on self-interest now? The answer, it may be argued, is that the governance structure within banks has changed. In the periods just considered banks, although sometimes quite large, were smaller than now and, very important, in more concentrated ownership. Further, those who managed the banks usually had a large amount of their wealth in the bank.

So why not reform "governance"? Why not require bank management to hold their wealth, in increasing proportions as they become more senior, in the Bank's equity? This would start to produce the alliance of desired outcome with incentive that we saw in the past.

Nonetheless, it cannot be denied that there is a problem with relying on that alone. Banks nowadays often operate across many jurisdictions. Some bank failures are so significant relative to the size of the economy (for example, in Finland in the 1990s) that re-capitalisation is required. (Re-capitalisation is *not* the same as a bail-out, as a bail-out involves saving an insolvent institution while a recapitalisation involves capital being supplied to an institution which is still solvent, albeit fragile.)

Often such re-capitalisation requires at least some taxpayer funds, and governments and regulators understandably want to minimise these costs, at least for their own citizens. Hence, to prevent squabbling, delay, and economic problems following major international bank failures, a simple course could be adopted.

To ensure a minimum amount of capital, the principles of the US Federal Deposit Insurance Corporation Act (FDICIA) could be used to supplement governance.

A basic level of capital is set. But it is *not* a minimum. Rather, a move below it requires a series of pre-prescribed actions, quasi-automatic penalties such as not paying dividends or bonuses, and the requirement to raise more capital in a prescribed period.

In sum, because of the international nature of banks, governance reform alone is probably not a satisfactory substitute for detailed bank regulation: but in conjunction with some simple capital rules it is.

12.2.2 Investment Trust Regulation

In the UK, the Financial Services Authority (FSA) proposed in 2003 a set of changes to the rules governing investment trusts. These were the consequence of a particular problem. To understand these proposed changes, it is necessary first to describe the background to that problem, and then the problem itself.

The UK stock market had by late 2000 witnessed a remarkable "bull run" that had lasted for almost ten years, starting in the early in the 1990s. The Financial Times Stock Exchange (FTSE) All Share Index stood at 960 in October 1990. By September 2000 it had reached 3,266, an increase of some 240 per cent.

What about the people who were "creating" all of this wealth, the management, and executives of the companies? Many of these managers, or the relevant boards of directors, decided to introduce remuneration packages linked to the share price of their company. We now had an additional element in the spiralling process. Management who were previously focussed on producing sustainable high quality earnings focussed instead on strategies aimed at boosting shares prices in the short term, thus increasing both their own remuneration and the value of shareholders' funds. (These remuneration arrangements by failing to distinguish between company performance and market performance were themselves a failure of corporate governance.)

In 2000 the market hesitated, stopped altogether, and then dived. The size and longevity of the fall took most by surprise. Thousands of people who had lost money on their savings, their pensions, and their endowment policies looked to ways of making good their losses. They often asserted that they were either not told of the risks involved or that they did not understand the risk when it had been mentioned.

Mis-selling became the single most important issue facing both the FSA and the investment management industry. The claims of mis-selling of endowment and pension products are well documented. There are similarities with the possible mis-selling of split capital investment trusts ("splits"), of trusts with different classes of shares, usually one class getting the capital gain and the other class the dividends. In the case of splits, some products were sold as low risk. There were allegations that a small number of people had deliberately orchestrated a situation whereby, through a series of cross holdings, the share prices of some trusts had been artificially maintained.

Following its own investigations, comment from independent analysts, and increasing interest in the financial press, the FSA decided to gather information on 113 Split Capital Closed End Funds (i.e. investment trusts) at the end of September 2001. The FSA then issued a Discussion Paper in December 2001 and a Policy Statement in May 2002.

Following discussions with a number of investment trust practitioners the FSA produced a consultation paper in January 2003, in which it laid out what it saw as the main causes of the problems within the investment trust industry, and what it saw as the abuses perpetrated. These were as follows: Gearing, Cross Holding, Ineffectual Boards, and Dominant investment managers.

All investment trusts were, to varying degrees, affected by at least some of the changes proposed in response to the diagnosis. But these changes themselves caused problems. Gearing can enhance the returns to shareholders when managed effectively; arbitrarily restricting gearing is not inevitably in the interests of shareholders. Preventing investment trusts from investing in other investment trusts could, far from reducing the market risk to shareholders, actually increase the risk; for a means of risk diversification would no longer be available. Proposed changes to the eligibility of certain directors to remain on the board and the total exclusion of a representative from the investment manager being a director would lead to a reduction of industry-experienced directors being available.

These regulations were aimed at a particular set of recent problems. But the events surrounding the "splits crisis" were not unprecedented and will surely occur again in the future. Buoyant markets and bull market expectations produced an environment that encouraged over-optimism and downplayed risk.

The response by the FSA to the crisis might well have been different had the FSA been in existence for a number of years before the market fall. By then the FSA's ability to monitor and react might have been more developed. In particular, it may well have had an opportunity to remind directors of investment trusts of their responsibilities. Directors should ensure: that managements do not undertake self-serving actions, for example buying shares in one trust in the expectation of that trust in turn buying some of their shares; that the risks of gearing are fully understood by the managers and explained to the shareholders (who then have the choice of selling their shares if they are unhappy with the increased risk); and that any advertising literature issued on behalf of the trust is accurate. All these *already existing* responsibilities clearly implied that directors should ensure their organisations maintain good governance. Had directors paid greater heed to that, the splits crisis, if it happened at all, would have been very much smaller.

As it is, the response, more and tighter regulation, deals with a particular set of problems but does nothing to prevent different problems developing in the future (and creates some new problems). This is in contrast with insisting on good governance, which would have kept better aligned the interests of shareholders and management. Again, as in the capital regulation of banks, governance rather than regulation would have produced a more flexible and therefore more durable outcome.

Now to our third example.

12.2.3 Accountants and Accountancy

The two examples discussed so far have in common a feature not so far remarked on in this chapter; there was, or was thought to be, a problem for which no existing remedy existed, so new regulations had to be introduced. Accountancy shares that feature. The dangers of suddenly discovering a problem can be significant.

British (and North American) accounting both derive from the same tradition. The original purpose – and still probably the primary purpose – of company accounts is as follows:

> ...in law the object of annual accounts is to assist shareholders in exercising control of the company by enabling them to judge how its affairs have been conducted
>
> (Caparo Industries plc. V Dickman and others: House of Lords, 8th February 1980; Lord Jaunay)

Such accounting originated from the practice of "accounting for ventures" – for discrete operations, such as a voyage to the Indies – and evolved into accounting for the stewardship of going concerns. In the first, the returns, if any, were at the conclusion of the venture divided among the shareholders. Going concern accounting required regular measurement of profit to determine how much a company could distribute to the "shareholders" without diminishing its capital. These dividends might equal profits if there were no retention of profit in the business.

The one-year accounting period is a convention around which other conventions have evolved – annual tax payments, for example. There are arguments for a longer accounting period or periods (Myddleton, 2004), but the accounting period is now so intertwined with other aspects of life that change would be difficult. But be that as it may, what matters for our purposes is that the annual accounting period emerged originally as a convention, just as accounting emerged from accounting for stewardship of a venture to accounting for that of a going concern.

In 1966 there was in the USA a proposal (from the American Accounting Association) to move away from stewardship accounting to accounting for decision-making (Myddleton, op. cit., p36). This was followed up by the US Financial Accounting Standards Board:

> Financial Accounting should provide information that is useful to present and potential investors and creditors and other users in making rational investment, credit and similar decisions.
>
> (p37)

There is thus disagreement about the purpose of accounts, and invariably, as we shall see, disagreement about what kind of regulation of them might be sensible.[5]

For over 50 years British law has required that company accounts provide a "true and fair view" of the state of a company's affairs and of its profit or loss for the financial year. Thus, so long as the procedure is revealed, different companies can depending on the nature of the business do different things – for writing down old or damaged stock, for allowing for bad debts, for depreciating capital. It is, and this is a point and distinction returned to, a requirement over outputs rather than over inputs or processes.

Formal accounting standards, restricting the use of judgement, started to be discussed in the UK after the 1967 takeover of Associated Electrical Industries (AEI) by the General Electric Company. (Before then, there had been "Recommendations on Accounting Principles" – voluntary guidelines on best practice which often described several possible approaches.) After the takeover, AEI's projected profit of £10 million for the year turned out to be a loss of £4.5 million. (Note that no less two-thirds of the turn round was the result of a different judgement about the prospective outcome of long-term contracts.)

But what was laid down was still not a set of standards; rather it was a basic framework from which departures were expected to be disclosed and explained. They were not a code of rigid rules. The over-riding requirement remained to give a "true and fair view".

International accounting standards have emerged in the last 30 years. There are two basic templates: International Financial Reporting Standards (IFRS) and US Generally Accepted Accounting Principles (GAAP).

The differences can be summarised as follows. IFRS is more principle-based standards than detailed prescriptions. Under it, "true and fair" is the over-riding rule. Alternative treatments are allowed rather than a single one being prescribed.

US accounting is more authoritarian. This, Myddleton (2004) suggests, is a result of the much greater influence there of government agencies over the subject. As a result,

> In the USA 'presenting fairly' requires absolute compliance with US GAAP even if it might lead to a misleading view. There is no provision in law or practice for any equivalent of the UK's 'true or fair 'override'.

What can be said about the positions? What are the arguments for and against imposing a common set of rules?

First the "for". Six arguments for accounting standards are as follows: they prevent dishonesty by preparers of accounts: auditors can lack independence; investors may be damaged without standards; accounting decisions can be complex; uniformity in words and layout is helpful; standards will facilitate cross company comparisons.

Now, how strong are these arguments? All have encountered criticism. It *pays* insiders to provide information to outsiders. Auditors' incomes depend in the long run on their honesty. So long as accounts provide a clear account of stewardship they can give no further guidance. As to uniformity, a sufficient degree tends to evolve. To quote an example from a related area, "Prospectuses in the UK (fell) voluntarily into a reasonably uniform format because users liked it that way" (Myddleton, op. cit., p91). Regulation could freeze practice when evolution is desired.[6]

As well as these "negative" arguments against imposed standards, there are "positive" ones. They can stifle or even forbid independent judgement. They can reduce competition in ideas and restrict evolution. They may legitimise bad accounting; and they can mislead by raising expectations unduly. In a voluntary regime, views on the treatment of difficult issues can evolve slowly; disclosure of the method is what matters. As for compelling bad accounting, many argue (for example) that the treatment of research expenditure under Statements of Standard Accounting Practice (SSAP) requires just that (Myddleton, op. cit., p104). And finally, people can be confused by the clear implication that the presentation of accounts has no grey areas. Not everything is black or white; but compulsory standards imply that it is.

But be all that as it may, as with the previous examples, capital standards in banking and the regulation of investment trusts, it is clear that governance has for a long time done a good job – governance in this present context being a situation where auditors who prepare and check company accounts prosper by being independent, honest, and providing information helpful to the users of the accounts.

At least in those three areas, governance appears to trump regulation. Now, one cannot generalise simply from three cases. But in fact there is a well-developed body of analysis, neglected in this area, which is helpful in exploring the issues further and to which we turn in the next section of the chapter.

12.3 A Neglected Approach

So far it has been maintained in three cases that detailed prescription of processes will not necessarily produce desired outcomes. Even if they do produce such outcomes initially, they are unlikely to do so in the long term, when circumstances change (that including people finding their way round the regulation). What can be done apart from continually changing the regulations?

The alternative implied by the above discussion is to consider what kind of behaviour is desired and then put in place the appropriate "governance" within the firm so as to promote that behaviour. In the three cases examined the behaviour desired is respectively: to avoid becoming insolvent; to behave as if the manager of the investment trust had the same objectives as the holders of shares in the trust; and to provide accounts which, so far as the data permit, allow an accurate appraisal of the financial performance of a firm over the time period covered by the accounts.

We can, in other words, specify the objective. Can we design contracts to deliver these objectives?

Contract design has received a good deal of attention over the years from economists. It is usually discussed nowadays under the heading of, "The Principal-Agent Problem", the nomenclature invented by Steve Ross in 1973. The "principal" is the person who wants something done, the "agent" is the person employed to do it.

The "problem" can arise for a variety of reasons. A little background from the history of economics is helpful in showing both the difficulties – the problem – and the solutions to it.

Adam Smith touched on the subject in some detail. This he did at several points. For example:

> ... the work done by slaves, though it appears to cost only their maintenance, is in the end the dearest of any. A person who can acquire no property, can have no interest but to eat as much, and labour as little as possible.
> (Smith, 1776, book 1, chapter 8)

But his most detailed, and best known, discussion arises in the context of his explanation for the decline of agriculture in Europe after the fall of the Roman Empire. The system was one where the land was worked by "metayers":

> The Landlord furnished them with the seed, cattle, and instruments of husbandry. The produce was divided equally between the proprietor and the farmer.
> (Book 3, chapter 2)

Now, what was the problem? Smith identified two problems – there would be underinvestment and there would be misuse of resources.

> It could never, however, be the interest even of this last species of cultivators (the metayers) to lay out, in the further improvement of the land, any part of the little stock they might save from their own share of the produce, because the lord, who laid out nothing, was to get one-half of whatever it produced ... It *might* be the interest of metayer to make the land produce as much as could be brought out of it by means of the stock furnished by the proprietor; but it could never be in his interest to mix any part of his own with it. In France ... the proprietors complain that their metayers take every opportunity of employing the master's cattle rather in carriage than in cultivation; because in the one case they get the whole profits for themselves, in the other they share them with their landlords.
> Smith (1776, bk. 3, chap 2, p367)

Contract design has appeared in various contexts over the years, both before that famous discussion and after it. Hume (1740) seems to have been the first to state the free rider problem.

> Two neighbours may agree to drain a meadow, which they possess in common; because it is easy for them to know each other's mind; and each must perceive that the immediate consequence of his failing in his part, is the abandoning the whole project. But it is very difficult, and indeed impossible, that a thousand persons shou'd agree in any such action; it being difficult for them to concert so complicated a design, and still more difficult for them to execute it; while each seeks a pretext to free himself of the trouble and expence, and wou'd lay the whole burden on others.
>
> Hume (1740, p538)

This was followed up in nineteenth-century discussions of public finance – on the "benefit approach" and the "ability to pay approach" to taxation. Various writers, notably Pantaleoni and de Viti de Marco, advocated the benefit approach. Wicksell pointed out what became known subsequently as the free rider problem with this approach.

> If the individual is to spend his money for private and public uses so that his satisfaction is maximized he will obviously pay nothing whatsoever for public purposes. ... Whether he pays much or little will affect the scope of public service so slightly, that for all practical purposes, he himself will not notice it at all. Of course, if everyone were to do the same, the State will soon cease to function.
>
> Wicksell (1896, p81)

In other words, it can be advantageous to the individual to conceal preference. That, too, is a problem for contract design.

This "voting" problem has been tackled by various authors: Borda, Bowen, and Vickrey are the best known. Borda (1781) showed he was aware of the problem – but, as he acknowledged, his "solution" was a purely academic one: "My scheme is intended only for honest men". Bowen (1943) proposed a sequential voting procedure, but one which depended on myopia. Each voter voted according to his time preferences at each stage – but only because the voter did not look beyond that stage. Vickrey (1960) was led to the conjecture that there is no way of aggregating individual preferences by voting that cannot be distorted by strategic behaviour. (A formal proof of this was provided by Gibbard in 1973.)

The problem of monopoly regulation has also been recognised as essentially one of contract design. This was done by Loeb and Marget (1979) who recognised that (as with the voting problem above) the difficulty is lack of information. The regulator, in advance of setting the regulation, knows less about costs (and possibly demand) than does the regulated firm.

The problem of concealment (or non-disclosure) of course also lies behind the problem of moral hazard that has been recognised for centuries in insurance. A number of economists have grappled with how to design contracts for this – see, for example, Arrow (1963), Pauly (1974), and Grossman and Hart (1983).

The possibility of concealment also inhibits price discrimination. This was discussed in the context of infrastructure provision by Dupuit (1844).

> The best of all tariffs would be the one which would make pay those which use a way of communication a price proportional to the utility they derive from using this service .... I do not have to say that I do not believe in the possible application of this voluntary tariff; it would meet an insurmountable obstacle in the universal dishonesty of passants, but it is the kind of tariff one must try to approach by a compulsory tariff.
>
> Dupuit (1844, p223)

It arises too in economic planning. Hayek and Robbins had both pointed out the difficulty of such an activity – a market was needed before the information a planner needed would be disclosed. As late as 1967, Lange did not acknowledge this point. "Were I to rewrite my essay today my task would be much simpler. My answer to Hayek and Robbins would be: so what's the trouble? Let us put the simultaneous equations on an electronic computer and we shall obtain the solution in less than a second. The market process with its cumbersome tatonnements appears old fashioned" (Lange, 1967, p158).[7]

If we stand back to see the problems of contract design that economists have grappled with since Hume and Smith what do we find?

We see first why the subject temporarily (for at least a hundred years) vanished from view.

In a large economy, with many buyers and many sellers and no entry barriers to a particular activity, the problems vanish. Rational individual behaviour translates into profit maximisation for firms' owners. This leads to cost minimisation and hence to productive efficiency. Similarly, consumers facing exogenous prices have the appropriate incentives for utility maximisation.

But that treated the firm as a "black box". How did the owners of firms align the interests of the various members of the firm (workers, managers) with profit maximisation? The moment that question returned to view, we came to the issue of contract design. The extensive and often complex literature which has examined contract design problems, touched on above, faces difficulties and sometimes reaches impasses because of three main types of information problem – adverse selection, moral hazard, and non-verifiability. The first is when the agent has private knowledge (about cost or valuation) that is not available to the principal. The second is when the agent can take action (of a type the principal would not wish) unknown to the principal. The third is when both principal and agent have the same information after the event, but no third party can observe it – so even after the event the information cannot be used for contract enforcement in, for example, a court of law.

Now, do these three difficulties arise in the examples above?

12.4 Relevance in the Examples

Consider the three examples – banking system stability, appropriate information disclosure and behaviour towards investors, and accountants and auditors producing "accounts of stewardship" which are fit for that purpose.

Banking sector instability can be all too visible. The kind of behaviour that was problematic in the "splits crisis" can certainly be seen after the event, at least in part. Risk disclosure, for example, can be objectively reviewed ex post. Similarly the results of faulty audits reveal themselves. Not necessarily immediately, but in due course. In all three cases there is ex post visibility which can be verified by a third party. So one of our problems is not present. What about adverse selection and moral hazard?

Neither of these is relevant. For we are concerned only with observable outcomes *after* the event, and not at all with what goes on *inside* the firms; and we can observe the outcomes.

Now, what goes on inside these firms is of course of concern for their owners, and there may be problems of contract design there. But that is no concern of ours. We need to specify only that the contracts have characteristics which regardless of their other features will produce the kind of behaviour the authorities regard as desirable.

An example shows how this might be done.

Charles Goodhart has proposed (though we fear his she me will not be adopted) that the Chairman of any bank which gets into difficulties should be put in the stocks outside the Bank of England, and then, as was traditional with those placed in the stocks, be pelted with rotten fruit.[8] This, he suggests, would sharpen their attention to the stability of their respective banks. He is surely right. But would any prospective British government adopt that measure?

Another course, much more plausible, is however prompted by the proposal. The proposal was designed to make senior management focus on stability. This could be done by insisting that contracts do not grant options with no risk of loss; that management have to place their wealth, the more senior they are the higher the proportion, in the bank's stock, and that stock be held, untradeable, by trustees until, say, five years after retirement of the respective manager (and that any contract designed to offset the risk be unenforceable at law); and, if it were so wished, to sharpen incentives also for the owners double or even triple liability for each shareholder could be reintroduced.

In other words, the nature of the contract design problem allows relatively straightforward solutions – not necessarily optimal, whatever that is thought to mean in this context, but certainly one free of the problem of the regulator continually chasing the regulated. Similar suggestions can be made for investment trusts and accounting. One has, indeed, already been implied for investment trusts – rigorously enforce the existing body of company law and in particular that part of it governing the conduct of directors.

Governance can do a better job than regulation in these areas, provided we are willing to intervene in that part of the firm rather than be equally intrusive (at the least) in other parts.

Now, where does that lead in general? What general lessons can be drawn?

12.5 General Conclusion

Regulation has invariably led to attempts to circumvent it. Accordingly, it is surely worth considering an approach which aligns the interests of the regulated with the regulators, rather than the latter simply telling the former what to do. There is extensive work by economists on contract design. It is worth attempting to draw on that. This claim is surely reinforced by the work of lawyers – notably Richard Posner – showing how judicial interpretations under common law tend to evolve towards economically efficient outcomes. Law, a form of governance, has worked. Why not try it again?

As the economic literature discussed above has shown, there can sometimes be substantial problems with attempting to do so. But so long as there is public concern only with observable outcomes, governance can at least in principle replace regulation. It should certainly replace regulation as the first resort of governments seeking to influence the behaviour of firms. It will be more durable in its effects, and relying on it, and thus focussing on outcomes rather than processes, will ensure that the regulated firms seek the most economically efficient way of doing what the government wants. We would thus be exploiting the most fundamental of all economic insights, one stated by Adam Smith and reiterated by Hayek in his famous "The Use of Knowledge in Society". Each individual knows more about his own situation, interests, and desires than any outside observer can. This insight has (with the exception of the work of Stephen Littlechild, for example, 1978, 2017) been neglected in the field of regulation. Ending this neglect might well prove productive.

Notes

1 The Bank of England was unique. It was founded as a joint stock company (in 1694) and retained that form until its nationalisation in 1946.

2 We are indebted to Richard Epstein for an extensive discussion of the concepts of regulation and governance and their possible differences.

3 This would be a classic Lender of Las Resort (LoLR) action, as described for example in Wood (2000).

4 This was the case even before the mid-twentieth century, by when UK banks were a well-capitalised and well-diversified cartel.

5 It is worth observing that there is little evidence that company accounts are good at predicting future profits – except of course when they provide evidence of fraudulent or incompetent stewardship (Benston, 1969).

6 Some have argued that on those grounds common law is a superior basis for commerce to Roman law.

7 A good overview of this debate is given in Boettke (2000).
8 So far as we know he has never proposed this in writing, but has done so several times in lectures and seminars.

References

Arrow, K. (1963) 'Research in Management Controls: A Critical Synthesis', in C. Bonini, R. Jaecliche, and H. Wagner (eds) *Management Controls: New Directions in Basic Research*, pp317–327 McGraw-Hill, New York.
Benston, G.J. (1969) 'The Effectiveness and Effects of the SEC's Accounting Disclosure Requirements', in H. Manne (ed) *Economic Policy and the Regulation of Corporate Securities* AEI, Washington, DC.
Boettke, Peter (2000). *Socialism and the Market: The Socialist Calculation Debate Revisited.* Routledge, London.
Borda, J.C. de (1781) *Mémoire sur les Elections au Scrutin Histoire de l'Academie Royale des Sciences*, Imprimerie Royale, Paris.
Bowen, H. (1943) "The Interpretation of Voting in the Allocation of Economic Resources". *Quarterly Journal of Economic* 58: 27–48.
Crafts, N.F.R. and Harley, C.K. (1992) "Output Growth and the British Industrial Revolution: A Restatement of the Crafts-Harley View". *Economic History Review* 45: 703–730.
Dupuit, J. (1844) "De la Mesure de L'utilité des Travaux Publics". Annales des Ponts et Chaussées. Scientifiques et Medicales Elsevier, Paris.
Gibbard, Allan (1973) "Manipulation of Voting Schemes: A General Result". *Econometrica* 41: 587–601.
Grossman, S. and Hart, O. (1983) "An Analysis of the Principal-Agent Problem". *Econometrica* 51: 7–45.
Hume, D. (1740) *Treatise of Human Nature*. Oxford University Press, Oxford.
Lange, O. (1967) 'The Computer and the Market', in C. H. Feinstein (ed) *Socialism, Capitalism, and Economic Growth: Essays Presented to M. Dobb.* Cambridge University Press, Cambridge.
Levine, Ross (1997) "Financial Development and Economic Growth: Views and Agenda". *Journal of Economic Literature* 35(2): 688–726.
Littlechild, Stephen (1978) *Fallacy of the Mixed Economy*: 80 (Hobart Papers) Paperback IEA, London.
Littlechild, Stephen (2017) "Regulation and the Nature of Competition". *Journal of Air Transport Management* 67: 10–24.
Loeb, M. and Marget, W. (1979) "A Decentralised Method of Utility Regulation". *Journal of Law and Economics* 22: 399–404.
Myddleton, D. (2004) *Unshackling Accounts*. Institute of Economic Affairs, London. Available at https://iea.org.uk/publications/research/unshackling-accountants
Pauly, M.V. (1974) "Over Insurance and Public Provision of Insurance: The Roles of Moral Hazard and Adverse Selection". *Quarterly Journal of Economics* 88: 44–62.
Rockoff, Hugh (1991) "Lessons from the American Experience with Free Banking' and James Dorn Comment on Rockoff', in Capie and Wood (eds), *Unregulated Banking; Chaos or Order?* Macmillan, New York
Ross, S. (1973) "The Economic Theory of Agency; The Principle's Problem". *American Economic Review* G3: 134–139.
Rousseau, Peter (2003) "Historical perspectives on financial development and economic growth". *Federal Reserve of St Louis Review* 84(4): 81–105.
Smith, A. (1776) *The Wealth of Nations* The Modern History, New York
Stigler, G.J. (1975) *The Citizen and the State* University of Chicago Press, Chicago

Vickrey, W. (1960) "Utility, Strategy and Social Decision Rules". *Quarterly Journal of Economics* 74: 507–535.

White, Lawrence H, (1984) *Free banking in Britain; Theory, Experience, and Debate, 1800–1845* Cambridge University Press, Cambridge

Wicksell, K. (1896, 1967) 'A New Principle of Just Taxation', in Richard A. Musgrave and Alan T. Peacock (eds) *Classics in the Theory of Public Finance* St Martin's Press, New York. Originally published in Fiananztheoretische Untersuchungen, Jena, 1896.

Wood, Geoffrey (2000) "The Lender of Last Resort Reconsidered". *Journal of Financial Services Research* 18(2/3): 203–227.

Index

MIX
Papier | Fördert gute Waldnutzung
FSC® C083411

Kolibri 360 GmbH
Ferdinand-Jühlke-Straße 7
99095 Erfurt, Deutschland
produktsicherheit@kolibri360.de